The Literary Life

THE LITERARY LIFE

*A Scrapbook Almanac
of the Anglo-American
Literary Scene from
1900 to 1950*

*by Robert Phelps
and Peter Deane*

Chatto and Windus
London
1969

Contents

Foreword

"This whole book is but a draft,—nay, but the draft of a draft. Oh, Time, Strength, Cash, and Patience!"

—HERMAN MELVILLE

". . . I enjoy reading railroad timetables, recipes, or, indeed, any kind of list."

—W. H. AUDEN

What follows is unofficial, non-specialist, homegrown. In its original form, it was even handmade. It began with a scrapbook called *The Poet's Face,* into which miscellaneous pictures and clippings were glued or Scotch-taped, with relevant dates, quotations, and biographical details scribbled in the margins. When one volume was filled up, another was begun. The poet's face led to his desk, his family, his travels, finances, love affairs—anything germane to his vocation. In the same way, poets came to include not only writers but composers, painters, any expressive maker. It was all very personal and capricious, often indiscreet, and swaddled throughout in hero-worship for the creative life.

In its present form, the hero-worship remains. But we have tried to temper the indiscretion and to introduce some useful order. There is now a structure, partly chronological, partly categorical. There are patterns, rubrics, groupings. The result is a calendar view of literature in England and America as it happened from year to year over the first half of our century.

It begins, in 1900, with three emblematic acts: Mark Twain's expatriation after a decade of living abroad, Henry Adams diagnosing the dynamo at the Paris Exposition, the death of martyred Oscar Wilde, and with at least three books that speak for their epoch and continue to survive: *Sister Carrie, Lord Jim, The Oxford Book of English Verse.* It advances into three decades of the great upthrust of maverick creativity called Modernism, whose slogan was Ezra Pound's "Make It New," whose landmark crests were *The Waste Land* and *Ulysses,* both in 1922, and whose *hic jacet* is *The Unquiet Grave,* in 1944. Symmetrically, it concludes with three more representative *gestes* in 1950: Dylan Thomas coming to America and, as someone said, finalizing the marriage between the Poet and the Academy with a blood sacrifice; James Agee going to Hollywood, with a more or less analogous immolation to come; and the death of ancient G. B. Shaw, at ninety-four, one of the very few men-of-letters, along with Maugham and Santayana (no Americans!), whose life and published works span the entire fifty years. As for three surviving books, it is too soon to say. W. H. Auden's *Poets of the English Language* has certainly redressed the late Victorian canon of Anglo-American verse, as established by Sir Arthur Quiller-Couch. But, for instance, will Paul Goodman (*The Dead of Spring*) and Angus Wilson (*Such Darling Dodos*) be seen in another generation to stand in the same relation to 1950 as Dreiser and Conrad, respectively, do to 1900?

Anyway, there the half century lies—lambent with its novelty and glamorous names, sibilant with its warnings and whispered asides. Is it a transition? A silver age? A finale? A renaissance? At most, we have gathered some of the evidence. Every reader must frame the indictment and render a verdict for himself.

As a reference book, this Almanac belongs with (and humbly claims lineage from) the Oxford University Press's little *Annals of English Literature,* and those inspired chronologies which Auden has included in so many of his anthologies: the *Greek Reader,* the *Poets of the English Language,* etc. His strategy could not be simpler—titles and events laid out in columns by calendar years. But the result is inexhaustibly rewarding, a tonic, a literal restorative. For the most part, these specialist days, we are given literary history in separate strands. We examine a particular writer's achievement, a single literary form, a certain movement or regional group. We evaluate Graham Greene, or the decline of the novel, or the Southern Gothic school, and we see them in isolation. In actuality, they all happened at once. They co-transpired. Auden's chronologies reaffirm this fact, and what our Almanac has done is expand the possibilities of Auden's basic device.

Thus each year from 1900 to 1950 (fifty-one in all) accounts for itself, as follows:

1 A list of books (classified as fiction, verse-drama, and non-fiction) published in Great Britain and the United States, or elsewhere by citizens thereof. This includes, first, all the works of those writers who, as of 1968, seem most likely to be remembered in another century—Hardy, Frost, Eliot, Joyce, Hemingway, Shaw, etc.; and then selected titles by lesser lights. In choosing the latter, we favored the author's prestige as a total entity over individual works. Hence we included everything by Gertrude Stein, even though much of it may remain forever unread, and everything by

Robert Graves, even though many of his titles may be forgotten. Authors like Galsworthy, Wells, Howells, Marquand were heavily pruned.

2   A necrology—not only of writers but of anyone else productive of, or related to, the arts.

3   A selection of books in languages other than English—the emphasis here being upon those which influenced the English-language product (Rilke or Cavafy) rather than those which were perhaps better known on their native ground (D'Annunzio or Géraldy).

4   A selection of works in the other arts.

5   A catch-all calendar of goings-on in the literary life: travels, laurels, gestures, losses, triumphs, bons mots; in other words, gossip, the stuff out of which legends are made, myths nourished.

What this layout yields at a glance (Instant Perspective!) is a rich cross-section of the creating matrix. Any bibliography of D. H. Lawrence will tell you that he published *Sons and Lovers* in 1913; and any biography will tell you where he was living and what Frieda was saying. Only this Almanac will tell you that in those same twelve months

Virginia Woolf, a bride of one year, was suffering her
first nervous breakdown;

Marcel Duchamp's *Nude Descending a Staircase* was
shown at the Armory in New York;

Robert Frost, at 38, had his first book published—
in England;

Charles Chaplin appeared in his first film,
Making a Living;

Baron Corvo died and Ambrose Bierce forever vanished
into the wilds of revolutionary Mexico;

Stravinsky's *Sacre du Printemps* had its première
in Paris;

Joyce Cary was working as a cook in the Montenegrin Army;

Proust published *Du Côté de chez Swann,* Apollinaire published *Alcools,* Thomas Mann published *Der Tod in Venedig,* E. C. Bentley published *Trent's Last Case,* Eleanor Hodgman Porter published *Pollyanna;*

T. S. Eliot played the role of *Lord Bantok* in a Harvard production of *Fanny and the Servant Problem,* which perhaps helped inspire the line about "the damp souls of housemaids. . . ."

Such a book is necessarily incomplete. The omissions are rife, and having corrected the proofs, we can already imagine indignant queries. Where, for instance, is Hilaire Belloc's novel, *Mr. Clutterbuck's Election* (1908)? Or William Faulkner's privately printed *Idyll in the Desert* (1931)? What about Katherine Anne Porter's (apocryphal or otherwise) novel, *My Chinese Marriage,* which was signed "M.T.F." and published in New York in 1921? Or *Beechen Vigil* (1925), the first book of verse by our new Poet Laureate, C. Day Lewis?

The answer is patent. This Almanac had better be owned, not borrowed; and its owner must use it possessively, aggressively, with fountain pen in hand. He must cover the margins with further details, other titles, with events from political history, sports, movies, whatever obsesses him personally. He must thicken the plot, add to the soup, make his own copy unique, and thereby reclaim a little more of the total truth about our first half century's progress.

And while his pen is in hand, there is something else he can try, another use to which such an Almanac as this can be put. Or perhaps "use" is too serious a word; perhaps "game" is better, a personal game, to be played by one reader at a time, for his own sake, his own self-knowing. What it amounts to is relating the main-stream of Anglo-American literature to his own secret history. This is not as frivolous as it may sound. For each of us—in his own re-membering, at least—cannot help coloring all the august public events with his own homely private ones.

Take a milestone from your own annals—your birthday, your graduation from college, your loss of virginity; a broken leg, a trip to Paris, your first cigarette—and see what was going on simultaneously around you that same year, or month, or week. It is an ego-centric but also an exhilarating, harmless, and curiously satisfying experience. What it makes—or recovers—is a connection, a modest link, between your own life and literature's, a community, you might say, that has always been waiting there. Speaking for our-selves, we were profoundly moved to find that one of us was born the very week that Proust died, and that the other came into the world while Cesare Pavese was translating Gertrude Stein into Italian, and Ford Madox Ford, holed up in Michigan, was scrib-bling the massive love letter to world literature which has given this Almanac its motto.

Self-absorbed? Perhaps. Precious? Not at all. Romantic? Cer-tainly, absolutely, by all means. This whole book is romantic, hopelessly, unabashedly so. It presupposes a love of books, and a belief in their making, which may very well be anachronistic, but for which we cannot apologize.

We have already been warned that ours will probably be the century in which the printed word—literary expression in the form of *books*—will pass, become obsolete. In 1978—only a decade away—we shall celebrate the 500th anniversary of Caxton's *editio princeps* of the *Canterbury Tales*. There was literature before that, but it existed without benefit of the printed word. It circulated in handwritten forms, or by word of mouth. With William Caxton, we began five centuries of making books.

Things moved slowly at first. Shakespeare's sonnets were read in someone's holograph until his celebrity as a playwright made it worth a printer's while to set them up in type. That was in 1609. By 1715, all of London was eagerly waiting for Pope's translation of the *Iliad*. Dr. Johnson's *Dictionary* was a best-seller, and a century later Dickens had his own magazine, with an entire nation alert for the first of the month and the next installment of his current serial. Very soon after come those sumptuously imposing Collected Editions, in dozens of volumes numbered in gilt Roman numerals, an upper-middle-class *beau geste* which was only to last two or three generations, but which authors loved while it lasted. Finally, in the twentieth century, literature declared its independence of commercial publishing, and we find a sudden flurry of valiant printing schemes: Gertrude Stein selling a Picasso to finance the Plain Edition of her own unwanted works; D. H. Lawrence publishing *Lady Chatterley's Lover* in Florence at his own expense; *Ulysses* set up by French printers in Dijon and paid for by Sylvia Beach; Norman Douglas selling his own books by private subscription; and most ambitious of all, Virginia and Leonard Woolf, with a hand press at first, and then a real publishing house which issued their own books and those of two generations of their contemporaries—Katherine Mansfield, T. S. Eliot (*The Waste Land* itself!), Christopher Isherwood, Henry Green.

As of 1968, we are still publishing, of course. We still have books—real books, paperback books, mimeographed books, Xeroxed books. (There is even one young man in New York who sells his own first novel in photostat form, and at $40, bless him.) But the end has been predicted by experts. As recently as 1950, we thought it was the atomic bomb which would change the world.

Now it appears that the real changes will be less violent, but more radical. The book, which we have taken for granted all these years, may be passing. By A.D. 2068, it may be only a curiosity. Collectors will scour Sussex and New England for copies. Books will find their way into the interior decorator's vocabulary, and, instead of waxy grapes and pears, under glass bells there will be *Lord Weary's Castle, The Pilgrim Hawk, Party-Going, The Song of the Cold*. Not to be handled, of course; or read (use closed-circuit Videolex for that); but for historical interest, for whimsy, along with butter churns and foot warmers, for the antiquarian touch no well-appointed room can be without.

In that case, this Almanac (long out of print) will have a claim, however retroactive, to more than reference use. It will be plain that, all along, it was also a loving elegy, a larky swansong, a doting, dotty, but undaunted Souvenir Album for books, books, books, and for all the men and women who ever believed in making them.

Robert Phelps
and Peter Deane

A FOOTNOTE FOR OWLS: In compiling the annual booklists, we used, when available, only individual studies of each author: definitive bibliographies (those delicious Soho ones, for instance) when they existed, otherwise a minimum per author of three checklists in critical or biographical studies devoted to him. With some younger, or less important, writers, we had to rely on general literary histories, and often found that with a given book, we pretty much had our pick of dates. Tracking down the publication of Stephen Spender's *The Destructive Element*, for instance, we found 1934 given in Stanley Kunitz's *Twentieth Century Au-*

thors; 1935 in *The Concise Cambridge Bibliography of English Literature;* no mention in the *Oxford Annals of English Literature;* 1936 in the Select Bibliography included in Alan Ross's *Poetry, 1945–1950,* published for the British Council; and 1936, again, in the Select Bibliography compiled by "W.M." as an appendix to Spender's *Poetry Since 1939.* In Mr. Spender's autobiography, *World Within World* (or at least in the American edition), he himself gives 1936, while the British Museum General Catalogue of Printed Books gives 1935. A check of the original reviews of the book turned up notices by Cyril Connolly and Edwin Muir in, respectively, *The New Statesman and Nation* and *The Spectator*—both in May 1935. So we settled for 1935.

In all such instances (not always this tangled), conflicting dates have been checked against the Library of Congress Catalog, or the British Museum Catalogue, to confirm at least the copyright date; and then, where possible, against the first reviews, to determine whether the book might actually have appeared in the early winter preceding the copyright year, or some time after the New Year following it.

There have also been some exceptions (necessary to all good rules), which shall remain a secret for all time.

R.P. *and* P.D.

The Literary Life

1900

Great Britain

FICTION

Winston S. Churchill: *Savrola: A Tale of the Revolution in Laurania*
Joseph Conrad: *Lord Jim*
R. B. Cunninghame Graham: *Thirteen Stories*
G. B. Shaw: *Love Among the Artists* (U.S.)
John Sinjohn (John Galsworthy): *Villa Rubein*
H. G. Wells: *Love and Mr. Lewisham*

Samuel Butler: translation of Homer's *Odyssey*

VERSE AND DRAMA

Thomas Edward Brown: *Collected Poems* (in the Manx dialect)
G. K. Chesterton: *Graybeards at Play; The Wild Knight and Other Poems*
William Ernest Henley: *For England's Sake*
Ford Madox Hueffer: *Poems for Pictures*
Sir Arthur Quiller-Couch, ed.: *The Oxford Book of English Verse: 1250–1900*
W. B. Yeats: *The Shadowy Waters*

W. B. Yeats

NON-FICTION

W. H. Hudson: *Nature in Downland*
Ford Madox Hueffer: *The Cinque Ports: A Historical and Descriptive Record*
Walter Raleigh: *Milton*
Mark Rutherford (William Hale White): *Pages From a Journal with Other Papers*
George Saintsbury: *A History of Criticism and Literary Taste in Europe* (concluded 1904)

❧ ❧ *"Words alone are certain good."*
WILLIAM BUTLER YEATS

Joseph Conrad

United States

FICTION

Lyman F. Baum: *The Wonderful World of Oz*
Stephen Crane: *Whilomville Stories; Wounds in the Rain: War Stories*
Theodore Dreiser: *Sister Carrie*

Paul Laurence Dunbar: *The Strength of Gideon and Other Stories; The Love of Landry*
Ellen Glasgow: *The Voice of the People*
Henry Harland: *The Cardinal's Snuff Box*
Henry James: *The Soft Side*
Jack London: *The Son of the Wolf*
Frank Norris: *A Man's Woman*
Booth Tarkington: *Monsieur Beaucaire*
Mark Twain (Samuel L. Clemens): *The Man That Corrupted Hadleyburg and Other Stories and Essays*
Edith Wharton: *The Touchstone* (G.B. title: *A Gift from the Grave*)

VERSE AND DRAMA

Joaquin Miller (Cincinnatus Hiner Miller): *Chants for the Boer*
William Vaughn Moody: *The Masque of Judgment*
Edmund Clarence Stedman, ed.: *An American Anthology: 1787–1900*

NON-FICTION

Finley Peter Dunne: *Mr. Dooley's Philosophy*
William Dean Howells: *Literary Friends and Acquaintance: A Personal Retrospective of American Authorship*

Josiah Royce: *The World and the Individual*
George Santayana: *Interpretations of Poetry and Religion*

❦❦ *"An artist, I think, is nothing but a powerful memory that can move itself at will through certain experiences sideways, and every artist must be in some things powerless as a dead snake."*
STEPHEN CRANE

Related Events

DEATHS

Stephen Crane: American short-story writer and journalist; age 29; of tuberculosis: in Badenweiler, Germany, on June 5. As an undergraduate at Nebraska State University, Willa Cather had helped copy-edit *The Red Badge of Courage* when it was serialized in a local paper. Now, under the pseudonym "Henry Nicklemann," she memorialized Crane in the June 23 issue of

Mark Twain

Stephen Crane

Library: ". . . it occurs to me that all his life was a preparation for sudden departure. I remember once when he was writing a letter, he stopped and asked me about the spelling of a word, saying carelessly, 'I haven't time to learn to spell.' Then, glancing down at his attire, he added with an absent-minded smile, 'I haven't time to dress either; it takes an awful slice out of a fellow's life.' "

Oscar Wilde: Irish dramatist, verse writer, and storyteller; age 44; of "an intercranial complication of suppurative *otitis media*, or middle-ear disease"; in a small hotel on the rue d'Alsace, in Paris, on November 30. "*Sept personnes suivirent l'enterrement*," wrote André Gide, "*encore n'accompagnèrent-elles pas toutes jusqu'au bout le funèbre convoi. Sur la bière, des fleurs, des couronnes; une seule, m'a-t-on dit, portait une inscription: c'était celle du propriétaire de l'hôtel: on y lisait ces mots:* A MON LOCATAIRE."

Other Deaths:

Richard Blackmore, British novelist
Ernest Dowson, British poet
Friedrich Nietzsche, German poet and philosopher
John Ruskin, British essayist
Sir Arthur Sullivan, British composer

IN OTHER LANGUAGES

Henri Bergson: *Le Rire*
Sigmund Freud: *Traumdeutung* (*The Interpretation of Dreams*)
Gerhardt Hauptmann: *Michael Kramer*
Jules Renard: *Poil de Carotte* (stage adaptation)
Willy (Henri Gauthiers-Villars and Gabrielle Colette): *Claudine à l'École* (sequels through 1903)

IN OTHER ARTS

Music: Gustave Charpentier: *Louise* ‖ Edward Elgar: *The Dream of Gerontius* ‖ Giacomo Puccini: *Tosca* ‖ Jan Sibelius: *Finlandia*
Stage: Frank Harris: *Mr. and Mrs. Daventry* (starring Mrs. Pat Campbell, and based on an idea purchased from Oscar Wilde) ‖ Henrik Ibsen: *Når Vi Döde Vågner* (*When*

Henry James and his dachshund Max

Oscar Wilde

Colette and Willy

Ernest Dowson

We Dead Waken) || Stephen Phillips: *Herod* || Edmond Rostand: *L'Aiglon* (written for Sarah Bernhardt) || The Floradora Girls in a New York musical of the same name

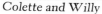

IN THE MARGIN

Joseph Conrad finishes *Lord Jim:* "I sent wife and child out of the house (to London) and sat down at 9 A.M. with a desperate resolve to be done with it. Now and then I took a walk around the house, out at one door, in at the other. Ten-minute meals. A great hush. Cigarette ends growing into a mound similar to a cairn over a dead hero. Moon rose over the barn, looked in at the window and climbed out of sight. Dawn broke, brightened. I put the lamp out and went on, with the morning breeze blowing the sheets of ms. all over the room. Sun rose. I wrote the last word and went into the dining room. Six o'clock I shared a piece of cold chicken with Escamillo [the dog] . . . Felt very well, only sleepy; had a bath at seven and at 1:30 was on my way to London . . ."

In Paris, **Henry Adams** visits the Exposition Universelle: "It is a new century and what we used to call electricity is its God. I can already see that the scientific theories and laws of our generation will, to the next, appear as antiquated as the Ptolemaic system, and that the fellow who gets to 1930 will wish he hadn't . . . You are free to deride my sentimentality if you like, but I assure you that I—a monk of St. Dominic, absorbed in the Beatitudes of the Virgin Mother—go down to the Champs de Mars and sit by the hour over the great dynamos, watching them run as noiselessly and as smoothly as the planets, and asking them—with infinite courtesy—where in Hell they are going."

Mark Twain returns to the United States after a decade's residence abroad and is hailed on the front page of *The New York Times* as "the Hero as Man of Letters."

Five years into his second marriage, and still seeking "a complete loveliness of bodily response," **H. G. Wells** makes an arrangement with his wife which leaves him free to become what he later calls a "Don Juan of the intelligentsia."

Theodore Dreiser, stricken by *Sister Carrie's* poor reviews and even poorer sales, begins to circulate the long-popular myth that because his publisher's wife was "horrified" by the novel's frankness, the entire edition had been locked away in the office basement and "no copies ever sold." As of 1928, however, Doubleday's files showed that of the 1,008 copies printed, 456 had been sold, 423 remaindered, and 129 sent out for review, with puffs from Frank Norris. Moreover, as early as 1901, Dreiser received a royalty statement for $68.40. Shortly thereafter, he suffered a nervous breakdown.

In the Wings:

Walter de la Mare, 27, is working for the Liverpool office of the Anglo-American Oil Company and preparing his first book of poems, to be published under the name of "Walter Ramal."

Robert Frost, 26 and recently settled with his wife and baby daughter on a New Hampshire farm (bought for him by his grandfather), is raising chickens and writing poems "with a view to a volume some day."

John Millington Synge, 29 and based in Paris as a literary critic, makes his third trip to the Aran Islands, where he had originally been sent by Yeats with the advice to live as "one of the people themselves [and] express a life that has never found expression . . ."

In the Great World:

Count Ferdinand von Zeppelin builds his first dirigible
The Boxer Rebellion in China
The Boer War in South Africa

1901

Great Britain

FICTION

Samuel Butler: *Erewhon Revisited*
Joseph Conrad and Ford Madox Hueffer: *The Inheritors*
George Gissing: *Our Friend the Charlatan*
Rudyard Kipling: *Kim*
W. Somerset Maugham: *The Hero*
George Moore: *Sister Teresa*
Normynx (Mr. and Mrs. Norman Douglas): *Unprofessional Tales*

Rudyard Kipling

VERSE AND DRAMA

Laurence Binyon: *Odes*
John Davidson: *The Testament of a Man Forbid*
Thomas Hardy: *Poems of the Past and the Present*
George Meredith: *A Reading of Life and Other Poems*
Alice Meynell: *Later Poems*
Arthur Symons: *Poems*

G. B. Shaw: *Three Plays For Puritans* (*The Devil's Disciple*, produced 1897, Albany, New York; *Captain Brassbound's Conversion*, produced 1902; *Caesar and Cleopatra*, produced 1906, Berlin)

NON-FICTION

George Gissing: *By the Ionian Sea*
W. H. Hudson: *Birds and Man*
James Joyce: "The Day of the Rabblement," in *Two Essays* (privately printed, Dublin)

❦ ❦ *"For the work of man's mind there is one test, and one alone, the judgment of generations yet unborn. If you have written a great book, the world will come to know it . . ."*

GEORGE GISSING

United States

FICTION

Winston Churchill: *The Crisis*
Bret Harte: *Under the Redwoods*
William Dean Howells: *A Pair of Patient Lovers*
Henry James: *The Sacred Fount*
Sarah Orne Jewett: *The Tory Lover*
Jack London: *The God of His Fathers*
Frank Norris: *The Octopus: A Story of California*
Alice Hegan Rice: *Mrs. Wiggs of the Cabbage Patch*
Upton Sinclair: *Springtime and Harvest: A Romance*
Edith Wharton: *Crucial Instances*

VERSE AND DRAMA

Bliss Carman and Richard Hovey: *Last Songs from Vagabondia*
Edwin Markham: *Lincoln and Other Poems*
William Vaughn Moody: *Poems*
George Santayana: *A Hermit of Carmel and Other Poems*

NON-FICTION

Stephen Crane: *Great Battles of the World*
Lafcadio Hearn: *A Japanese Miscellany*
Booker T. Washington: *Up From Slavery*

Thomas Hardy

G. B. Shaw

❧❧ *". . . the Great American Novel is not extinct like the Dodo, but mythical like the Hippogriff . . . the thing to be looked for is not the Great American Novelist, but the Great Novelist who shall also be American."*

FRANK NORRIS

Related Events

DEATHS

Queen Victoria: British monarch and diarist; age 81; at Osborne, Isle of Wight, on January 22. "I will be good" (age 11, to her tutor).

Other Deaths:

January 27: Giuseppe Verdi
September 9: Henri de Toulouse-Lautrec
September 14: United States President William McKinley, after being shot twice by an assassin on the 6th

IN OTHER LANGUAGES

André Gide: *Le Roi Candaule*
Thomas Mann: *Buddenbrooks*
August Strindberg: *Dödsdansen (The Dance of Death)*

IN OTHER ARTS

Stage: Anton Chekhov: *Tri Sestre (The Three Sisters)*: produced at the Moscow Art Theatre, with the author's bride-to-be, Olga Knipper, playing the role of Masha
Music: Sergei Rachmaninoff: *Piano Concerto in C Minor* ‖ Arnold Schoenberg: *Gurre-Lieder* (finished 1911) ‖ Under the pseudonym of "Monsieur Croche," Claude Debussy begins to write music criticism in the *Revue blanche*

IN THE MARGIN

Change of Scene: William James arrives in Edinburgh to deliver the Gifford Lectures at the university (published as *Varieties of Religious Experience*, 1902) ‖ In Toul, France, Hilaire Belloc finishes his book on Robespierre and on the same evening, with a new book in mind, sets out on a walking tour,

Frank Norris

Lafcadio Hearn

following the "path to Rome" || William Sydney Porter (O. Henry) is released on July 24 from the Ohio Penitentiary, in Columbus, Ohio, after serving three years and three months of a five-year sentence for embezzlement

Publishing: Oxford "World Classics" begun || *McClure's Magazine* founded in New York (until 1912) || *Samhain,* an occasional review edited by Yeats to promote the Irish Literary Theatre, appears in Dublin

In the Wings: James Joyce, age 19 and an undergraduate at Dublin University, attacks the proposed National Theatre for Ireland in a two-penny pamphlet called "The Day of the Rabblement": "No man . . . can be a lover of the true or the good unless he abhors the multitude; and the artist, though he may employ the crowd, is very careful to isolate himself . . ."

In the Great World: Edward VII becomes King of England || Theodore Roosevelt becomes 26th President of the United States || Guglielmo Marconi sends the first wireless message—from Cornwall, England, to Newfoundland, North America—on December 12

Thomas Mann

Queen Victoria

James Joyce

1902

Great Britain

FICTION

Arnold Bennett: *Anna of the Five Towns* (dedicated to Joseph Conrad); *The Grand Babylon Hotel*
Joseph Conrad: *Youth and Two Other Stories*
R. B. Cunninghame Graham: *Success*
Arthur Conan Doyle: *The Hound of the Baskervilles*
W. H. Hudson: *El Ombú*
Rudyard Kipling: *Just So Stories*
W. Somerset Maugham: *Mrs. Craddock*
Beatrix Potter: *The Tale of Peter Rabbit*

Lady Gregory: translation, *Cuchulain of Muirthemne: The Story of the Men of the Red Branch of Ulster, Arranged and Put into English* (Preface by W. B. Yeats)

VERSE AND DRAMA

John Masefield: *Salt-Water Ballads*
Walter Ramal (Walter de la Mare): *Songs of Childhood*

W. B. Yeats: *Cathleen ni Hoolihan: A Play in One Act; Where There Is Nothing: A Play in Five Acts*

NON-FICTION

Hilaire Belloc: *The Path to Rome*
Ford Madox Hueffer: *Rossetti*
W. B. Yeats: *The Celtic Twilight*, revised edition (originally published in 1893)

❧❧ *"My credentials are those of a field naturalist who has observed men: all their actions and mentality."*
W. H. HUDSON

"*Mr. Holmes, they were the footprints of a giant hound!*" (Arthur Conan Doyle's The Hound of the Baskervilles)

United States

FICTION

Stephen Crane: *Last Words* (edited by Cora Crane; G.B.)
Ellen Glasgow: *The Battle-Ground*
Bret Harte: *Openings in the Old Trail*
Lafcadio Hearn: *Kotto*
Henry James: *The Wings of the Dove*
Jack London: *Children of the Frost; A Daughter of the Snows*
Mark Twain: *A Double-Barrelled Detective Story*
Edith Wharton: *The Valley of Decision*
Owen Wister: *The Virginian: A Horseman of the Plains* (dedicated to Theodore Roosevelt)

VERSE AND DRAMA

George Cabot Lodge: *Poems 1899–1902*
E. A. Robinson: *Captain Craig*
Trumbull Stickney: *Dramatic Verses*

NON-FICTION

William Dean Howells: *Literature and Life: Studies*
William James: *The Varieties of Religious Experience: A Study in Human Nature* (Gifford Lectures, 1901–2)

Logan Pearsall Smith: *Trivia* (privately printed, G.B.; trade edition, 1918)
Henry David Thoreau: *The Service* (edited by Frank B. Sanborn)
Woodrow Wilson: *A History of the American People*

❧ ❧ *"What the American public always wants is a tragedy with a happy ending."*
WILLIAM DEAN HOWELLS

Related Events

DEATHS

Samuel Butler: British novelist and essayist; age 67; of intestinal catarrh and pernicious anemia; in London, on June 18. According to his own wish, his ashes were not preserved, but buried in the crematorium garden without a marker.
Lionel Johnson: British poet and critic; age 35; of a fractured skull, incurred in falling off a barstool; in London, October 3.

John Masefield

"When you call me that, smile."
(Owen Wister's The Virginian)

Frank Norris: American novelist; age 32; of peritonitis, in San Francisco, on October 25.
Emile Zola: French novelist and polemicist; age 62; of asphyxiation from carbon monoxide fumes due to a debris-filled chimney; in Paris, on September 29.

Other Deaths:

Lord Acton, June 19, in Bavaria
Bret Harte, May 5, in Surrey
Frank R. Stockton, April 20, in Washington, D.C.

IN OTHER LANGUAGES

André Gide: *L'Immoraliste*
Hugo von Hofmannsthal: *Brief des Lord Chandos* (Letter of Lord Chandos)
Rainer Maria Rilke: *Das Buch der Bilder* (The Book of Pictures)

IN OTHER ARTS

Stage: James Barrie: *Quality Street; The
    Admirable Chrichton*
Music: Claude Debussy: *Pelléas et Mélisande*
Films: Georges Méliès: *Le Voyage dans la Lune*

IN THE MARGIN

Jan. 17: First issue of *The Times Literary
    Supplement*
June 1: End of the Boer War
July: American poets William Vaughn Moody,
    age 32, and Trumbull Stickney, age 28, both
    destined to die of brain tumors within the
    decade, spend the summer together in Paris
    reading the complete Greek drama.
Sept.: Trying to save enough from his ten-
    shilling-a-week private income to pay for
    printing his first book of poems, W. H. Davies
    leaves the Ark, a London Salvation Army
    shelter, and resumes the tramping life he had
    been forced to abandon in 1899 after losing a
    leg in a train-hopping accident in Canada.
Sept. 3: While out for a ride on her 53rd birthday,
    Sarah Orne Jewett is thrown from her carriage,
    sustaining head and spinal injuries which
    virtually end her writing career. For over a year
    she was unable even to sit at a desk, and long
    afterward suffered violent headaches and
    vertigo. It was not until 1908 that she could
    write to Willa Cather that she had found a
    verse among her papers which she was sending
    to *McClure's Magazine* as a "sign": "No story
    yet, but I do not despair; I begin to dare to
    think that if I could get a quiet week or two, I
    could really get something done for you . . ."
    Six months later, she suffered the brain
    hemorrhage which ended all hope.
Oct. 21: Amy Lowell, age 28, returns from a
    performance by Eleonora Duse in Boston and
    suddenly finds herself compelled to write her
    first poem: "I knew nothing whatever about
    the technique of poetry . . . I was as ignorant

E. A. Robinson

as anyone could be. I sat down, and with
infinite agitation wrote this poem. It has, I
think, every cliché and every technical error
which a poem can have, but it loosed a bolt
in my brain and I found out where my true
function lay . . ."

Great Britain

FICTION

Samuel Butler: *The Way of All Flesh*
Joseph Conrad: *Typhoon and Other Stories* (dedicated to R. B. Cunninghame Graham)
Joseph Conrad and Ford Madox Hueffer: *Romance*
George Gissing: *The Private Papers of Henry Ryecroft*
George Moore: *The Untilled Field*
Beatrix Potter: *The Tailor of Gloucester*

VERSE AND DRAMA

Laurence Binyon: *The Death of Adam and Other Poems*
Robert Bridges: *Now in Wintry Delights*
Rudyard Kipling: *The Five Nations*
John Masefield: *Ballads*

Sturge Moore: *The Centaur's Booty; The Rout of the Amazons*
Thomas Traherne: *Poetical Works* (edited and published by Bertram Dobell)
W. B. Yeats: *In the Seven Woods: Being Poems Chiefly of the Irish Heroic Age*

G. B. Shaw: *Man and Superman* (produced 1905)

NON-FICTION

E. K. Chambers: *The Medieval Stage*
G. K. Chesterton: *Robert Browning*
Richard Garnett and Edmund Gosse: *English Literature: An Illustrated Record*
W. H. Hudson: *Hampshire Days*
G. E. Moore: *Principia Ethica*
Walter Raleigh: *Wordsworth*
W. B. Yeats: *Ideas of Good and Evil*

❧ ❧ *"Art is interesting only insofar as it reveals an artist."*

SAMUEL BUTLER

Samuel Butler

United States

FICTION

Stephen Crane and Robert Barr: *The O'Ruddy: A Romance*
Bret Harte: *Trent's Trust*
William Dean Howells: *Questionable Shapes; Letters Home*
Henry James: *The Ambassadors; The Better Sort*
Jack London: *The Call of the Wild*
Frank Norris: *The Pit: A Story of Chicago; A Deal in Wheat, and Other Stories of the Old and the New World*
Edith Wharton: *Sanctuary*
Kate Douglas Wiggin: *Rebecca of Sunnybrook Farm*

VERSE AND DRAMA

Ambrose Bierce: *Shapes of Clay*
Willa Cather: *April Twilights*
Paul Laurence Dunbar: *Lyrics of Love and Laughter*
H. L. Mencken: *Ventures into Verse*
Joaquin Miller: *As It Was in the Beginning*

NON-FICTION

Bliss Carman: *The Kinship of Nature*
Henry James: *William Wetmore Story and His Friends*
Jack London: *The People of the Abyss*
Frank Norris: *The Responsibilities of the Novelist and Other Literary Essays*

❧❧ *"The frank yet graceful use of 'I' distinguishes a good writer from a bad . . ."*

AMBROSE BIERCE

Jack London

Related Events

DEATHS

William Ernest Henley: British poet; age 54; of tuberculosis and injuries resulting from a fall while getting off a train; in Woking, on July 11
George Gissing: British novelist and man-of-letters; age 46; of double pneumonia compounded by cirrhosis of the lungs; in Saint-Jean-de-Luz, on December 28

Gertrude Stein in the Luxembourg Gardens

Other Deaths:

Hugo Wolf, February 22
Paul Gauguin, May 8
James Whistler, July 7
Pope Leo XIII, July 20
Herbert Spencer, December 8

George Gissing

IN OTHER LANGUAGES

Sarah Bernhardt: *Ma Double Vie*

Hugo von Hofmannsthal: *Ausgewählte Gedichte (Selected Poems)*

Thomas Mann: *Tristan* (including *Tonio Kröger*)

Académie Goncourt established in Paris on January 19, by the will (1896) of Edmond de Goncourt

IN OTHER ARTS

Stage: W. Somerset Maugham: *A Man of Honour*

Films: Edwin S. Porter (director): *The Great Train Robbery*

Music: Erik Satie: *Trois Morceaux en Forme de Poire*

Other: Alfred Stieglitz: *Camera Work*

IN THE MARGIN

On the Move: After five years of marriage and two sons, Norman Douglas, 35, is divorced, explores Capri and decides to build a villa there ‖ W. B. Yeats, 38, begins a lecture tour of America in November

In the Money: Arthur Conan Doyle accepts $5,000 apiece for six or more stories bringing Sherlock Holmes back from the death he had allegedly suffered in "The Adventure of the Final Problem" ‖ Theodore Dreiser stacks planks for the New York Central Railroad at 15¢ an hour

In the Wings: In October, Gertrude Stein, 29, settles with her brother Leo in Paris, at 27 rue de Fleurus, at the same time finishing her first novel, *Q.E.D.* (*Quod Erat Demonstrandum*, published posthumously in 1950 as *Things As They Are*) ‖ Aged 14 and attending a girl's school in England, New Zealander Kathleen Beauchamp chooses her future *nom de plume:* Katherine Mansfield ‖ Lytton Strachey, 23, publishes his first professional piece in the *Independent Review*, declaring that "the greatest misfortune that can happen to a witty man is to be born out of France"

In the Great World: On June 14, the Ford Motor Company is founded in Detroit, Michigan, operating in a converted ice house ‖ On December 17, Orville Wright is airborne for 12 seconds at Kitty-Hawk, North Carolina

W. H. Hudson

G. K. Chesterton

Great Britain

FICTION

G. K. Chesterton: *The Napoleon of Notting Hill*
Joseph Conrad: *Nostromo: A Tale of the Seaboard*
Baron Corvo (Frederick William Rolfe): *Hadrian the Seventh*
John Galsworthy: *The Island Pharisees*
George Gissing: *Veranilda*
W. H. Hudson: *Green Mansions: A Romance of the Tropical Forest*
Rudyard Kipling: *Traffics and Discoveries* (stories and poems)
W. Somerset Maugham: *The Merry-Go-Round*
Walter Ramal (Walter de la Mare): *Henry Brocken*
Forrest Reid: *The Kingdom of Twilight*
May Sinclair: *The Divine Fire*

Howard Sturgis: *Belchamber*
W. B. Yeats: *Stories of Red Hanrahan*

Lady Gregory: *Gods and Fighting Men: The Story of the Tuatha de Danaan and of the Fianna of Ireland, Arranged and Put into English* (Preface by W. B. Yeats)

VERSE AND DRAMA

Æ (George William Russell): *The Divine Vision and Other Poems*
Thomas Hardy: *The Dynasts, First Part* (completed 1908)
Ford Madox Hueffer: *The Face of the Night*
Rudyard Kipling: *The Muse Among the Motors* (U.S.)
Alfred Noyes: *Poems*
Algernon Charles Swinburne: *A Channel Passage; Collected Poems*

Henry James

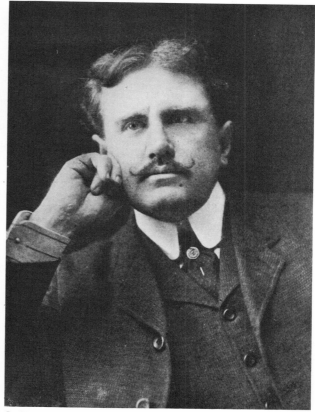

O. Henry

W. B. Yeats: *The Hour-Glass and Other Plays;
The King's Threshold and On Baile's Strand*

NON-FICTION

Max Beerbohm: *The Poet's Corner*
A. C. Bradley: *Shakespearean Tragedy*
Samuel Butler: *Essays in Life, Art and Science*
Vernon Lee: *Hortus Vitae*
Herbert Spencer: *Autobiography*
Arthur Symons: *Studies in Prose and Verse*

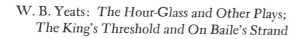 *"J'écris avec peine, lentement,
raturant sans cesse. Quel métier de chien!
'C'est un art trop difficile,' comme ce cher
et bon Henry James me dit (chaque fois
que nous nous voyons) en levant les bras
au ciel . . ."*

JOSEPH CONRAD

United States

FICTION

James Branch Cabell: *The Eagle's Shadow*
Ellen Glasgow: *The Deliverance*
Lafcadio Hearn: *Kwaidan*
O. Henry (William Sydney Porter): *Cabbages
and Kings*
William Dean Howells: *The Son of Royal
Langbrith*
Henry James: *The Golden Bowl*
Jack London: *The Sea Wolf*
Edith Wharton: *The Descent of Man and Other
Stories*

VERSE AND DRAMA

Joel Chandler Harris: *Tar-Baby and Other
Rhymes of Uncle Remus*
George Cabot Lodge: *Cain, a Drama*

1904

Peter Pan, *by James M. Barrie*

William Vaughn Moody: *The Fire-Bringer*
Charles A. (Carl) Sandburg: *In Reckless Ecstasy*
(Asgard Press, the home-basement operation
of a Lombard College professor with whom
Sandburg had studied)

NON-FICTION

Henry Adams: *Mont-Saint-Michel and Chartres*
(privately printed; trade edition 1913)
Lafcadio Hearn: *Japan: An Attempt at
Interpretation*
Paul Elmer More: *Shelburne Essays* (11 volumes
through 1921)
Walt Whitman: *An American Primer* (edited by
Horace Traubel)
Edith Wharton: *Italian Villas and Their Gardens*

❧ ❧ *"The fascination of the silent
midnight, the veiled lamp, the smouldering
fire, the white paper asking to be covered
with elusive words; the thoughts grouping
themselves into architectural forms, and
slowly rising into dreamy structures,
constantly changing, shifting, beautifying
their outlines,—this is the subtlest of
solitary temptations, and the loftiest of the
intoxications of genius."*

HENRY ADAMS

Related Events

DEATHS

Sir Leslie Stephen: British man-of-letters and
father of Virginia Woolf; 72; of cancer; in
London, on February 22
Anton Chekhov: Russian dramatist and short-
story writer; 44; of tuberculosis; in
Badenweiler, Germany, on July 2
Lafcadio Hearn: American man-of-letters; 54; of
heart disease; in Tokyo, on September 27
Trumbull Stickney: American poet; 30; of a brain
tumor; in Boston, on October 11

IN OTHER LANGUAGES

Sigmund Freud: *Zur Psychopathologie des
Alltagslebens* (*The Psychopathology of
Everyday Life*)
Hermann Hesse: *Peter Camenzind*
Rainer Maria Rilke: *Geschichten vom Lieben
Gott* (*Little Stories of God*)
Romain Rolland: *Jean-Christophe* (finished
1912)
Frank Wedekind: *Die Büchse der Pandora*
(*Pandora's Box*)

IN OTHER ARTS

The Abbey Theatre is born: Miss Annie E. F. Horniman takes out a 99-year lease on Dublin's Music Hall and an adjacent morgue, offering them rent-free to Yeats and the Irish Literary Theatre. Yeats accepts ("I am confident . . . The stars are quiet and fairly favorable . . ."), and the Abbey Theatre opens on December 27, with Lady Gregory's *Spreading the News* and Yeats's *On Baile's Strand.* "We do not desire propagandist plays," he declared, "nor plays written mainly to serve some obvious moral purpose; for art seldom concerns itself with those interests or opinions that can be defended by argument, but with realities of emotion and character that become self-evident when made vivid to the imagination."

Premières:

Moscow: Chekhov's last play, *Vishnyovy Sad* (*The Cherry Orchard*)
Milan: Giacomo Puccini's *Madame Butterfly*
Paris: Maurice Ravel's song cycle, *Shéhérazade*
London: James Barrie's *Peter Pan*
Dublin: John Millington Synge's *Riders to the Sea*

IN THE MARGIN

Travels: Spanish-born Pablo Picasso settles in Paris ‖ American-born Henry James sails from Southampton on August 24 to visit his native land for the first time in 23 years ‖ British-born Ford Madox Hueffer, suffering from neurasthenia, goes to Germany for treatment and rest. It was not (reportedly) until the following year, when Conrad's doctor told him he had only one month to live, that Hueffer began to recover

Milestones: Ex-Rough-Rider and occasional man-of-letters Theodore Roosevelt is elected 26th President of the United States ‖ The American Academy of Arts and Letters is founded ‖ On June 16, "Bloomsday," the events presently to be recorded in James Joyce's *Ulysses* come to pass ‖ In his Journal for May 27, Arnold Bennett notes: "Today I am thirty-seven. I have lived longer than I shall live. My new series begins in the *Windsor.* My name is not on the cover. Anthony Hope's stands there alone. And I am thirty-seven. Comment is needless"

Anton Chekhov

E. M. Forster

1904

Rewards: A Civil List Pension of £74 is awarded to George Gissing's two minor sons, by way of posthumously acknowledging their father's literary gifts || Thanks apparently to his claim that dairymen were poisoning the local citizenry, G. B. Shaw comes in next-to-last in the London County Council elections || In Paris, Henry Adams buys an 18 hp Mercedes, to "run about the country hunting 16th century glass windows" || E. M. Forster, 25, receives the £8,000 bequest left him when he was 18 by his great aunt Marianne Thornton: ". . . she and no one else made my career as a writer possible, and her love, in a most tangible sense, followed me beyond the grave"

Ronald Firbank

1905

H. G. Wells

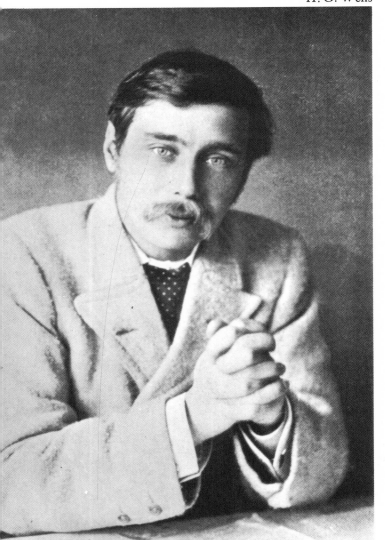

Great Britain

FICTION

G. K. Chesterton: *The Club of Queer Trades*
Arthur Conan Doyle: *The Return of Sherlock Holmes*
Arthur (Ronald) Firbank: *Odette d'Antrevernes and A Study in Temperament*
E. M. Forster: *Where Angels Fear to Tread*
George Gissing: *Will Warburton*
W. H. Hudson: *A Little Boy Lost*
Ford Madox Hueffer: *The Benefactor*
John Masefield: *A Mainsail Haul*
George Moore: *The Lake*
Baroness Orczy: *The Scarlet Pimpernel*
Forrest Reid: *The Garden God: A Tale of Two Boys* (dedicated to Henry James)
G. B. Shaw: *The Irrational Knot*
Algernon Charles Swinburne: *Love's Cross-Currents*
Edgar Wallace: *The Four Just Men*
H. G. Wells: *Kipps*

VERSE AND DRAMA

Laurence Binyon: *Penthesilea*
Robert Bridges: *Demeter, a Mask*
John Davidson: *Selected Poems*
W. H. Davies: *The Soul's Destroyer and Other Poems* (published at the author's own expense)
Ernest Dowson: *Poems* (edited by Arthur Symons)

G. B. Shaw: *Passion, Poison and Petrifaction, or the Fatal Gazogene* (produced 1905)
John Millington Synge: *In the Shadow of the Glen and Riders to the Sea* (produced 1903 and 1904); *The Well of the Saints* (Introduction by W. B. Yeats; produced 1905)

Willa Cather

Edith Wharton

NON-FICTION

G. K. Chesterton: *Heretics*
Ford Madox Hueffer: *The Soul of London; Hans Holbein*
Vernon Lee: *The Enchanted Wood, and Other Essays on the Genius of Place*
W. Somerset Maugham: *The Land of the Blessed Virgin: Sketches and Impressions in Andalusia*
Oscar Wilde: *De Profundis*

❦❦ *"Literary! Literary! Now that is the last thing that verse should ever be . . ."*
FORD MADOX HUEFFER

Sigmund Freud

United States

FICTION

James Branch Cabell: *The Line of Love*
Willa Cather: *The Troll Garden*
Thomas Dixon: *The Clansman* (source for
    D. W. Griffith's film, *Birth of a Nation*)
Joel Chandler Harris: *Told By Uncle Remus:
    New Stories of the Old Plantation*
Lafcadio Hearn: *The Romance of the Milky Way*
William Dean Howells: *Miss Bellard's
    Inspiration*
Edith Wharton: *The House of Mirth*

VERSE AND DRAMA

Van Wyck Brooks and John Hall Wheelock:
    Verses by Two Undergraduates
Bliss Carman: *Collected Poems*
George Cabot Lodge: *The Great Adventure*

Trumbull Stickney: *Poems* (edited by William
    Vaughn Moody, George Cabot Lodge, and
    John Ellerton Lodge)

NON-FICTION

William Dean Howells: *London Films*
James Huneker: *Iconoclasts: A Book of
    Dramatists*
Henry James: *The Question of Our Speech and
    The Lesson of Balzac; English Hours*
H. L. Mencken: *George Bernard Shaw: His Plays*
George Santayana: *The Life of Reason, or The
    Phases of Human Progress*

❧❧ *". . . I am no believer in pampered
vocations . . ."*

EDITH WHARTON

Related Events

DEATHS

General Lew Wallace: American novelist (*Ben
    Hur*) and friend of Billy the Kid; 78; in
    Crawfordsville, Indiana, on February 15
Jules Verne: French novelist (*Tour du Monde
    en Quatre-Vingts Jours*); 77; at his home in
    Amiens, France, on March 24
Henry Harland: St. Petersburg-born, American
    novelist (*The Cardinal's Snuff Box*); 44; in
    San Remo, Italy, on December 20

IN OTHER LANGUAGES

Albert Einstein: "Elektrodynamik bewegter
    Körper," in *Annalen der Physik* (first paper on
    special relativity)
Sigmund Freud: *Drei Abhandlungen zur
    Sexualtheorie* (Three Contributions to
    the Theory of Sexuality)
Rainer Maria Rilke: *Das Stunden-Buch* (Book
    of Hours)

New York: Alfred Stieglitz opens his "291" Gallery, introducing the work of Rodin, Picasso, Matisse, Lautrec to America. (Became "An American Place" in 1929.) || Largely through the agitations of Anthony Comstock, who denounced Shaw as an "Irish smut-dealer" (and from whose name, in turn, Shaw derived the neologism "Comstockery"), the first public performance of *Mrs. Warren's Profession* ends with the arrest of everyone, from the theater owner to the entire cast

Paris: Claude Debussy's tone poem *La Mer* || First exhibition of *Les Fauves* at the Salon d'Automne

Vienna: Première of Richard Strauss's opera *Salomé*

Patronage: President Theodore Roosevelt secures poet Edwin Arlington Robinson, 36, a job in the New York Custom House of the U. S. Treasury Department, at $2,000 a year. Although Robinson found himself better off than he had been when working for the New York subway system, he soon had complaints: ". . . my chief duty as a pillar of the government appears to consist in remaining a prisoner in Room 408. This is particularly rotten just now, as I am in a mood for work (work with me means studying the ceiling and my navel for four hours and then writing down perhaps four lines—sometimes as many as seven and again none at all) . . ." In 1909, he resigned

Laurels: George Meredith receives the Order of Merit || George Moore appointed High Sheriff of Mayo County, Ireland || W. H. Hudson receives a fan letter from Australia, sent by a young clerk in a Melbourne counting-house "who got two friends to join him in spending all their week-ends in a log hut in a lonely spot forty miles from the town where they go in for a simple natural life with nature and read Jefferies, Thoreau, and my poor books . . ."

In the Wings: Recently admitted to the bar and set up in his own law firm, Wallace Stevens writes to his future bride: "Are you really fond of books—paper valleys and far countries, paper gardens, paper men and women? . . . I live with them constantly"

In the Great World: Russia: the October Revolution and the Potemkin Mutiny || Ireland: the National Council of Sinn Fein established

Albert Einstein

John Galsworthy

Thomas Hardy: *The Dynasts, Second Part*
W. B. Yeats: *Poems, 1899–1905*; ed.: *Poems of Spenser*

NON-FICTION

Lord Acton: *Lectures on Modern History*
Robert Browning and Alfred Domett: *Letters* (edited by F. G. Kenyon)
G. K. Chesterton: *Charles Dickens*
Joseph Conrad: *The Mirror of the Sea: Memories and Impressions*
H. W. and F. G. Fowler: *The King's English*
Ford Madox Hueffer: *The Heart of the Country* (dedicated to Henry James)
George Moore: *Memoirs of My Dead Life*
George Saintsbury: *History of English Prosody* (through 1910)
G. B. Shaw: *Dramatic Opinions and Essays* (Preface by James Huneker)

❦ ❦ *"I had rather be called a journalist than an artist, that is the essence of it . . ."*
H. G. WELLS

Great Britain

FICTION

John Galsworthy: *The Man of Property*
George Gissing: *The House of Cobwebs and Other Stories*
Ford Madox Hueffer: *The Fifth Queen* (dedicated to Joseph Conrad)
Rudyard Kipling: *Puck of Pook's Hill* (stories and poems)
W. Somerset Maugham: *The Bishop's Apron*
H. G. Wells: *In the Days of the Comet*

VERSE AND DRAMA

Æ: *By Still Waters*
Walter de la Mare: *Poems*
Charles M. Doughty: *The Dawn in Britain*

Ford Madox Hueffer and his daughter Christina

Upton Sinclair

United States

FICTION

Ellen Glasgow: *The Wheel of Life*
O. Henry: *The Four Million*
Jack London: *White Fang*
Upton Sinclair: *The Jungle*
Mark Twain: *The $30,000 Bequest and Other Stories*

NON-FICTION

Ambrose Bierce: *The Cynic's Wordbook* (later called *The Devil's Dictionary*)
Mark Twain: *What Is Man?* (published anonymously)

❧❧ "*. . . I'd rather win a water-fight in a swimming pool, or remain astride a horse that is trying to get out from under me, than write the great American novel.*"
JACK LONDON

Related Events

DEATHS

Paul Laurence Dunbar: American poet; 34; in Dayton, Ohio, on February 9
Henrik Ibsen: Norwegian dramatist; 78; in Christiania, Norway, on May 23
Paul Cézanne: French painter; 67; in Aix-en-Provence, on October 22

IN OTHER LANGUAGES

Paul Claudel: *Partage de Midi*
Robert Musil: *Die Verwirrungen des Zöglings Törless* (*Young Torless*)
Rainer Maria Rilke: *Die Weise von Liebe und Tod des Cornets Christoph Rilke* (*The Lay of the Love and Death of Cornet Christopher Rilke*)

IN OTHER ARTS

John Galsworthy: *The Silver Box*
E. W. Hornung: *Raffles* (adapted for the stage by Gerald du Maurier and Lawrence Irving)

Ambrose Bierce

1906

Arnold Schoenberg: *Kammersymphonie*
  (*Chamber Symphony*; performed 1913)
Pablo Picasso paints his portrait of Gertrude Stein

IN THE MARGIN

Relocations: Mr. and Mrs. G. B. Shaw settle in
  the New Rectory at Ayot St. Lawrence,
  Hertfordshire, henceforth known as "Shaw's
  Corner" || Monsieur Marcel Proust moves
  to 102 boulevard Hausseman and has the walls
  of his bedroom lined with cork || Mrs.
  Edith Wharton rents an apartment in the rue
  Varenne, and remains a resident of Paris for
  the next twenty years

Milestones: Everyman's Library begins
  publication || On April 18, San Francisco
  is shaken by an earthquake, with five
  succeeding days of fires

America! America!: January: Planning his first
  tour of the United States, young H. G. Wells
  asks Henry James for help: "I shall be very
  grateful if you can give me any letters to
  typical people. I suppose you know no one in
  Salt Lake City?" || April: Maxim Gorky,
  arriving in New York to raise money for the
  Russian revolutionary movement, is
  enthusiastically hailed by Mark Twain,
  William Dean Howells, and Finley Peter
  Dunne—until they discover that the lady
  accompanying him is not Madame Gorky ||
  August: Pausing in Newport in the course of
  his own first visit to North America, Ford
  Madox Hueffer is miserable: "It is hot, dusty,
  dull, and uninspiring, and the expenses are
  appalling!"

In the Wings: Vachel Lindsay, 27 and on a
  tramping tour through Florida and Georgia,
  tries to exchange copies of his poems for food
  and shelter || D. H. Lawrence, 21, enters
  the University College in Nottingham on a
  scholarship grant—commuting daily by train
  from Eastwood. He was especially interested
  in botany and a French course given by
  Professor Ernest Weekley, with whose wife
  Lawrence was to elope in 1912 || James

Henrik Ibsen

Paul Cézanne

Joyce, 24, protests to Grant Richards, who has abandoned plans to publish *Dubliners:* "It is not my fault that the odor of ashpits and old weeds and offal hangs round my stories. I seriously believe that you will retard the course of civilization in Ireland by preventing the Irish people from having one good look at themselves in my nicely polished looking glass"

Poets and Politics: Running for the House of Commons from South Salford and warned to avoid the "religious question," Hilaire Belloc begins his first campaign speech by taking a rosary out of his pocket and announcing: "Gentlemen, I am a Catholic. As far as possible, I go to Mass every day . . . As far as possible, I kneel down and tell these beads every day. If you reject me on account of my religion, I shall thank God that He has spared me the indignity of being your representative."

Belloc was elected by a majority of 852 ‖ Upton Sinclair's exposé of Chicago slaughter houses in *The Jungle* results in the passing of the Pure Food and Drug Act in the United States, and in England provokes a full-throated review by Winston Churchill: "It has . . . disturbed in the Old World and the New the digestions, and perhaps the consciences, of mankind . . ."

D. H. Lawrence

Great Britain

FICTION

Arnold Bennett: *The Grim Smile of the Five Towns*
Joseph Conrad: *The Secret Agent*
E. M. Forster: *The Longest Journey*
John Galsworthy: *The Country House*
Ford Madox Hueffer: *Privy Seal*
W. Somerset Maugham: *The Explorer*

VERSE AND DRAMA

Hilaire Belloc: *Cautionary Tales for Children*
Padraic Colum: *Wild Earth*
James Elroy Flecker: *The Bridge of Fire*
Wilfrid Gibson: *The Stonefolds*
Ralph Hodgson: *The Last Blackbird and Other Lines*
Ford Madox Hueffer: *From Inland and Other Poems* (selected by Edward Garnett)
James Joyce: *Chamber Music*

Laurence Binyon: *Attila*

G. B. Shaw: *Major Barbara* (produced 1905);
John Bull's Other Island (produced 1904);
How He Lied to Her Husband (produced
1904, New York)

John Millington Synge: *The Playboy of the
Western World* (produced 1907)

W. B. Yeats: *Deirdre* (produced 1906)

NON-FICTION

Max Beerbohm: *A Book of Caricatures*

Edmund Gosse: *Father and Son* (published
anonymously)

Ford Madox Hueffer: *The Spirit of the People;
The Pre-Raphaelite Brotherhood*

Edward Lear: *Letters* (edited by Lady Strachey)

Walter Raleigh: *Shakespeare*

Arthur Symons: *William Blake* (dedicated to
Auguste Rodin)

John Millington Synge: *The Aran Islands*

Queen Victoria: *Letters*

W. B. Yeats: *Discoveries* (Dun Emer Press)

❦❦ *"When your Daemon is in charge, do
not try to think consciously. Drift, wait,
and obey."*

RUDYARD KIPLING

United States

FICTION

James Branch Cabell: *Gallantry*

Joel Chandler Harris: *Uncle Remus and Brer
Rabbit*

O. Henry: *The Trimmed Lamp*

William Dean Howells: *Through the Eye of a
Needle; Between the Dark and the Daylight*

Henry James: *Novels and Tales* (New York
Edition, 24 vols.)

Mark Twain: *A Horse's Tale*

Edith Wharton: *Madame de Treymes; The Fruit
of the Tree*

VERSE AND DRAMA

Joaquin Miller: *Light: A Narrative Poem*

Sara Teasdale: *Sonnets to Duse and Other Poems*

NON-FICTION

Henry James: *The American Scene*

William James: *Pragmatism: A New Name for
Some Old Ways of Thinking*

Mark Twain: *Christian Science with Notes
Containing Corrections to Date*

Rudyard Kipling

Henry and William James

Max Beerbohm, as seen by Joseph Simpson

*John Millington Synge, as seen by
Jack B. Yeats, the poet's brother*

❦ ❦ *"Remember that every life is a special
problem, which is not yours but another's;
and content yourself with the terrible
algebra of your own."*

HENRY JAMES

Related Events

DEATHS

Joris Karl Huysmans, May 12
Edvard Grieg, September 4
Francis Thompson, November 13

IN OTHER LANGUAGES

Henri Bergson: *L'Évolution Créatrice*
Stefan George: *Der Siebente Ring* (The Seventh
   Ring)
Maxim Gorky: *Mat* (Mother)
Rainer Maria Rilke: *Neue Gedichte* (New
   Poems; second volume in 1908)

IN OTHER ARTS

Music: Maurice Ravel: *Histoires Naturelles*
   (based on prose poems by Jules Renard) ||
   Nikolai Rimski-Korsakov: *Le Coq d'Or*
   || Ralph Vaughan Williams: Whitman's
   "Toward the Unknown Region"

Stage: W. Somerset Maugham: *Lady Frederick* || August Strindberg: *Spöksonaten* (*The Ghost Sonata*) || John Millington Synge: *The Playboy of the Western World* || First *Ziegfeld Follies*

Painting: Pablo Picasso: *Les Demoiselles d'Avignon*

IN THE MARGIN

Rudyard Kipling, 42, becomes the youngest man ever to receive the Nobel Prize for Literature

The MacDowell Colony founded in Peterboro, New Hampshire, by Mrs. Edward MacDowell. "An artist in any field, with something really to say, can say and do more in the four months of quiet and seclusion it affords than in four years of hand to mouth uncertainty and constant interruption and unrest" (E. A. Robinson)

In March, **Thomas Hardy**, who had nearly abandoned *The Dynasts* after its poor critical reception in 1904, finishes the Third Part on Good Friday Eve, noting in his diary: "Critics can never be made to understand that the failure may be greater than the success . . . To have the strength to roll a stone weighing a hundredweight to the top of a mount is a success, and to have the strength to roll a stone of ten hundredweight only halfway up that mount is a failure. But the latter is two or three times as strong a deed"

In April, **Jack London** sets sail from San Francisco in his newly built 45-foot ketch *The Snark* on a projected seven-year cruise around the world; the expedition was abandoned in the Solomon Islands when London and his wife came down with malaria and skin ulcers

In June, **Theodore Dreiser**, 36, takes over the editorship of Butterick Publications, interlarding poetry with dress patterns and advice to the Jenny Wren Club

Pablo Picasso

Jack London

In September, **John Millington Synge** enters a Dublin hospital for his second operation on an "enlarged neck gland," the symptom of a malignancy that was to take his life a year later

On October 22, the Knickerbocker Trust Company in New York closes its doors, precipitating the panic of 1907 and, among other things, causing the failure of **Henry James's** lovingly revised, plum-colored, twenty-four-volume New York Edition of his novels.

In the Wings: **Ezra Pound,** 22 and an instructor in Spanish and French at Wabash College, in Crawfordsville, Indiana, is asked to resign after a girl from a burlesque show spends the night in his room. Early the following year, he leaves for Venice—"an excellent place to come to from Crawfordsville, Indiana"

Ford Madox Hueffer

Rainer Maria Rilke

1908

Great Britain

FICTION

Arnold Bennett: *Buried Alive; The Old Wives' Tale*

G. K. Chesterton: *The Man Who Was Thursday: A Nightmare*

Joseph Conrad: *A Set of Six*

E. M. Forster: *A Room with a View*

Kenneth Grahame: *The Wind in the Willows*

Ford Madox Hueffer: *Mr. Apollo; The Fifth Queen Crowned*

W. Somerset Maugham: *The Magician*

Arnold Bennett

NON-FICTION

Hilaire Belloc: *On Nothing*
G. K. Chesterton: *Orthodoxy*
W. H. Davies: *The Autobiography of a Super-Tramp* (Preface by G. B. Shaw)
W. H. Hudson: *The Land's End: A Naturalist's Impressions in West Cornwall*
Rudyard Kipling: *Letters to the Family: Notes on a Recent Trip to Canada* (essays and poems; Toronto)
Algernon Charles Swinburne: *The Age of Shakespeare*
Oscar Wilde: *Works* (14 volumes)

❧❧ *". . . happiness is a very difficult thing to do in art, and what novelists have put it across convincingly? It only arrives through music."*

E. M. FORSTER

VERSE AND DRAMA

Lascelles Abercrombie: *Interludes and Poems*
William Barnes: *Selected Poems* (edited by Thomas Hardy)
John Davidson: *The Testament of John Davidson*
Thomas Hardy: *The Dynasts, Third Part*
Lionel Johnson: *Selected Poems*
Algernon Charles Swinburne: *The Duke of Gandia*
Francis Thompson: *Selected Poems* (with a memoir by Wilfrid Meynell)
W. B. Yeats: *Collected Works in Verse and Prose*

John Millington Synge: *The Tinker's Wedding* (produced 1909, London)
W. B. Yeats and Lady Gregory: *The Unicorn from the Stars and Other Plays*

W. B. Yeats

William Dean Howells

Van Wyck Brooks: *The Wine of the Puritans: A Study of Present-Day America* (G.B.)
Henry James: *Views and Reviews*
H. L. Mencken: *The Philosophy of Friedrich Nietzsche*
Edith Wharton: *A Motor Flight Through France*

❧❧ *"It is well understood that 'all the truth' cannot be told in print . . . but how about 'nothing but the truth'?"*

O. HENRY

United States

FICTION

Ellen Glasgow: *The Ancient Law*
O. Henry: *Voice of the City; The Gentle Grafter*
William Dean Howells: *Fennell and Rue*
Jack London: *The Iron Heel*
Mary Roberts Rinehart: *The Circular Staircase*
Edith Wharton: *The Hermit and the Wild Woman, and Other Stories*

VERSE AND DRAMA

Ezra Pound: *A Lume Spento* (Venice); *A Quinzaine for This Yule* (G.B.)
George Cabot Lodge: *Herakles*

Ezra Pound

Related Events

DEATHS

January 8: Edmund Clarence Stedman, American poet and anthologist

January 23: Edward MacDowell, American composer

January 25: Ouida (Louise de la Ramée), British novelist

June 20: Nikolai Rimski-Korsakov, Russian composer

July 3: Joel Chandler Harris, American tale-teller

August 21: George Cabot Lodge, American poet

IN OTHER LANGUAGES

Colette: *Les Vrilles de la Vigne*
Anatole France: *L'Isle des Pingouins*
Friedrich Nietzsche: *Ecce Homo* (written 1888)

IN OTHER ARTS

Music: Maurice Ravel: *Rhapsodie Espagnole* ‖ Arnold Schoenberg: *Buch der Hängenden Gärten* (*Book of the Hanging Gardens*—to fifteen poems by Stefan George)

Stage: James Barrie: *What Every Woman Knows* ‖ W. Somerset Maugham, 34, has four plays running simultaneously on the London stage: *Mrs. Dot, The Explorer, Jack Straw,* as well as *Lady Frederick* from the previous year

Other: New York's "Ashcan School" has its first show ‖ George Herriman begins his *Krazy Kat* cartoon strip

IN THE MARGIN

Milestones: William Howard Taft is elected 27th President of the United States ‖ Penny post (called "two-cent postage" in America) is set up between Great Britain and the United States ‖ The First International Congress of Psychoanalysis is held in Salzburg, and attended by Freud, Brill, Adler, and Jung

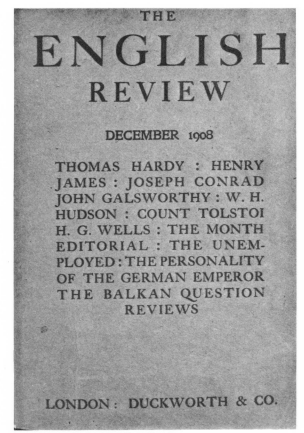

First issue of The English Review

Cartoon in Punch, January 24, 1908

La vie littéraire: T. E. Hulme founds his Wednesday night "Poetry Club" in London, with the credo "Never, never, never a simple statement. It has no effect. One must always have analogies, which make another world" || In New York, George H. Doran begins publishing under his own name || First issue (December) of *The English Review*, founded (according to Ford Madox Hueffer) to publish Thomas Hardy's poem "A Sunday Morning Tragedy"; originally financed by Hueffer and his friend Arthur Marwood, each putting up about £2500; and edited by Hueffer himself, with help from, among others, Joseph Conrad || G. B. Shaw sends £250 to the ill and financially desperate John Davidson to free him from hack work for six months so that he can write the "great poem" Shaw believed him capable of. Overwhelmed, Davidson resolved to repay Shaw by writing a money-making melodrama instead. "The result," wrote Shaw, "was disastrous. . . . He forgot that if he could not do this for himself, he could not do it for me. . . . He had thrown away his big chance; and instead of asking me for another £250, which I would have given him, he drowned himself"

In the Wings: Ring Lardner, 23, joins the staff of the Chicago *Tribune* and is assigned to cover the Cubs baseball team || Breaking himself in on a seventeen-volume edition of Thackeray, Charles Williams, 22, goes to work as a proofreader for the Oxford University Press, presently meeting Wilfrid and Alice Meynell, who subsidize his first book of poetry, *The Silver Stair* (1912)

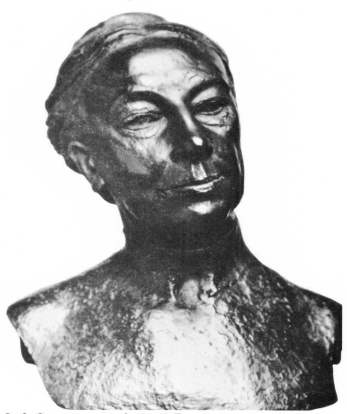

Lady Gregory, as seen by Jacob Epstein

Great Britain

FICTION

Hilaire Belloc: *A Change in the Cabinet*
R. B. Cunninghame Graham: *Faith*
John Galsworthy: *Fraternity*
Ford Madox Hueffer: *The "Half Moon"*
Rudyard Kipling: *Abaft the Funnel* (stories, letters, articles); *Actions and Reactions* (stories and poems)
George Meredith: *Collected Works* (Memorial Edition, 27 vols. through 1911)
Hugh Walpole: *The Wooden Horse*
H. G. Wells: *Ann Veronica; Tono Bungay*
P. G. Wodehouse: *Enter Psmith*

VERSE AND DRAMA

Matthew Arnold: *Poems, 1840–1867* (edited by Humphrey Mitford, with an Introduction by Arthur Quiller-Couch)
Laurence Binyon: *England and Other Poems*

Gertrude Stein, as seen by Pablo Picasso

John Davidson: *Fleet Street and Other Poems*
Thomas Hardy: *Time's Laughingstocks and Other Verses*
George Meredith: *Last Poems*
James Stephens: *Insurrections* (dedicated to Æ)
John Millington Synge: *Poems and Translations* (edited by W. B. Yeats; Cuala Press)

Lady Gregory: *Seven Short Plays*
G. B. Shaw: *The Admirable Bashville, or Constancy Unrewarded* (produced 1905)

NON-FICTION

Max Beerbohm: *Yet Again*
A. C. Bradley: *Oxford Lectures on Poetry*
Thomas and Jane Welsh Carlyle: *Love Letters* (edited by A. Carlyle)
G. K. Chesterton: *George Bernard Shaw; Tremendous Trifles*
Frank Harris: *The Man Shakespeare and His Tragic Life Story*

Algernon Charles Swinburne: *Three Plays of Shakespeare*
Francis Thompson: *Shelley*

❧❧ *"The real, if unavowed, purpose of fiction is to give pleasure by gratifying the love of the uncommon in human experience, mental or corporeal."*
THOMAS HARDY

United States

FICTION

James Branch Cabell: *Chivalry; The Cords of Vanity*
Ellen Glasgow: *The Romance of a Plain Man*
O. Henry: *Options; Roads of Destiny*
Henry James: *Julia Bride*
Jack London: *Martin Eden*
Frank Norris: *The Third Circle*
Gertrude Stein: *Three Lives: Stories of the Good Anna, Melanctha, and the Gentle Lena*
Mark Twain: *Extract from Captain Stormfield's Visit to Heaven*

VERSE AND DRAMA

Ezra Pound: *Personae* (G.B.); *Exultations of Ezra Pound* (G.B.)
Edith Wharton: *Artemis to Actaeon and Other Verses*
William Carlos Williams: *Poems* (privately printed)

NON-FICTION

Ambrose Bierce: *The Shadow on the Dial; Write It Right: A Little Blacklist of Literary Faults; Collected Works* (12 vols.)
Ralph Waldo Emerson: *Journals: 1820–1832* (10 volumes through 1914)
James Huneker: *Egotists: A Book of Supermen*

Henry James: *Italian Hours*
William James: *A Pluralistic Universe; The
    Meaning of Truth: A Sequel to "Pragmatism"*
Mark Twain: *Is Shakespeare Dead?*

❧❧ *"The normal process of life contains
moments as bad as any of those which
insane melancholy is filled with, moments
in which radical evil gets its innings and
takes its solid turn . . ."*

WILLIAM JAMES

André Gide

Virginia Stephen (Woolf)

Related Events

DEATHS

John Davidson: British poet and man-of-letters;
52; disappears on March 23 after leaving his house
to mail the manuscript of *Fleet Street*. A suicide
note was soon discovered, and his body was found
floating in Mousehole Bay, near Penzance,
Cornwall, six months later, on September 18.
"Except to the poet, the age of poetry is always
past."

John Millington Synge: Irish dramatist; 38; of
lymphatic sarcoma; in Dublin, on March 24. "The
drama, like the symphony, does not prove
anything. Analysts with their problems, and
teachers with their systems, are as old-fashioned
as the pharmacopaeia of Galen—look at Ibsen
and the Germans—but the best pages of Ben
Jonson and Molière can no more go out of fashion
than the blackberries on the hedges."

Algernon Charles Swinburne: British poet and man-of-letters; 72; of pneumonia, in Putney, London, on April 10. "He was the greatest of our lyric poets," said Meredith, who had also once described him as "a sea blown to storm by a sigh."

George Meredith: British novelist and poet; 81; of a chill contracted while out for his daily drive in a donkey cart; at Box Hill, on May 18. "It was characteristic of him," wrote Siegfried Sassoon, "that, a few hours before the action of his heart failed, he drank a bottle of beer and smoked a cigar."

Sarah Orne Jewett: American novelist and short-story writer; 60; after a cerebral hemorrhage, at her home in South Berwick, Maine, on June 24. "To work in silence and with all one's heart, that is the writer's lot . . ."

IN OTHER LANGUAGES

Charles Baudelaire: *Oeuvres Posthumes*
André Gide: *La Porte Étroite*
Gerhart Hauptmann: *Griselda*
Maurice Maeterlinck: *L'Oiseau Bleu*
Thomas Mann: *Königliche Hoheit* (*Royal Highness*)
Filippo Marinetti: *Manifeste du Futurisme*
First issue of the *Nouvelle Revue Française* (February)

IN OTHER ARTS

Music: Maurice Ravel: *Gaspard de la Nuit* || Arnold Schoenberg: *Drei Klavierstücke* (*Three Pieces for Pianoforte*) || Richard Strauss: *Elektra* || First season of the Diaghilev Ballet Russe in Paris

Stage: John Galsworthy: *Strife* || Thomas Hardy's *Far from the Madding Crowd* adapted for stage in Dorchester, with eight-year-old Maurice Evans making his debut in the cast || W. Somerset Maugham: *Smith; Penelope* || Ferenc Molnar: *Liliom*

Algernon Charles Swinburne

IN THE MARGIN

Milestones: U. S. Copyright Code is modified: books may now be copyrighted for 28 years plus an additional 28 years, if renewed || First practical portable typewriter || Admiral Peary reaches the North Pole

Faits Divers: A Civil List Pension of £100 enables Walter de la Mare to leave his job with Anglo-American Oil || Oscar Wilde's body is moved to Père Lachaise Cemetery in Paris, with Jacob Epstein's monument to mark his tomb || Under the management of James Joyce, four cinema houses open in Dublin and elsewhere during the week of Christmas || Sigmund Freud arrives in the U.S. for a lecture tour of New England and Canada, concluding at the end of his trip: "America is a mistake; a gigantic mistake, it's true, but none the less a mistake"

1910

George Meredith

In the Wings: Ronald Firbank, recently converted to the Roman Catholic Church, leaves Cambridge University without a degree ‖ Dressed entirely in black, Katherine Mansfield marries a singing teacher eleven years her senior, and abandons him the following morning ‖ As an anonymous contributor to *The Times Literary Supplement*, Virginia Stephen (Woolf) reviews, among other books of the year, *The Love Letters of Thomas Carlyle and Jane Welsh*, *The Cookery Book of Lady Clark of Tillypronie*, and *The Girlhood of Queen Elizabeth*, by Frank A. Mumby

Great Britain

FICTION

Arnold Bennett: *Clayhanger*
John Buchan: *Prester John* (U. S. title: *The Great Diamond Pipe*)
R. B. Cunninghame Graham: *Hope*
Walter de la Mare: *The Return; The Three Mulla-Mulgars* (later retitled *The Three Royal Monkeys*)
E. M. Forster: *Howards End*
Ford Madox Hueffer: *A Call; The Portrait*
Rudyard Kipling: *Rewards and Fairies* (stories and poems)
George Meredith: *Celt and Saxon* (unfinished)
H. G. Wells: *The History of Mr. Polly*
P. G. Wodehouse: *Psmith in the City*

VERSE AND DRAMA

Hilaire Belloc: *Verses*
James Elroy Flecker: *Thirty-Six Poems*
Ford Madox Hueffer: *Songs from London*
John Masefield: *Ballads and Poems*
Thomas Traherne: *Poems of Felicity*
W. B. Yeats: *The Green Helmet and Other Poems* (Cuala Press; trade edition 1912)
Andrew Young: *Songs of Night*

John Millington Synge: *Deirdre of the Sorrows* (produced 1910); *Collected Works*

NON-FICTION

Matthew Arnold: *Essays in Criticism: Third Series* (U.S.)
G. K. Chesterton: *William Blake; Alarms and Discursions*
W. H. Hudson: *A Shepherd's Life: Impressions of the South Wiltshire Downs*
William Morris: *Collected Works*

Bertrand Russell and Alfred North Whitehead: *Principia Mathematica* (3 volumes through 1913)

Mark Rutherford: *More Pages from a Journal with Other Papers*

Eleventh Edition of the Encyclopaedia Britannica

❧ ❧ *"Many of the older poets, such as Villon and Herrick and Burns, used the whole of their personal life as their material, and the verse written in this way was read by strong men, and thieves, and deacons, not by little cliques only."*

JOHN MILLINGTON SYNGE

United States

FICTION

O. Henry: *Strictly Business; Whirligigs*
Henry James: *The Finer Grain*
Sarah Orne Jewett: *Stories and Tales* (7 vols.)
Edith Wharton: *Tales of Men and Ghosts*

VERSE AND DRAMA

John A. Lomax, ed.: *Cowboy Songs and Other Frontier Ballads* (Prefatory Letter by Theodore Roosevelt)
Ezra Pound: *Provença* (selected from *Personae, Exultations,* and *Canzoniere*; first U.S. publication of Pound's poems)
E. A. Robinson: *The Town Down the River*

John Millington Synge

Sarah Orne Jewett

T. S. Eliot

Ezra Pound: *The Spirit of Romance: An Attempt to Define Somewhat the Charm of the Pre-Renaissance Literature of Latin Europe* (G.B.)

Mark Twain: *Mark Twain's Speeches* (Introduction by William Dean Howells)

❧ ❧ *"Even you won't tell the black heart's truth. The man who could do it would be famed to the last day the sun shone upon."*
WILLIAM DEAN HOWELLS, TO
MARK TWAIN

Related Events

DEATHS

Mark Twain (Samuel L. Clemens): American novelist, man-of-letters and lecturer; 75; of angina pectoris, in Redding, Connecticut, on April 21. "I am persuaded," G. B. Shaw had once written him, "that the future historian of America will find your works as indispensable to him as a French historian finds the political tracts of Voltaire."

Jules Renard: French diarist, short-story writer, and playwright; 46; of arteriosclerosis; in Paris, on May 22. *"Il y a les conteurs et les écrivains,"* he once wrote. *"On conte ce qu'on veut; on n'écrit pas ce qu'on veut: on n'écrit que soi-même . . ."*

Leo Tolstoi: Russian novelist, autobiographer, religious polemicist, and troubled landowner; 82; following a siege of bronchitis and a heart attack; in Astapovo, Russia, on November 20. A few days before, he had quarreled with his wife over a secret will in which he had tried to renounce his copyrights. "I will go somewhere," he had cried, "where no one can interfere with me."

NON-FICTION

Irving Babbitt: *The New Laokoön: An Essay on the Confusion of the Arts*

William Dean Howells: *My Mark Twain: Reminiscences and Criticisms*

James Huneker: *Promenades of an Impressionist*

Other Deaths:

O. Henry (William Sydney Porter), June 5
William James, August 26
Winslow Homer, September 30
William Vaughn Moody, October 17

IN OTHER LANGUAGES

Paul Claudel: *Cinq Grandes Odes*
Colette: *La Vagabonde*
Benedetto Croce: *Problemi de Estetica*
　　(*Aesthetics*)
Sigmund Freud: *Über Psychoanalyse* (*Five*
　　Lectures on Psychoanalysis)
André Gide: *Oscar Wilde*
Rainer Maria Rilke: *Die Aufzeichnungen des*
　　Malte Laurids Brigge (*The Notebooks of*
　　Malte Laurids Brigge)
Arnold Schoenberg: *Harmonielehre* (*Theory of*
　　Harmony)

IN OTHER ARTS

January 13: Première at the Abbey Theatre,
　　Dublin, of John Millington Synge's
　　posthumous drama, *Deirdre of the Sorrows*,
　　the acting text having been assembled, from
　　Synge's manuscripts, by Yeats, Lady Gregory,
　　and Molly Allgood, the actress who played
　　Deirdre and to whom Synge had been engaged
　　at the time of his death
June 25: Diaghilev's Ballet Russe presents first
　　production of Igor Stravinsky's *L'Oiseau de*
　　Feu, in Paris
December 10: Giacomo Puccini's *La Fanciulla*
　　del West, with a libretto based on David
　　Belasco's *The Girl of the Golden West*, sung
　　at the Metropolitan Opera House, in New
　　York

IN THE MARGIN

Laurels: The Order of Merit to Thomas Hardy ‖
　　Civil List Pensions to Yeats (£150) and
　　Conrad (£100)

Travels: On his way home after a year of
　　pediatrics in Leipzig, William Carlos Williams
　　visits Ezra Pound in London, finding him

Mark Twain

"very much in love with someone whose
picture he kept on his dresser, with a candle
perpetually lighted before it" ‖ Max
Beerbohm marries and settles for life in
Rapallo, Italy ‖ In America for the first
time, Somerset Maugham has dinner with
Henry James, who is spending the winter with
his recently widowed sister-in-law in
Cambridge. "I wander about these great empty
streets of Boston," declared the Master, "and
I never see a soul. I could not be more alone in
the Sahara"

Milestones: Upon the death of Edward VII on
　　May 6, George V becomes King of England

Leo Tolstoi

White Peacock, an advance copy of which he is able to put into his mother's hands before her death in December ‖ T. S. Eliot studying at the Sorbonne, attending lectures of Henri Bergson, and being tutored by Alain-Fournier ‖ Sinclair Lewis, 25, working as a ghost for Jack London: "I was very glad to receive your note suggesting that you are willing to look at some short story plots, etc. I am enclosing a big bunch, at the completion of which I've been working day AND night since hearing from you . . ." To which London replied: "Your plots came in last night, and I have promptly taken nine (9) of them, for which same, according to invoice, I am remitting you herewith check for $52.50" ‖ Aldous Huxley, 16, suffers an attack of *keratitis punctata* which leaves him almost totally blind for eighteen months, after which he is able to read "tolerably well" only with the aid of special glasses and the dilatant atropine

‖ Halley's Comet appears on schedule, 75 years after the birth of Mark Twain ‖ In December, the first English exhibition of postimpressionists is held at the Grafton Gallery, including Van Gogh, Cézanne, Matisse. Sizing up the show for *New Age*, Arnold Bennett concluded: ". . . supposing some young writer were to come along and do in words what these men have done in paint . . . I might have to begin again"

In the Wings: Willa Cather working as an editor for *McClure's Magazine* in New York ‖ D. H. Lawrence teaching near London and correcting the proofs of his first novel, *The*

1911

Great Britain

FICTION

Max Beerbohm: *Zuleika Dobson, or An Oxford Love Story*

Arnold Bennett: *Hilda Lessways; The Card* (U. S. title: *Denry the Audacious*)

G. K. Chesterton: *The Innocence of Father Brown*

Ivy Compton-Burnett: *Dolores*

Joseph Conrad: *Under Western Eyes*

E. M. Forster: *The Celestial Omnibus and Other Stories*

John Galsworthy: *The Patrician*

Ford Madox Hueffer: *Ladies Whose Bright Eyes*

D. H. Lawrence: *The White Peacock*

Compton Mackenzie: *The Passionate Elopement*

Max Beerbohm

Katherine Mansfield

Katherine Mansfield (Kathleen Mansfield
    Beauchamp): *In a German Pension*
Forrest Reid: *The Bracknels: A Family Chronicle*
Saki (H. H. Munro): *Chronicles of Clovis*
Hugh Walpole: *Mr. Perrin and Mr. Traill*
H. G. Wells: *The New Machiavelli*

VERSE AND DRAMA

Rupert Brooke: *Poems*
G. K. Chesterton: *The Ballad of the White
    Horse*
Digby Mackworth Dolben: *Poems* (edited, with a
    memoir, by Robert Bridges)
James Elroy Flecker: *Forty-Two Poems*
John Masefield: *The Everlasting Mercy*

G. B. Shaw: *The Doctor's Dilemma* (produced
    1906); *The Shewing-Up of Blanco Posnet*
    (produced 1909, Dublin); *Getting Married*
    (produced 1908)

NON-FICTION

Norman Douglas: *Siren Land* (revised 1923)
Ford Madox Hueffer: *The Critical Attitude;
    Ancient Lights* (U.S. title: *Memories and
    Impressions*)
Lionel Johnson: *Post Liminium*
George Moore: *Ave* (Vol. I of *Hail and
    Farewell*)
W. B. Yeats: *Synge and the Ireland of His Time*
    (Cuala Press)

❦ ❦ *"Life as we see it is so haphazard that
it is only by picking out its key situations
and arranging them in their significant
order (which is never how they actually
occur) that it can be made intelligible."*

G. B. SHAW

United States

FICTION

Theodore Dreiser: *Jennie Gerhardt*
Ellen Glasgow: *The Miller of Old Church*
O. Henry: *Sixes and Sevens*
Henry James: *The Outcry*
Edith Wharton: *Ethan Frome*

VERSE AND DRAMA

George Cabot Lodge: *Poems and Dramas*
   (Introduction by Theodore Roosevelt)
Ezra Pound: *Canzoni of Ezra Pound* (G.B.)
Sara Teasdale: *Helen of Troy and Other Poems*

William Vaughn Moody: *The Great Divide*
   (produced 1906)

NON-FICTION

Henry Adams: *The Life of George Cabot Lodge*
Lafcadio Hearn: *Leaves from the Diary of an
   Impressionist* (Introduction by Ferris
   Greenslet)
William James: *Memories and Studies* (edited by
   Henry James, Jr.)
Sarah Orne Jewett: *Letters* (edited by Anne
   Fields)
Jack London: *The Cruise of the Snark*

❦❦ *"We live in an age in which the
impact of materialized forces is well-nigh
irresistible; the spiritual nature is
overwhelmed by the shock."*
              THEODORE DREISER

Sara Teasdale

Theodore Dreiser

1911

Related Events

DEATHS

Gustav Mahler, Austrian composer and
conductor, on May 18
Sir William S. Gilbert, British poet and librettist,
on May 29
Joseph Pulitzer, American journalist, on October
29

IN OTHER LANGUAGES

Guillaume Apollinaire: *Le Bestiaire, ou Cortège
d'Orphée* (woodcuts by Raoul Dufy)
André Gide: *C.R.D.N.* (published anonymously
in Bruges: first edition of what was later called
Corydon)
Saint-John Perse (Alexis Saint-Léger Léger):
Éloges

IN OTHER ARTS

Irving Berlin: *Alexander's Ragtime Band*
W. C. Handy: *Memphis Blues*
Maurice Ravel: *L'Heure Espagnole*; *Valses
Nobles et Sentimentales*
Richard Strauss: *Der Rosenkavalier*
Igor Stravinsky: *Petrouchka*

IN THE MARGIN

Geographical: Lady Gregory and Yeats take the
Abbey Theatre on a tour of America, in the
course of which the cast of *The Playboy of the
Western World* is (a) potatoed by Irish
"patriots" in New York, (b) arrested under
the McNichol Act (covering "lascivious,
sacrilegious, obscene or indecent plays") in
Philadelphia, and (c) almost banned by the
City Council in Chicago ‖ Ronald Firbank
sees the Nile for the first time: "I daresay,
dear, you can't judge of Egypt by *Aida* . . ."
‖ Claiming that he had obtained a German
divorce, Ford Madox Hueffer goes to Belgium
with Violet Hunt, where he introduces her to
the press as the second Mrs. Hueffer. As a
result, the first—and only—Mrs. Hueffer filed
suit against the *Daily Mail* in London,
provoking a scandal which seriously affected
Hueffer's literary as well as personal reputation.
Very soon, for instance, he found himself not
only on Henry James's blacklist, but alienated
from the Conrads and the Garnetts, cut out of
the will of a wealthy aunt, and forced to claim
bankruptcy ‖ A. E. Housman appointed to
the Chair of Latin at Trinity College,
Cambridge, which he holds for the remaining
25 years of his life ‖ Returning from
Europe, Marianne Moore begins teaching at
the U. S. Indian School in Carlisle,
Pennsylvania

Historical: The Nobel Prize for Literature is
awarded to Belgian Maurice Maeterlinck ‖
On June 22, King George V and Queen Mary
are crowned at Westminster Abbey ‖ On
December 14, Captain Roald Amundsen
reaches the South Pole

Robert Bridges

1912

Great Britain

FICTION

Arnold Bennett: *The Matador of the Five Towns*
Daniel Chaucer (Ford Madox Hueffer): *The New Humpty-Dumpty*
G. K. Chesterton: *Manalive*
Joseph Conrad: *'Twixt Land and Sea: Tales*
R. B. Cunninghame Graham: *Charity*
Thomas Hardy: *The Wessex Novels* (revised text: through 1931)
D. H. Lawrence: *The Trespasser*
Compton Mackenzie: *Carnival*
Forrest Reid: *Following Darkness* (dedicated to E. M. Forster; revised in 1937 as *Peter Waring*)
Saki: *The Unbearable Bassington*
James Stephens: *The Crock of Gold*

Constance Garnett: translation of Dostoevsky's *The Brothers Karamazov*, first of 13 volumes (through 1920) comprising all of Dostoevsky's fiction.

Walter de la Mare

VERSE AND DRAMA

Robert Bridges: *Later Poems and Poems in Classical Prosody*
Walter de la Mare: *The Listeners and Other Poems*
Ford Madox Hueffer: *High Germany*
Edward Marsh, ed.: *Georgian Poetry 1911–12* (published by Harold Monro at his Poetry Bookshop; four more volumes through 1922)
George Meredith: *Poetical Works* (edited by G. M. Trevelyan)
Isaac Rosenberg: *Night and Day* (published at the author's expense)
Charles Williams: *The Silver Stair*

Rabindranath Tagore: his own translation into English of his *Gitanjali* (Introduction by W. B. Yeats)

NON-FICTION

Max Beerbohm: *A Christmas Garland*
Hilaire Belloc: *The Servile State*
Samuel Butler: *Note-Books* (edited by Henry Festing Jones)
Joseph Conrad: *Some Reminiscences* (U. S. title: *A Personal Record*)
Norman Douglas: *Fountains in the Sand*
George Meredith: *Letters* (edited by W. M. Meredith)
George Moore: *Salve* (Vol. II of *Hail and Farewell*)
George Saintsbury: *History of English Prose Rhythm*

1912

Lytton Strachey: *Landmarks of French Literature*
H. L. Tomlinson: *The Sea and the Jungle*
W. B. Yeats: *The Cutting of an Agate*

❧❧ *"An Author with a grievance is of all God's creatures the most tedious."*
MAX BEERBOHM

Virginia and Leonard Woolf

United States

FICTION

Edgar Rice Burroughs: *Tarzan of the Apes* (serial; book 1914)
Willa Cather: *Alexander's Bridge*
Theodore Dreiser: *The Financier*
Tom Graham (Sinclair Lewis): *Hike and the Aeroplane*
Zane Grey: *Riders of the Purple Sage*
O. Henry: *Rolling Stones*
Edith Wharton: *The Reef*

VERSE AND DRAMA

Robinson Jeffers: *Flagons and Apples* (published at the author's expense)
Vachel Lindsay: *Rhymes to Be Traded for Bread* (privately printed)
Amy Lowell: *A Dome of Many-Colored Glass*
William Vaughn Moody: *Poems and Plays* (edited by John M. Manly)
Ezra Pound: *Ripostes: Whereto Are Appended the Complete Poetical Works of T. E. Hulme* (dedicated to William Carlos Williams; G.B.)

Ezra Pound: translation of *The Sonnets and Ballads of Guido Cavalcanti*

NON-FICTION

William James: *Essays in Radical Empiricism* (edited by Ralph Barton Perry)

Tarzan's debut in All-Story Magazine (book published in 1914)

Rebecca West

Related Events

August Strindberg: Swedish dramatist and poet; 63; of cancer, in Stockholm, on May 14

❧ ❧ *"Pay no attention to the criticisms of men who have never themselves written a notable work."*

EZRA POUND

Gottfried Benn: *Morgue*
Paul Claudel: *L'Annonce Faite à Marie*
Sigmund Freud: *Totem und Tabu* (*Totem and Taboo*)
Hugo von Hofmannsthal: *Ariadne auf Naxos* (*Ariadne on Naxos*)

Carl Jung: *Wandlungen und Symbole der Libido* (*Psychology of the Unconscious*)

IN OTHER ARTS

Maurice Ravel: *Daphnis et Chloé* (Paris, June 18)

Arnold Schoenberg: *Pierrot Lunaire* (Berlin, October 16)

IN THE MARGIN

Magazines, Little and Otherwise: First issue (October) of *Poetry: A Magazine of Verse,* edited in Chicago by Harriet Monroe and Alice Corbin Henderson || First issue (January) of *The Poetry Review,* edited in London by Harold Monro || In October, Norman Douglas becomes assistant editor of *The English Review,* serving until April, 1916 || Cicily Isabel Fairchild, 20, begins writing under the pen name Rebecca West, contributing 44 articles and reviews to the *New Freewoman* and the *Clarion* between February and December || Edna St. Vincent Millay, a teen-age contributor to the *St. Nicholas Magazine* from 1906 to 1910, makes her adult debut at 20 with a poem, "Renascence," in the poetry contest anthology *The Lyric Year*

To Have and to Hold: On April 11, Katherine Mansfield, 24, and John Middleton Murry begin to share quarters at 69 Clovelly Mansions || On May 3, D. H. Lawrence, 27, elopes with Mrs. Frieda von Richthofen Weekley, staying at Metz, Germany, where local authorities arrest Lawrence as a spy || On August 10, Virginia Stephen, 30, marries Leonard Woolf at the St. Pancras Register office, "in a room which, in those days, looked down into a cemetery . . ."

Milestones: Woodrow Wilson elected 28th President of the United States || The Nobel Prize for Literature awarded to German dramatist and novelist Gerhart Hauptmann,

aged 50 || After striking an iceberg the night of April 14, the S. S. *Titantic* sinks off Newfoundland on her maiden voyage from Southampton to New York. Theodore Dreiser was almost among the passengers but, for economy's sake, took another ship instead. Henry Adams, who had actually booked passage for the return trip, suffered a stroke ten days after the disaster

Another Part of the Forest: Sherwood Anderson, 36 and head of his own mail-order paint firm in Elyria, Ohio, suffers a nervous breakdown on November 27 || E. M. Forster, 43, visits India for the first time || Robert Frost, 37, moves with his family to Buckinghamshire, England, "within a mile or two of where Milton finished *Paradise Lost* . . . a mile or two of where Gray lies buried . . . and within as many rods as furlongs of the house where Chesterton tries truth to see if it won't prove as true upside down as it does right side up"

D. H. Lawrence

1913

Great Britain

FICTION

E. C. Bentley: *Trent's Last Case*

John Galsworthy: *The Dark Flower*

Thomas Hardy: *A Changed Man and Other Tales*

Ford Madox Hueffer: *The Young Lovell*

Rudyard Kipling: *Collected Works* (Bombay Edition, 31 vols. through 1938)

D. H. Lawrence: *Sons and Lovers* (dedicated to Edward Garnett)

Compton Mackenzie: *Sinister Street* (Vol. I)

Forrest Reid: *The Gentle Lover: A Comedy of Middle Age*

Hugh Walpole: *Fortitude*

Compton Mackenzie

VERSE AND DRAMA

Æ: *Collected Poems*

Walter de la Mare: *Peacock Pie*

James Elroy Flecker: *The Golden Journey to Samarkand*

Ford Madox Hueffer: *Collected Poems*

D. H. Lawrence: *Love Poems and Others*

Alice Meynell: *Collected Poems*

Francis Thompson: *Works* (edited by Wilfrid Meynell)

NON-FICTION

G. K. Chesterton: *The Victorian Age in Literature*

W. H. Hudson: *Adventures Among Birds*

Ford Madox Hueffer and Violet Hunt: *The Desirable Alien*

Mark Rutherford: *The Early Life of Mark Rutherford by Himself*

Algernon Charles Swinburne: *Charles Dickens*

❦❦ *". . . all rules of construction hold good only for novels which are copies of other novels. A book which is not a copy of other books has its own construction . . ."*

D. H. LAWRENCE

United States

FICTION

Willa Cather: *O Pioneers!* (dedicated to Sarah Orne Jewett)

Ellen Glasgow: *Virginia*

William Dean Howells: *New Leaf Mills*

Jack London: *John Barleycorn*

Eleanor Hodgman Porter: *Pollyanna*

Edith Wharton: *The Custom of the Country*

VERSE AND DRAMA

William Rose Benét: *Merchants from Cathay*
Paul Laurence Dunbar: *Complete Poems*
John Gould Fletcher: *The Dominant City*
    (G.B.)
Robert Frost: *A Boy's Will* (G.B.)
Vachel Lindsay: *General William Booth Enters*
    into Heaven and Other Poems
William Carlos Williams: *The Tempers*
    (Introductory Note by Ezra Pound)

NON-FICTION

Brooks Adams: *The Theory of Social Revolutions*
Henry Adams: *Mont-Saint-Michel and Chartres*
    (trade edition)
Randolph Bourne: *Youth and Life*
Van Wyck Brooks: *The Malady of the Ideal:*
    Obermann, Maurice de Guérin, and Amiel
    (G.B.)
Theodore Dreiser: *A Traveller at Forty*
Henry James: *A Small Boy and Others*
George Santayana: *Winds of Doctrine: Studies*
    in Contemporary Opinion

❧ ❧ *"I give you a new definition of a*
sentence: A sentence is a sound in itself
on which other sounds called words may
be strung."

ROBERT FROST

Robert Frost

William Carlos Williams

Related Events

DEATHS

Ambrose Bierce: American short-story writer and journalist; 71. It remains uncertain to this day just when or where or how Bierce died. He was traveling as an observer with Pancho Villa's army in Mexico when a letter to his secretary, dated December 26, said he would proceed from Chihuahua to Ojinaga. Ojinaga was besieged the following week. Bierce was never heard from again.

Other Deaths:
Baron Corvo (Frederick William Rolfe), October 26
Joaquin Miller (Cincinnatus Hiner Miller), February 17
Mark Rutherford (William Hale White), March 14

Igor Stravinsky

IN OTHER LANGUAGES

Alain-Fournier (Henri Fournier): *Le Grand Meaulnes*
Guillaume Apollinaire: *Alcools. Poèmes 1898–1913*
Maxim Gorky: *Detstvo (My Childhood)*
Thomas Mann: *Der Tod in Venedig (Death in Venice)*
Marcel Proust: *Du coté de chez Swann*
Miguel Unamuno: *Del Sentimiento Trágico de la Vida (The Tragic Sense of Life)*

IN OTHER ARTS

Music: Manuel de Falla's opera *La Vida Breve (The Short Life)* (written 1904–5) is produced in Nice ‖ Maurice Ravel finishes his *Trois Poèmes de Stéphane Mallarmé* ‖ Arnold Schoenberg's *Gurre-Lieder* sung in Vienna ‖ Igor Stravinsky's ballet, *Le Sacre du Printemps*, with choreography by Nijinsky, provokes a riot at its première in Paris. Gertrude Stein attends the second performance

Theater: Professor George Pierce Baker begins his "47 Workshop" in play-writing and production at Harvard ‖ G. B. Shaw's *Pygmalion* is given its world première in Vienna

Other: Charles Chaplin shooting his first film, *Making a Living* ‖ Marcel Duchamp's *Nude Descending a Staircase* is shown at the Armory in New York

IN THE MARGIN

Laurels: The Nobel Prize for Literature awarded to Rabindranath Tagore ‖ Robert Bridges appointed Poet Laureate to succeed Alfred Austin

Turning Points: Edith Wharton divorces her husband, a move which even Henry James regarded as "the only thing to save her life." Besides alcohol and fiscal mismanagement, Mr. Wharton was also prone to showing off his gold garters in public ‖ Having "written rather desultorily a number of books—a great number, but all in the nature of *pastiches*," Ford Madox Hueffer sits down on December 17, his 40th birthday, "to show what I can do," and begins writing *The Good Soldier* ‖ Richard Aldington, 21, marries Hilda Doolittle, 27

Magazines: In April, the *New Statesman* is founded by G. B. Shaw, Sidney and Beatrice Webb, and others, with Clifford Sharp as editor ‖ In May, the *Blue Review* is founded by John Middleton Murry and Katherine Mansfield, lasting until July

La vie littéraire: Joseph Conrad, 56, firmly lays down the law to a young Doubleday editor named Alfred A. Knopf, who had proposed becoming his American publisher: "There are two methods in the publishing business. The first is speculative. A book is a venture. Hit or miss. To a certain extent it must be so. But here and there a writer may be taken up as an investment. An investment must be attended to, it must be nursed—if one believes in it. I can't develope much feeling for a publisher who takes me on the 'hit or miss' basis. A gamble is not a connection. What position I have attained I owe to no publisher's efforts. Sixteen years of hard work begin to tell. The question for me is: Has the Doubleday, Page Co. simply bought two books of mine or is it to be a connection?" ‖ In San Francisco, about to embark for Samoa and Tahiti, Rupert Brooke reflects on America: "Everywhere in this extraordinary country, I am welcomed with open arms when I say I know Masefield! . . . Their wide-mouthed awe at England is so touching—they really are merely a colony of ours still. That they should be speaking to a man who knows Lowes Dickinson, who has met Galsworthy, who once saw Belloc plain!"

In the Wings: Having finished her first novel in February, Virginia Woolf, 31, succumbs in September to an attack diagnosed as neurasthenia. "Her mental breakdown," wrote her husband, "lasted in an acute form from the summer of 1913 to the autumn of 1915, but it was not absolutely continuous . . ." ‖ Unknown to each other, T. S. Eliot, a graduate student, and e. e. cummings, a sophomore, appear in a Harvard production of *Fanny and the Servant Problem.* Eliot had the role of Lord Bantock; cummings played his second footman ‖ "Eager for any sort of adventure," Joyce Cary serves as a cook in the Montenegrin Army in the First Balkan War, receiving a gold medal for his participation in the final campaign

In the Great World: Federal Income Tax Amendment becomes law in the U. S.

Charles Chaplin

1914

Great Britain

FICTION

G. K. Chesterton: *The Wisdom of Father Brown; The Flying Inn*
Joseph Conrad: *Chance: A Tale in Two Parts*
James Joyce: *Dubliners*

James Joyce and his son Giorgio in Trieste

D. H. Lawrence: *The Prussian Officer and Other Stories*
Compton Mackenzie: *Sinister Street* (Vol. II)

VERSE AND DRAMA

Robert Bridges: *Poems Written in 1913*
Thomas Hardy: *Satires of Circumstance*
W. B. Yeats: *Responsibilities* (Cuala Press; trade edition 1916)

D. H. Lawrence: *The Widowing of Mrs. Holroyd*
G. B. Shaw: *Misalliance* (produced 1910); *The Dark Lady of the Sonnets* (produced 1910); *Fanny's First Play* (produced 1911)

NON-FICTION

Clive Bell: *Art*
Havelock Ellis: *Impressions and Comments*
Lady Gregory: *Our Irish Theatre: A Chapter of Autobiography*
Ford Madox Hueffer: *Henry James*
George Moore: *Vale* (Vol. III of *Hail and Farewell*)

❦❦ *". . . A literary movement consists of five or six people who live in the same town and hate each other cordially."*
GEORGE MOORE

Gertrude Stein and her friend Alice B. Toklas in Venice

United States

FICTION

Theodore Dreiser: *The Titan*
Sinclair Lewis: *Our Mr. Wrenn*
Frank Norris: *Vandover and the Brute* (edited
    by Charles Norris, who discovered the
    manuscript in a trunk which had survived the
    San Francisco fire)
Booth Tarkington: *Penrod*

VERSE AND DRAMA

Conrad Aiken: *Earth Triumphant and Other
    Tales in Verse*
Emily Dickinson: *The Single Hound: Poems of a
    Lifetime* (edited by Martha D. Bianchi)
Robert Frost: *North of Boston* (G.B.)
Vachel Lindsay: *The Congo and Other Poems*
Amy Lowell: *Sword Blades and Poppy Seeds*
James Oppenheim: *Songs for the New Age*
Ezra Pound, ed.: *Des Imagistes: An Anthology*
    (fifth number of *The Glebe*)
Gertrude Stein: *Tender Buttons: Objects, Food,
    Rooms*

E. A. Robinson: *Van Zorn: A Comedy in Three
    Acts*

NON-FICTION

Van Wyck Brooks: *John Addington Symonds: A
    Biographical Study*
Lafcadio Hearn: *Fantastics and Other Fancies*
    (edited by Charles W. Hutson)
Henry James: *Notes on Novelists; Notes of a Son
    and Brother*
Vachel Lindsay: *Adventures While Preaching the
    Gospel of Beauty*

❧ ❧ *"It takes a lot of time to be a genius,
you have to sit around so much doing
nothing."*

GERTRUDE STEIN

Related Events

DEATHS

Adelaide Crapsey: American poet; 38; of
    tuberculosis, at Saranac Lake, New York; on
    October 8
Charles Péguy: French poet; 41; killed in action
    at Villeroy, France, on September 5
Alain-Fournier (Henri Fournier): French
    novelist; 28; killed in action at Eparges, France,
    on September 22

IN OTHER LANGUAGES

Anatole France: *La Révolte des Anges*
Stefan George: *Der Stern des Bundes* (*The Star
    of the Covenant*)

Thomas and the second Mrs. Hardy

André Gide: *Les Caves du Vatican* (published anonymously)

May 26: Igor Stravinsky's opera, *Le Rossignol*
September 14: W. C. Handy's *St. Louis Blues*
November: Granville-Barker's stage production of Thomas Hardy's *The Dynasts*, adapted by Hardy himself, with a special Prologue and Epilogue

Just Married: February: Thomas Hardy, 74, for the second time, to his secretary, Miss Florence Dugdale || April: Ezra Pound, 32, to Miss Dorothy Shakespear || July: D. H. Lawrence, 29, to Mrs. Frieda von Richthofen Weekley, in Kensington, with Katherine Mansfield, John Middleton Murry, and Gordon Campbell as witnesses. After the ceremony, Frieda presented Katherine with the ring from her first marriage, which Miss Mansfield wore for the rest of her life

In Uniform and Out: Aged 19, Robert Graves begins training with the Royal Welch Fusiliers, following his graduation from Charterhouse || Traveling in Austria, Joseph Conrad and his family are almost interned when war breaks out in August, but manage to escape by way of Italy || In November, G. B. Shaw publishes a pamphlet, *Common Sense About the War*, in which he proposes that soldiers of all armies shoot their officers and go home, provoking H. G. Wells to call him "an idiot child screaming in a hospital" || Attached to a Red Cross ambulance unit in France, Somerset Maugham, 37, meets Gerald Haxton, an American who becomes his traveling companion and co-resident until Haxton's death 30 years later in Washington, D.C.

Magazines: January: first issue of *The Egoist: an individualist review*, edited by Dora Marsden and (after July) by Harriet Shaw Weaver. In

Wyndham Lewis

its second issue, James Joyce's novel, *A Portrait of the Artist as a Young Man*, begins to appear serially, continuing until September 1915 || March: first issue of *The Little Review*, edited by Margaret C. Anderson (with Jane Heap after 1922) || June: first issue of *Blast: review of the great English vortex*, edited by Wyndham Lewis (second and final issue in July 1915) || November 7: first issue of *The New Republic* || December: H. L. Mencken and George Jean Nathan become co-editors of *The Smart Set*

Faits Divers: In London, John Singer Sargent's portrait of Henry James, hanging in the Royal Academy, is mutilated by a suffragette on the first day of its exhibition || In Chicago, while defending the local Waitresses' Union against a strike injunction, lawyer Edgar Lee Masters, 45, begins writing four to ten poems a week of the *Spoon River Anthology*, and publishing them serially under the pseudonym Webster Ford to protect his legal reputation ‖ In Brookline, Massachusetts, Amy Lowell sagely lays in a supply of 10,000 of her favorite Manila cigars against a possible wartime shortage

In the Great World: In June, the Archduke Ferdinand, heir to the Austrian throne, is assassinated at Sarajevo ‖ On July 28, Germany declares war on Russia, and on August 3, on France. The next day, August 4, Great Britain declares war on Germany

1915

Ford Madox Hueffer

Great Britain

FICTION

Arnold Bennett: *These Twain*
John Buchan: *The Thirty-Nine Steps*
Joseph Conrad: *Victory: An Island Tale; Within the Tides: Tales*
Arthur Conan Doyle: *The Valley of Fear*
Ronald Firbank: *Vainglory*
Ford Madox Hueffer: *The Good Soldier*
D. H. Lawrence: *The Rainbow* (expurgated edition in U.S., 1916)
Compton Mackenzie: *Guy and Pauline*
W. Somerset Maugham: *Of Human Bondage*
Forrest Reid: *At the Door of the Gate* (dedicated to Walter de la Mare)
Dorothy Richardson: *Pointed Roofs* (Vol. I of *Pilgrimage:* 11 successive volumes through 1938)
Virginia Woolf: *The Voyage Out*

VERSE AND DRAMA

Richard Aldington: *Images* (1910–1915)
Rupert Brooke: *1914 and Other Poems*
G. K. Chesterton: *Poems*
Ford Madox Hueffer: *Antwerp*
Lionel Johnson: *Poetical Works* (Preface by Ezra Pound)
Isaac Rosenberg: *Youth* (published at author's expense)
Edith Sitwell: *The Mother and Other Poems*

Richard Aldington: translation of *Latin Poems of the Renaissance*

NON-FICTION

Norman Douglas: *Old Calabria*
John Masefield: *John M. Synge: A Few Personal Recollections with Biographical Notes* (Cuala Press)
Forrest Reid: *W. B. Yeats: A Critical Study*
Mark Rutherford: *Last Pages from a Journal with Other Papers*

W. Somerset Maugham

Edgar Lee Masters

H. G. Wells: *Boon, The Mind of the Race, The Wild Asses of the Devil, and the Last Trump*

W. B. Yeats: *Reveries Over Childhood and Youth* (Cuala Press; trade edition 1916)

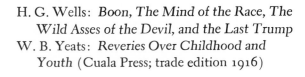 *"A painstaking woman who wishes to treat of life as she finds it, and to give voice to some of the perplexities of her sex, in plain English, has no chance at all."*

VIRGINIA WOOLF

United States

FICTION

James Branch Cabell: *The Rivet in Grandfather's Neck*

Willa Cather: *The Song of the Lark*

Theodore Dreiser: *The "Genius"*

Sinclair Lewis: *The Trail of the Hawk*

Harry Leon Wilson: *Ruggles of Red Gap*

VERSE AND DRAMA

Djuna Barnes: *The Book of Repulsive Women* (published by Bruno Guido as a 15¢ chapbook)

Adelaide Crapsey: *Verse* (reprinted in 1922 and 1934 with additional poems)

John Gould Fletcher: *Irradiations—Sand and Spray*

Alfred Kreymborg: *Mushrooms: Sixteen Rhythms*

Rupert Brooke

Henry James

Ring Lardner: *Bib Ballads*
Amy Lowell, ed.: *Some Imagist Poets* (also 1916, 1917)
Edgar Lee Masters: *Spoon River Anthology*
Ezra Pound, ed.: *Catholic Anthology 1914–15*
Sara Teasdale: *Rivers to the Sea*

E. A. Robinson: *The Porcupine: A Drama in Three Acts*

Ezra Pound: *Cathay—Translations for the most part from the Chinese of Rihaku, from the notes of the late Ernest Fenollosa, and the decipherings of the Professors Mori and Ariga.*

NON-FICTION

Van Wyck Brooks: *America's Coming of Age*
Lafcadio Hearn: *Interpretations of Literature* (edited by John Erskine)
James Huneker: *Ivory, Apes and Peacocks*

Vachel Lindsay: *The Art of the Moving Picture*
Amy Lowell: *Six French Poets*
Edith Wharton: *Fighting France: From Dunkerque to Belfort*

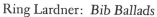 *". . . every great story . . . must leave in the mind of the sensitive reader an intangible residuum of pleasure; a cadence, a quality of voice that is exclusively the writer's own, individual, unique."*

WILLA CATHER

Amy Lowell

Related Events

DEATHS

Rupert Brooke: British poet and man-of-letters; 27; aboard the French hospital ship *Duguay-Trouin*, in Trebuki Bay, on Skyros, on April 23. Cause of death listed as "*oedème malin et septicémie foudroyante*," the blood poisoning resulting from an infected mosquito bite aggravated by sunstroke. Brooke was buried on Skyros. In a letter left to be opened after his death, he gave the capital from his allowance as well as his royalties to three poets: Wilfrid Gibson, 37; Lascelles Abercrombie, 34; and Walter de la Mare, 42, adding: "If I can set them free, to any extent, to write the poetry and plays and books they want to, my death will bring more gain than loss."

Other Deaths:

Anthony Comstock, American citizen and Secretary of the Society for the Suppression of Vice, who claimed to have been responsible for the destruction of over 160 tons of "obscene" literature; on September 21

James Elroy Flecker, British poet and career diplomat; age 31; of tuberculosis, at Davos Platz, Switzerland, on January 3

Rémy de Gourmont, French man-of-letters and novelist; age 57; of a cerebral hemorrhage, in Paris, on September 27

Alexander Scriabin, Russian composer; age 43; in Moscow, on April 15

IN OTHER ARTS

Stage: Sarah Bernhardt has her right leg amputated at the thigh

Music: Manuel de Falla: *El Amor Brujo* || Maurice Ravel: *Trio*

Films: David Wark Griffith: *Birth of a Nation*

IN THE MARGIN

James Joyce leaves Trieste in June and settles with his family in Zurich. Ezra Pound gives him an anonymous £25, and, with Yeats's help, secures him the grant of an additional £75 from the Royal Literary Fund.

In Paris, **Edith Wharton** serves as a fund raiser and directress for the Accueil Franco-Belge, gathering contributions from Stravinsky, Beerbohm, Renoir, Rodin, Monet, James, Conrad, Cocteau, and Yeats, among others, for the *Book of the Homeless.*

E. M. Forster (as of November) enlists as a volunteer with the International Red Cross in Egypt, stationed in a suburb of Alexandria, and presently becomes acquainted with Constantin Cavafy and his poetry.

Romain Rolland receives the Nobel Prize for Literature.

Prosecutions of "obscene" literature are facilitated in England by a new Indictments Act which no longer requires that the intent of an accused author necessarily be "to poison the minds of divers of the liege subjects of our said Lord the King, and to raise and create in them lustful desires, and to bring the said liege subjects into a state of wickedness, lewdness, and debauchery . . ."

D. H. Lawrence's fourth novel, *The Rainbow*, is declared obscene, the publisher Methuen is fined, and all existing copies of the book are ordered destroyed.

The S.S. *Lusitania* is torpedoed and sunk by a German U-boat within sight of the coast of Ireland on May 7.

With a capital of $3,000, **Alfred A. Knopf** and **Blanche Wolf** inaugurate their publishing house.

Alfred Kreymborg edits the first issue (July) of *Others: a magazine of the new verse*, with Marianne Moore, Conrad Aiken, Wallace Stevens, T. S. Eliot, and Ezra Pound among the contributors.

Henry James: The Master's Voice:

On July 10, in response to an irreverent attack by H. G. Wells (who, in a book called *Boon*, had compared James's prose "to a magnificent but painful hippopotamus resolved at any cost . . . upon picking up a pea") : "It is art that *makes* life, makes interest, makes importance, for our consideration and application of these things, and I know of no substitute whatever for the force and beauty of its process . . ."

On July 26, after taking the Oath of Allegiance to the country in which he had made his home for over 35 years: "Since 4:30 this afternoon, I have been able to say *Civis Britannicus sum!*"

On the morning of December 2, upon suffering a stroke and in expectation of his imminent death: "So this is it at last, the distinguished thing!"

Ronald Firbank

1916

Great Britain

FICTION

John Buchan: *Greenmantle*
Ronald Firbank: *Inclinations*
James Joyce: *A Portrait of the Artist as a Young Man* (U.S.; G.B. 1917)
George Moore: *The Brook Kerith: A Syrian Story*
Forrest Reid: *The Spring Song*
Dorothy Richardson: *Backwater*
H. G. Wells: *Mr. Britling Sees It Through*

Constance Garnett: translation of Anton Chekhov's stories, plays, and letters (through 1926)

VERSE AND DRAMA

Robert Bridges, ed.: *The Spirit of Man*
James Elroy Flecker: *Collected Poems* (edited by J. C. Squire)
Robert Graves: *Over the Brazier*
Aldous Huxley: *The Burning Wheel*
D. H. Lawrence: *Amores*
Charlotte Mew: *The Farmer's Bride* (U. S. title: *Saturday Market*)
Edith Sitwell, ed.: *Wheels: An Anthology of Verse*
Edith and Osbert Sitwell: *Twentieth Century Harlequinade and Other Poems*

G. B. Shaw: *Androcles and the Lion* (produced 1913); *Overruled* (produced 1912); *Pygmalion* (produced 1913, Vienna)

NON-FICTION

Rupert Brooke: *Letters From America* (Preface by Henry James); *John Webster and the Elizabethan Drama*
Norman Douglas: *London Street Games*
D. H. Lawrence: *Twilight in Italy*
Rebecca West (Cicily Isabel Fairfield): *Henry James*

❦ ❦ *"Every man who would tell of reality does it at his personal cost amidst a chorus of abuse."*

H. G. WELLS

United States

FICTION

Sherwood Anderson: *Windy McPherson's Son*
Ellen Glasgow: *Life and Gabriella*
William Dean Howells: *The Leatherwood God*
Ring Lardner: *You Know Me, Al*
Booth Tarkington: *Seventeen*

Mark Twain: *The Mysterious Stranger: A Romance*
Edith Wharton: *Xingu and Other Stories*

VERSE AND DRAMA

Conrad Aiken: *Turns and Movies and Other Tales in Verse; The Jig of Forslin: A Symphony; Nocturne of Remembered Spring and Other Poems* (G.B.)
H. D. (Hilda Doolittle): *Sea Garden*
John Gould Fletcher: *Goblins and Pagodas*
Robert Frost: *Mountain Interval*
Edgar Guest: *A Heap o' Livin'*
Robinson Jeffers: *Californians*
Sarah Orne Jewett: *Verses*
Alfred Kreymborg, ed.: *Others* (also 1917, 1920)
Amy Lowell: *Men, Women, and Ghosts*
Ezra Pound: *Lustra* (G.B.)
E. A. Robinson: *The Man Against the Sky*
Carl Sandburg: *Chicago Poems*

NON-FICTION

Theodore Dreiser: *A Hoosier Holiday*
Lafcadio Hearn: *Appreciations of Poetry* (edited by John Erskine)
William Dean Howells: *Years of My Youth*
Vachel Lindsay: *A Handy Guide for Beggars*

Charlotte Mew

H. L. Mencken: *A Little Book in C Major; A Book of Burlesques*

Ezra Pound: *Gaudier-Brzeska: A Memoir* (G.B.); *Certain Noble Plays of Japan: from the manuscripts of Ernest Fenollosa, Chosen and Finished by Ezra Pound* (Introduction by W. B. Yeats; Cuala Press)

❧❧ *"Ah, for the things I mayn't want to know, I promise you shall find me stupid."*
HENRY JAMES

Sherwood Anderson

Androcles and the Lion, *by G. B. Shaw*

Related Events

DEATHS

Henry James: American novelist and short-story writer, "lover and interpreter of the fine amenities of brave decisions"; 73; following a stroke, in his home at #21 Carlyle Mansions, Cheyne Walk, in Chelsea, London, on February 28

Saki (H. H. Munro): British short-story writer; 46; killed in action near Beaumont Hamel, France, on November 13

Jack London: American journalist, ex-oyster pirate, and prolific author of animal stories and proletarian novels; 40; of suicide by a calculated overdose of morphine which had been prescribed as a pain-killer for uremia; at his "Beauty Ranch" in Glen Ellen, California, on November 22

1916

Conrad Aiken

IN OTHER ARTS

W. B. Yeats's play, *At the Hawk's Well*, has its first performance on April 2, in the London drawing room of Lady Emerald Cunard, with masks designed by Edmund Dulac, and with both T. S. Eliot and Ezra Pound in the audience

David Wark Griffith: *Intolerance*

"Dada-Soirée," the first Dadaist exhibition, on July 14, in Zurich

In September the Provincetown Players come to New York, rent the parlor floor of a Greenwich Village brownstone, and produce a triple bill of one-act plays, including Eugene O'Neill's *Bound East for Cardiff*. A second O'Neill play, *Before Breakfast*, followed in December, with the author in the role of the off-stage husband, whose sole appearance is his trembling hand reaching for a bowl of shaving water and whose only "line" is a death gurgle as he slashes his throat with a razor

Manuel de Falla: *Noches en los Jardines de España (Nights in the Gardens of Spain)*

"Jazz Bands": In its issue of October 27, the American newspaper *Variety* notes: "Chicago has added another innovation to its list of discoveries in the so-called 'Jazz-Bands.' The Jazz Band is composed of three or more instruments and seldom plays regulated music . . ."

With Van Wyck Brooks and Waldo Frank among its editors, *The Seven Arts* commences publication in November

IN THE MARGIN

In Uniform: Robert Graves, severely wounded in the chest, is officially listed as dead, his obituary appearing in *The Times* ‖ Ford Madox Hueffer, following his enlistment at age 42, is commissioned second lieutenant in the Welch Regiment and badly gassed the following month (September) ‖ Joyce Cary is wounded during an attack on a German stronghold in the Nigerian bush

Laurels: To a contest sponsored by Newark, New Jersey, to celebrate its 250th anniversary, Ezra Pound submits a poem, "To a City Sending Him Advertisements," and is awarded one of the ten "Fourth Prizes" of $50 ‖ The Order of Merit to Henry James

Milestones: April 23: 300th anniversary of the death of William Shakespeare ‖ April 24: Easter Rebellion in Dublin

New Horizons: T. S. Eliot is married, settled in London, and teaching at the Highgate School ‖ Katherine Mansfield and John Middleton Murry move to Cornwall, taking a cottage next to the one occupied by D. H. Lawrence, who unsuccessfully urges Murry to join him in a *blutbruderschaft* ‖ Somerset Maugham, stopping briefly in New Jersey to marry Mrs. Gwendolen Syrie Barnardo Wellcome, proceeds, by way of San Francisco and Honolulu, on his first voyage to the South Seas ‖ Wallace Stevens joins the legal staff of the Hartford Accident and Indemnity Company, of which (in 1934) he becomes a vice-president ‖ James Joyce, teaching languages in Zurich, begins to receive (until 1918) 1,000 Swiss

first published appearance in *Bruno's Weekly* (September), with a poem titled after Oscar Wilde's number as a Reading Gaol prisoner: "C 33"

1917

John Gould Fletcher

francs a month from Mrs. Harold McCormick, the only daughter of John D. Rockefeller, Sr. Early the following year, Miss Harriet Weaver adds an additional monthly sum of 500 francs, and presently makes Joyce an outright gift of capital, from the interest on which he is then able to live without anxiety

In the Wings: Hart Crane, 17 and living with his grandparents in Cleveland, Ohio, makes his

Great Britain

FICTION

Joseph Conrad: *The Shadow Line*
Norman Douglas: *South Wind*
Arthur Conan Doyle: *His Last Bow*
Ronald Firbank: *Caprice*
Rudyard Kipling: *A Diversity of Creatures* (stories and poems)
Dorothy Richardson: *Honeycomb*
Frank Swinnerton: *Nocturne*
Virginia and Leonard Woolf: *Two Stories*

Eugene O'Neill

Joseph Conrad

VERSE AND DRAMA

Laurence Binyon: *For the Fallen and Other Poems*

Walter de la Mare: *The Sunken Garden and Other Poems*

Edward Eastaway (Edward Thomas): *Poems* (dedicated to Robert Frost)

Robert Graves: *Fairies and Fusiliers*

Thomas Hardy: *Moments of Vision and Miscellaneous Verses*

Ralph Hodgson: *Poems*

Aldous Huxley: *Jonah*

D. H. Lawrence: *Look! We Have Come Through!*

Alice Meynell: *A Father of Women*

Siegfried Sassoon: *The Old Huntsman and Other Poems* (dedicated to Thomas Hardy)

Edith Sitwell, ed.: *Wheels, Second Cycle*

Algernon Charles Swinburne: *Posthumous Poems*

W. B. Yeats: *The Wild Swans at Coole* (Cuala Press; trade edition 1919)

NON-FICTION

G. K. Chesterton: *A Short History of England*

Edward Garnett: *Turgenev*

Wyndham Lewis: *The Ideal Giant: The Code of a Herdsman: Cantelman's Spring Mate* (play, imaginary letter, and story)

Ezra Pound, ed.: *Passages from the Letters of John Butler Yeats*

George Saintsbury: *History of the French Novel*

❧ ❧ *"The whole secret of a living style and the difference between it and a dead style, lies in not having too much style—being, in fact, a little careless, or rather seeming to be, here and there . . ."*

THOMAS HARDY

United States

FICTION

Sherwood Anderson: *Marching Men*

James Branch Cabell: *The Cream of the Jest*

O. Henry: *Waifs and Strays; Complete Writings*

Henry James: *The Ivory Tower; The Sense of the Past*

Ring Lardner: *Gullible's Travels, Etc.*

Sinclair Lewis: *The Job; The Innocents*

Christopher Morley: *Parnassus on Wheels*

Edith Wharton: *Summer*

VERSE AND DRAMA

John Peale Bishop: *Green Fruit*

Witter Bynner: *Grenstone Poems*

e. e. cummings *et al.*: *Eight Harvard Poets*
(introducing cummings, S. Foster Damon,
John Dos Passos, Robert Hillyer, and others)

T. S. Eliot: *Prufrock and Other Observations*
(G.B.)

Vachel Lindsay: *The Chinese Nightingale and
Other Poems*

Archibald MacLeish: *Tower of Ivory*

Edna St. Vincent Millay: *Renascence and Other
Poems*

E. A. Robinson: *Merlin*

Sara Teasdale: *Love Songs*

Eunice Tietjens: *Profiles from China*

William Carlos Williams: *Al Que Quiere! A
Book of Poems*

NON-FICTION

T. S. Eliot: *Ezra Pound: His Metric and Poetry*
(published anonymously)

Hamlin Garland: *A Son of the Middle Border*

Ezra Pound

Lafcadio Hearn: *Life and Literature* (edited by
John Erskine)

Henry James: *The Middle Years*

Amy Lowell: *Tendencies in Modern American
Poetry*

H. L. Mencken: *A Book of Prefaces*

Ezra Pound and Ernest Fenollosa: *Noh, or
Accomplishment: A Study of the Classical
Stage of Japan* (G.B.)

Mark Twain: *Letters* (edited by Albert B. Paine);
What Is Man? and Other Essays

Ezra Pound: translation of *Dialogues of
Fontenelle*

Norman Douglas

H. L. Mencken

Paul Valéry

 ". . . no verse is free for the man who wants to do a good job."

T. S. ELIOT

Related Events

DEATHS

Edgar Degas, French painter
Auguste Rodin, French sculptor
Philip Edward Thomas, British poet and
    man-of-letters

IN OTHER LANGUAGES

Albert Einstein: *Uber die spezielle und die
    allgemeine Relativitatstheorie;
    gemeinverstandlich* (Relativity, the Special
    and General Theory: a Popular Exposition)
George Trakl: *Die Dichtungen* (Poetry)
Paul Valéry: *La Jeune Parque* (dedicated to
    André Gide)

IN OTHER ARTS

James Barrie: *Dear Brutus*
W. Somerset Maugham: *Our Betters*
    (New York)
Eugene O'Neill: *The Long Voyage Home*
Manuel de Falla's ballet *El Corregidor y la
    Molinera*, or, as later staged, *El Sombrero de
    Tres Picos* (The Three-Cornered Hat)
Erik Satie's ballet *Parade*, with décor by Picasso
    and libretto by Jean Cocteau

March 23: For £19.5s.5d., Leonard and Virginia Woolf buy a small hand press, set it up in the dining room of their house in Richmond, and print a 32-page pamphlet containing Virginia's *The Mark on the Wall* and Leonard's *Three Jews*. Calling themselves The Hogarth Press, they go on to do the same with Katherine Mansfield's *Prelude*, T. S. Eliot's *Poems*, E. M. Forster's *The Story of the Siren*, Gorky's *Reminiscences of Tolstoi*, etc.

April 6: United States declares war on Germany

May: Poetry Society (later Pulitzer) Prize for Poetry awarded to Sara Teasdale, for *Love Songs* ‖ Albert and Charles Boni join Horace Liveright to publish the Modern Library ‖ In France, Gertrude Stein and Alice B. Toklas buy a Ford and, with Miss Stein as the driver, serve as volunteers for the American Fund for the French Wounded (until May, 1919), delivering medical supplies and blankets in Perpignan and later in Alsace

July: Recently wounded, holder of the Military Cross, recommended for the D.S.C., and slated for home duty, Siegfried Sassoon refuses to serve any longer in the British Army, declaring that the war "is being deliberately prolonged by those who have the power to stop it." In order to prevent a probable court-martial, Robert Graves testifies on Sassoon's behalf before a medical board and succeeds in getting him transferred to a convalescent center for neurasthenics

September 27: e. e. cummings and William Slater Brown, assigned to the Section Sanitaire Vingt-et-Un of the Norton Harjes Ambulance Corps, are "dragged across France like criminals, and closely confined in a Concentration Camp at *La Ferté Macé*." The charge was Germanophilia, based on three of Brown's letters, which expressed the opinion that local French beer was undrinkable, that no one was enthusiastic about the war, and that the French probably hated the English more than the Germans anyway. After U. S. State Department intervention, cummings, who was "guilty" only by virtue of his friendship with Brown, was released on

December 19; Brown was held until the following February

October 21: After buying a stone tower at Ballylee for £35 (June), William Butler Yeats, 52, is married to Miss Georgie Hyde-Lees, who, to keep her illustrious husband happy, pretends to be the recipient of automatic writing. Yeats takes her "messages" seriously, and the result, over the next two decades, is *A Vision*

sans date: "The friends of Mr. Sherlock Holmes will be glad to learn that he is still alive and well, though somewhat crippled by occasional attacks of rheumatism. He has, for many years, lived in a small farm upon the Downs five miles from Eastbourne, where his time is divided between philosophy and agriculture . . ." —John H. Watson, M.D.

A Red Star Is Born:

March 15: Czar Nicholas II abdicates

April 16: Nikolai Lenin returns to Russia, arriving by way of the Finland Station in Petrograd

November 7: The Bolsheviks seize power; Stalin sets up the G.P.U.

Great Britain

FICTION

John Galsworthy: *Five Tales* (includes "The Apple Tree")

Wyndham Lewis: *Tarr*

Compton Mackenzie: *The Early Life and Adventures of Sylvia Scarlett*

Katherine Mansfield: *Prelude*

George Moore: *A Story-Teller's Holiday*

Forrest Reid: *A Garden by the Sea: Stories and Sketches*

Rebecca West: *The Return of the Soldier*

Lytton Strachey and Virginia Woolf

NON-FICTION

Æ: *The Candle of Vision*
Robert Bridges: *The Necessity of Poetry*
Bryher (Annie Winifred Ellerman): *Amy Lowell: A Critical Appreciation*
W. H. Hudson: *Far Away and Long Ago*
Lytton Strachey: *Eminent Victorians*
Algernon Charles Swinburne: *Letters* (edited by Edmund Gosse and T. J. Wise)
W. B. Yeats: *Per Amica Silentia Lunae*

❧❧ *"The worst and the best parts of us are the secrets we never reveal."*
LYTTON STRACHEY

VERSE AND DRAMA

Rupert Brooke: *Collected Poems* (with a memoir by Edward Marsh)
Walter de la Mare: *Motley and Other Poems*
Gerard Manley Hopkins: *Poems* (edited by Robert Bridges)
Ford Madox Hueffer: *On Heaven and Other Poems*
Aldous Huxley: *The Defeat of Youth and Other Poems*
D. H. Lawrence: *New Poems* (dedicated to Amy Lowell)
John Masefield: *Collected Poems and Plays*
Siegfried Sassoon: *Counter-Attack and Other Poems*
Edith Sitwell: *Clowns' Houses*
Edward Thomas: *Last Poems*

Arthur Waley: translation of *One Hundred and Seventy Chinese Poems*

James Joyce: *Exiles: A Play in Three Acts*

United States

FICTION

Willa Cather: *My Antonia*
Theodore Dreiser: *Free and Other Stories*
Henry James: *Gabrielle de Bergerac*
Booth Tarkington: *The Magnificent Ambersons*

VERSE AND DRAMA

Conrad Aiken: *The Charnel Rose; Senlin: A Biography; and Other Poems*
Sherwood Anderson: *Mid-American Chants*
John Gould Fletcher: *The Tree of Life; Japanese Prints*

George Moore and Edmund Gosse

Henry Adams

Amy Lowell: *Can Grande's Castle*
Carl Sandburg: *Cornhuskers*

NON-FICTION

Henry Adams: *The Education of Henry Adams*
(first published privately in 1907)
H. L. Mencken: *Damn! A Book of Calumny; In
Defense of Women*
Ezra Pound: *Pavannes and Divisions*
Logan Pearsall Smith: *Trivia* (first published
privately 1902, G.B.)

❧ ❧ *"The test of a vocation is the love of
the drudgery it involves."*
LOGAN PEARSALL SMITH

Related Events

DEATHS

Henry Adams: American autobiographer and
cultural antiquarian; 80; of a stroke, in
Washington, D.C., on March 27

Guillaume Apollinaire: French poet and
man-of-letters; 38; of influenza (during the
great epidemic) and a generally weakened
constitution due to a forehead wound (March
1916) which had required trepanning; in Paris,
on November 9
Claude Debussy: French composer; 56; of cancer,
in Paris, on March 26
Wilfred Owen: British poet; 25; killed in action
(machine-gunned) in France, on November 4
Isaac Rosenberg: British poet; 28; killed in action
in France, on April 19

IN OTHER LANGUAGES

Guillaume Apollinaire: *Calligrammes. Poèmes de
la Paix et de la Guerre* (1913–1916). With a
Portrait by Picasso
Federico García Lorca: *Impresiones y Paisajes*
(*Impressions and Landscapes*)
Thomas Mann: *Betrachtungen eines
Unpolitischen* (*Reflections of an Unpolitical
Man*)

Ernest Hemingway

Guillaume Apollinaire   *F. Scott Fitzgerald*   *Wilfred Owen*

Luigi Pirandello: *Cosi è (se vi pare)* (*Right You Are If You Think You Are*)

Marcel Proust: *À l'Ombre des Jeunes Filles en Fleurs*

Oswald Spengler: *Der Untergang des Abendlandes* (*The Decline of the West*)

André Gide: translation into French of Joseph Conrad's *Typhoon* and of Walt Whitman's *Oeuvres Choisies*

IN OTHER ARTS

Stage: Eugene O'Neill: *Where the Cross Is Made*; *The Moon of the Caribbees*; *The Rope*

Music: Sergei Prokofiev: *Classical Symphony*  Igor Stravinsky: *L'Histoire du Soldat*

Films: Charles Chaplin: *Shoulder Arms*

IN THE MARGIN

February: Katherine Mansfield, recuperating from pleurisy in Bandol, France, is found to have tuberculosis. In May, she and John Middleton Murry are married

March: The *Little Review* begins serializing James Joyce's *Ulysses*

June: Graduated from Vassar, Edna St. Vincent Millay is living in New York, supporting herself with stories and sketches published under the pseudonym "Nancy Boyd," and acting with the Provincetown Players

July: Stationed at Camp Sheridan, near Montgomery, Alabama, First Lieutenant

Francis Scott Fitzgerald, 22, meets Zelda Sayre at a country-club dance ‖ As a volunteer Red Cross ambulance driver on the Italian front, Ernest Hemingway, 19, tries to drag a wounded soldier back to the trenches near the village of Fossalta on the night of July 8, and suffers a shattered knee cap when a Mennenwerter shell explodes a few yards away

September: In London, Aldous Huxley attends the Russian Ballet, "which is pure beauty, like a glimpse into another world. We . . . had a great evening of it the other day: almost everybody in London was there, and we all went to the back afterwards to see Lopokova, the *première danseuse*, who is ravishing—finding there no less a person than André Gide, who looked like a baboon with the voice, manners and education of Bloomsbury in French . . ." ‖ From Abu el-Lissan near Akaba, T. E. Lawrence and the Arab camel cavalry set out on the final push to Damascus, entering the city on the last day of the month

November: As a Royal Canadian Air Force cadet, William Faulkner, 21, sustains a leg injury on Armistice Day when he and a buddy, after considerable victory celebration, pilot their plane through a hangar roof

In the Great World:
November 11: Armistice Day: end of World War I
An epidemic of influenza sweeps across Western Europe and the United States

Miss Daisy Ashford

1919

Great Britain

FICTION

Daisy Ashford: *The Young Visitors*
Max Beerbohm: *Seven Men*
John Buchan: *Mr. Standfast*
Joseph Conrad: *The Arrow of Gold: A Story Between Two Notes*
Ronald Firbank: *Valmouth*
W. Somerset Maugham: *The Moon and Sixpence*
Forrest Reid: *Pirates of the Spring*
Dorothy Richardson: *The Tunnel; Interim*
Hugh Walpole: *Jeremy*
Virginia Woolf: *Kew Gardens; Night and Day*

James Branch Cabell

Carl Sandburg

VERSE AND DRAMA

Richard Aldington: *Images of War*

Laurence Binyon: *The Four Years: War Poems Collected and Newly Augmented*

Walter de la Mare: *Flora* (drawings by Pamela Bianco, 13, with illustrative poems by de la Mare)

Thomas Hardy: *Collected Poems*

Rudyard Kipling: *Verse, Inclusive Edition, 1885–1918*

D. H. Lawrence: *Bay: A Book of Poems*

John Masefield: *Reynard the Fox: or the Ghost Heath Run*

Siegfried Sassoon: *Picture Show* (privately printed)

Edith Sitwell, ed.: *Wheels, Third Cycle; Wheels, Fourth Cycle*

G. B. Shaw: *Heartbreak House* (produced 1920, New York); *Great Catherine* (produced 1913); *Playlets of the War*

W. B. Yeats: *Two Plays for Dancers*

NON-FICTION

W. H. Hudson: *The Book of a Naturalist*

George Moore: *Avowals*

Algernon Charles Swinburne: *Contemporaries of Shakespeare*

❧ ❧ *"The great tragedy of life is not that men perish, but that they cease to love."*

W. SOMERSET MAUGHAM

United States

FICTION

Sherwood Anderson: *Winesburg, Ohio*
James Branch Cabell: *Jurgen*
Theodore Dreiser: *Twelve Men*
Henry James: *Travelling Companions*
Ring Lardner: *Own Your Own House*
Sinclair Lewis: *Free Air*
Christopher Morley: *The Haunted Bookshop*

VERSE AND DRAMA

Babette Deutsch: *Banners*
T. S. Eliot: *Poems* (G.B.)
Amy Lowell: *Pictures of the Floating World*
Ezra Pound: *Quia Pauper Amavi* (G. B.)
John Crowe Ransom: *Poems About God*

H. D.: translation of *Choruses from the Iphigeneia in Aulis and the Hippolytus of Euripides* (G. B.)

NON-FICTION

Conrad Aiken: *Skepticisms: Notes on Contemporary Poetry*
Irving Babbitt: *Rousseau and Romanticism*
Waldo Frank: *Our America*
Henry James: *Within the Rim and Other Essays, 1914–15* (G. B.)
H. L. Mencken: *The American Language: A Preliminary Inquiry into the Development of English in the United States; Prejudices* (6 volumes through 1927)
John Reed: *Ten Days that Shook the World*
Edith Wharton: *French Ways and Their Meaning*

❧ ❧ *"The great artists of the world are never Puritans, and seldom even ordinarily respectable."*

H. L. MENCKEN

Related Events

DEATHS

Theodore Roosevelt: 26th President of the United States and occasional man-of-letters; 61; of pulmonary embolism; in Oyster Bay, Long Island, on January 5

IN OTHER LANGUAGES

André Gide: *La Symphonie Pastorale*
Hermann Hesse: *Demian*
Hugo von Hofmannsthal: *Die Frau ohne Schatten* (*The Woman Without a Shadow*)
Thomas Mann: *Herr und Hund* (*Man and Dog*)

Sylvia Beach

1919

IN OTHER ARTS

The Bauhaus school of design opens in Germany, with Walter Gropius as Director. Paul Klee joined the staff in 1921; Wassily Kandinsky in 1922

Maurice Ravel: *Le Tombeau de Couperin*

W. Somerset Maugham: *Caesar's Wife*

IN THE MARGIN

Sylvia Beach opens her Shakespeare and Company bookstore in Paris at 8 rue Dupuytren (moving in 1921 to 12 rue de l'Odéon)

Robert Graves, demobilized, makes a vow "never to be under anyone's orders for the rest of my life. Somehow I must live by writing." In May, he begins publishing *The Owl*, editorially declaring "a love of honest work well done, and a distaste for short cuts to popular success"

Alfred Harcourt and Donald Brace found their publishing house in New York

Ford Madox Hueffer, separated from Violet Hunt, moves with Stella Bowen to West Sussex, and in an apparent attempt to simplify his personal life, has his surname changed to "Ford" by deed poll. (He did not, however, begin to sign his books as "Ford Madox Ford" until 1923.)

Carl Sandburg, working as the motion-picture reviewer for the Chicago *Daily News*, receives one half of the Poetry Society Prize for *Cornhuskers*

Francis Steloff opens her Gotham Book Mart in New York at 128 West 45 Street (later moving to 51 West 47 St.)

In the Wings:

Ignatius Roy Dunnachie (Zulu) Campbell, 18, settles in London (after a year in Oxford and a childhood in the South African bush), sharing quarters with "the great Mahatma of all misanthropy, Aldous Huxley, who was already famous for his verse . . . I felt ill at ease with this pedant who leeringly gloated over his knowledge of how crayfish copulated (through their third pair of legs) but could never have caught or cooked one; let alone broken in a horse, thrown and branded a steer,

Elizabeth Bowen

flensed a whale, or slaughtered, cut, cured, and cooked anything at all"

Vladimir Nabokov, 20, leaves the Soviet Union and, in October, enters Cambridge University

Elizabeth Bowen, 20, begins work in the attic of her aunt's villa in Harpenden on her first short stories: "The room, the position of the window, the convulsive and anxious grating of my chair on the board floor were hyper-significant for me: here were the sensuous witnesses to my crossing the margin of a hallucinatory world . . . For me reality meant the books I had read—and I turned around, as *I* was writing, from time to time, to stare at them, unassailable in the shelves behind me"

John Casey (Sean O'Casey to-be), 39, sends the Abbey Theatre his first play, written for economy's sake on odd assortments of paper rifled by friends from their various jobs and with a home-brewed purple ink made by boiling the lead of indelible pencils, also stolen. The play, called *Frost in the Flower*, was rejected

In the Great World:

The Treaty of Versailles concluded on June 28; rejected by the United States on November 19

1920

Great Britain

FICTION

Bryher: *Development* (Preface by Amy Lowell)
Joseph Conrad: *The Rescue: A Romance of the Shallows*

H. G. Wells

Galsworthy Lowes Dickinson: *The Magic Flute: A Fantasia*
Norman Douglas: *They Went*
John Galsworthy: *In Chancery*
W. H. Hudson: *Dead Man's Plack and An Old Thorn*
Aldous Huxley: *Limbo*
D. H. Lawrence: *Women in Love* (privately printed in New York; G. B., 1921); *The Lost Girl*
Katherine Mansfield: *Bliss and Other Stories*
Edith Sitwell: *Children's Tales from the Russian Ballet*

VERSE AND DRAMA

Edmund Blunden: *The Waggoner*
Robert Bridges: *October and Other Poems*
Walter de la Mare: *Poems: 1901–1918*
Robert Graves: *Country Sentiment*
Aldous Huxley: *Leda and Other Poems*

Katherine Mansfield

Sinclair Lewis

Van Wyck Brooks

Wilfred Owen: *Poems* (edited by Siegfried Sassoon)
Ruth Pitter: *First Poems*
Edith Sitwell: *The Wooden Pegasus;* ed., *Wheels, Fifth Cycle*
Edward Thomas: *Collected Poems* (Foreword by Walter de la Mare)

Ronald Firbank: *The Princess Zoubaroff*
D. H. Lawrence: *Touch and Go: A Play in Three Acts*

NON-FICTION

Max Beerbohm: *And Even Now*
G. K. Chesterton: *The Uses of Diversity*
Roger Fry: *Vision and Design*
W. H. Hudson: *Birds of La Plata*
H. G. Wells: *The Outline of History*
Jessie L. Weston: *From Ritual to Romance*

❧ ❧ *"No authentic child of man will fit into a novel. History is the place for such people; history, or oblivion."*
NORMAN DOUGLAS

United States

FICTION

Sherwood Anderson: *Poor White*
Willa Cather: *Youth and the Bright Medusa*
John Dos Passos: *One Man's Initiation—1917*
F. Scott Fitzgerald: *This Side of Paradise; Flappers and Philosophers*

William Dean Howells: *The Vacation of the Kelwyns*

James Huneker: *Painted Veils*

Henry James: *A Landscape Painter; Master Eustace*

Sinclair Lewis: *Main Street*

Vachel Lindsay: *The Golden Book of Springfield*

Edith Wharton: *The Age of Innocence*

VERSE AND DRAMA

Conrad Aiken: *The House of Dust: A Symphony*

T. S. Eliot: *Ara Vus Prec* (G. B.; U. S. title: *Poems*)

Vachel Lindsay: *The Golden Whales of California, and Other Rhymes in the American Language*

Edna St. Vincent Millay: *A Few Figs from Thistles* (first published as a whole issue of *Salvo*, edited by Frank Shay; trade edition 1923)

Ezra Pound: *Umbra* (G.B.); *Hugh Selwyn Mauberley* (G.B.)

E. A. Robinson: *The Three Taverns; Lancelot*

Carl Sandburg: *Smoke and Steel*

Sara Teasdale: *Flame and Shadow*

Glenway Wescott: *The Bitterns: A Book of Twelve Poems* (Evanston, Illinois)

NON-FICTION

Van Wyck Brooks: *The Ordeal of Mark Twain*

Theodore Dreiser: *Hey Rub-a-Dub-Dub*

T. S. Eliot: *The Sacred Wood: Essays on Poetry and Criticism*

James Huneker: *Steeplejack*

Henry James: *Letters* (edited by Percy Lubbock)

William James: *Letters* (edited by his son, Henry James); *Collected Essays and Reviews* (edited by Ralph Barton Perry)

H. L. Mencken and George Jean Nathan: *The American Credo*

Ezra Pound: *Instigations of Ezra Pound, Together with an essay on the Chinese Written Character by Ernest Fenollosa*

George Santayana: *Character and Opinion in the United States: With Reminiscenses of William James and Josiah Royce and Academic Life in America*

William Carlos Williams: *Kora in Hell: Improvisations* (Prologue by Ezra Pound)

❦ ❦ *"Civilization is perhaps approaching one of those long winters that overtake it from time to time. Romantic Christendom —picturesque, passionate, unhappy episode—may be coming to an end . . ."*
GEORGE SANTAYANA

Vachel Lindsay

Related Events

DEATHS

Mrs. Humphrey Ward: British novelist, niece of Matthew Arnold, and friend of Henry James; age 69; on March 24

William Dean Howells: American novelist, man-of-letters, and editor; age 83; on May 11

André Breton and Philippe Soupault: *Les Champs Magnétiques*

Colette: *Chéri*

Sigmund Freud: *Jenseits des Lustprinzips* (*Beyond the Pleasure Principle*)

André Gide: *Si le grain ne meurt . . .*

Ernst Jünger: *In Stahlgewittern* (*The Storm of Steel*)

Marcel Proust: *Le Côté de Guermantes*

Ernst Töller: *Masse Mensch* (*Man and the Masses*)

Miguel de Unamuno: *Tres Novelas Ejemplares* (*Three Exemplary Novels*)

Paul Valéry: *Le Cimetière Marin*

Jean Cocteau: *Le Boeuf sur le Toit, ou The Nothing Doing Bar*; with music by Darius Milhaud and décor by Raoul Dufy

Eugene O'Neill: *Beyond the Horizon; The Emperor Jones; Diff'rent*

Maurice Ravel: *La Valse*

Robert Wiene, director: *The Cabinet of Dr. Caligari*

The Provincetown Players produce, among other novelties, Djuna Barnes's *An Irish Triangle* and *Kurzy of the Sea*; Edna Ferber's *The Eldest*; and Wallace Stevens's *Three Travelers Watch a Sunrise*

"*Little Mags*": *Contact* (through June 1923), edited by William Carlos Williams and Robert McAlmon || *The Dial* (through July 1929), a monthly edited by Scofield Thayer and J. S. Watson, with successive editors including Gilbert Seldes, Kenneth Burke, Alyse Gregory, and Marianne Moore

Scandals: The 18th Amendment to the U. S. Constitution, prohibiting the sale of alcoholic beverages, becomes law || U. S. postal authorities seize copies of the *Little Review* containing the serialization of James Joyce's *Ulysses*; in December, John Sumner's Society

Katherine Anne Porter

for the Suppression of Vice prosecutes on an obscenity charge, and Margaret Anderson, the *Little Review*'s editor, is fined $100

Laurels: The Pulitzer Prize for Drama to Eugene O'Neill's *Beyond the Horizon* || The Dial Award to Sherwood Anderson

At the Lectern: Carl Sandburg travels to Cornell College in Mount Vernon, Iowa, to give his first poetry reading—and brings his guitar || Vachel Lindsay takes Oxford University by storm with a poetry reading arranged by Robert Graves: "By two minutes he had the respectable and intellectual and cynical audience listening. By ten, intensely excited; by twenty, elated and losing self-control; by half an hour completely under his influence; by forty minutes roaring like a bonfire. At the end of the hour they lifted off the roof and refused to disperse . . ."

In the Wings: Back in England after six years of service in Nigeria, Joyce Cary, 32, settles with his wife in Oxford on a combined private income of £900, and contributes ten short stories to the *Saturday Evening Post* under the pseudonym Thomas Joyce ‖ Katherine Anne Porter, 31, moves to Mexico "after a long absence, to study the renascence of Mexican art" ‖ Freshly graduated from Yale, Thornton Wilder, 23, arrives in Rome to study archaeology at the American Academy

In the Great World: On May 5, Nicola Sacco and Bartolomeo Vanzetti are arrested for the slaying of the paymaster and guard of a shoe company in South Braintree, Massachusetts ‖ In November, Warren G. Harding is elected 29th President of the United States ‖ The 19th Amendment gives American women the right to vote

Aldous Huxley: translation of Rémy de Gourmont's *Un Coeur Virginal* (*A Virgin Heart*)

VERSE AND DRAMA

Walter de la Mare: *The Veil and Other Poems*
Robert Graves: *The Pier-Glass*; ed., with Richard Hughes and Alan Porter: *Oxford Poetry, 1921*
Ford Madox Hueffer: *A House*
D. H. Lawrence: *Tortoises* (U.S.)
Edith Sitwell, ed.: *Wheels, Sixth Cycle*
W. B. Yeats: *Michael Robartes and the Dancer* (Cuala Press)

G. B. Shaw: *Back to Methuselah* (produced 1922, New York)
W. B. Yeats: *Four Plays for Dancers*

1921

Great Britain

FICTION

Walter de la Mare: *Memoirs of a Midget*
Ronald Firbank: *Santal*
John Galsworthy: *To Let*
Aldous Huxley: *Chrome Yellow*
W. Somerset Maugham: *The Trembling of a Leaf: Little Stories of the South Sea Islands*
George Moore: *Héloïse and Abélard*
Dorothy Richardson: *Deadlock*
Virginia Woolf: *Monday or Tuesday*

Aldous Huxley

NON-FICTION

Joseph Conrad: *Notes on Life and Letters*
Lawrence H. Davison (D. H. Lawrence):
    Movements in European History
Norman Douglas: *Alone*
W. H. Hudson: *A Traveller in Little Things*
Ford Madox Hueffer: *Thus to Revisit*
D. H. Lawrence: *Psychoanalysis and the
    Unconscious* (U.S.); *Sea and Sardinia* (U.S.)
Percy Lubbock: *The Craft of Fiction*
Lytton Strachey: *Queen Victoria*
W. B. Yeats: *Four Years: Reminiscences,
    1887–1891* (Cuala Press)

❧❧ *". . . why, we don't even know what
we are—in ourselves, I mean. And how
many of us have tried to find out?"*
                WALTER DE LA MARE

United States

FICTION

Sherwood Anderson: *The Triumph of the Egg*
James Branch Cabell: *Figures of Earth*
Stephen Crane: *Men, Women and Boats* (edited
    by Vincent Starrett)
John Dos Passos: *Three Soldiers*
William Dean Howells: *Mrs. Farrell*

VERSE AND DRAMA

Conrad Aiken: *Punch: The Immortal Liar,
    Documents in His History*
H. D.: *Hymen*
John Gould Fletcher: *Breakers and Granite*
Amy Lowell: *Legends*
Edna St. Vincent Millay: *Second April*
Marianne Moore: *Poems* (arranged by H. D. and
    Bryher; G.B.)
Ezra Pound: *Poems, 1918–1921*
E. A. Robinson: *Avon's Harvest*
William Carlos Williams: *Sour Grapes*

Yvor Winters: *The Immobile Wind*
Elinor Wylie: *Nets to Catch the Wind*

Edna St. Vincent Millay: *Aria da Capo; The
    Lamp and the Bell; Two Slatterns and a King*

NON-FICTION

John Gould Fletcher: *Paul Gauguin: His Life and
    Art*
Hamlin Garland: *A Daughter of the Middle
    Border*
Henry James: *Notes and Reviews* (edited by
    Pierre de Chaignon la Rose)
Don Marquis: *The Old Soak, and Hail and
    Farewell*
Logan Pearsall Smith: *More Trivia*
Raymond Weaver: *Herman Melville* (the first
    biography)

❧❧ *". . . after all there is the fact of life.
Its story wants telling and singing. That's
what I want,—the tale and the song of it."*
                SHERWOOD ANDERSON

Edna St. Vincent Millay

Walter de la Mare

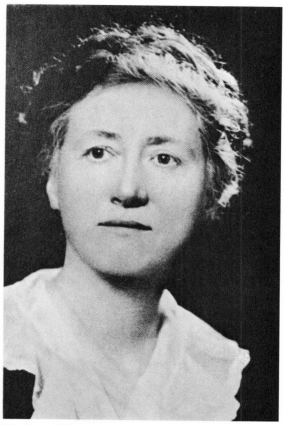

Marianne Moore

DEATHS

James Huneker: American man-of-letters; 61; of pneumonia; in Brooklyn, on February 9

IN OTHER LANGUAGES

Sigmund Freud: *Massenpsychologie und Ich-Analyse* (*Group Psychology and the Analysis of the Ego*)

Federico García Lorca: *Libro de Poemas*

Luigi Pirandello: *Sei Personaggi in Cerca d'Autore* (*Six Characters in Search of an Author*)

Marcel Proust: *Guermantes II—Sodome et Gomorrhe I*

IN OTHER ARTS

Jean Cocteau's mime-drama *Les Mariés de la Tour Eiffel,* with music by five members of *Les Six:* Germaine Tailleferre, Georges Auric, Arthur Honegger, Darius Milhaud, and Francis Poulenc

Somerset Maugham's *The Circle*

Anne Nichols's *Abie's Irish Rose*

Eugene O'Neill's *Anna Christie; The Straw; Gold*

Sergei Prokofiev's *Love for Three Oranges* (première in Chicago)

Edgar Varèse founds the International Composer's Guild

IN THE MARGIN

Laurels: James Tait Black Prize to D. H. Lawrence for *The Lost Girl* ‖ Pulitzer Prize for Fiction to Edith Wharton for *The Age of Innocence* ‖ Nobel Prize for Literature to Anatole France

Publishers: Jonathan Cape founds his own publishing company in London || *Broom, an International Magazine of the Arts,* edited by Harold Loeb (later Alfred Kreymborg, Matthew Josephson, Malcolm Cowley, etc.) in Rome, Berlin, and New York || *The Double-Dealer,* publishing the work of William Faulkner, Hart Crane, Allen Tate, John Crowe Ransom, and Sherwood Anderson, appears from January to May 1926 in New Orleans

Whereabouts: Sherwood Anderson (with expenses paid by Paul Rosenfeld) visits Paris and meets Gertrude Stein || After the failure of his short-lived dry-goods store, Robert Graves moves to a cottage in Islip purchased by his mother and rented to him for ten shillings a week. He is also helped by T. E. Lawrence, who gives him four chapters of *Seven Pillars of Wisdom* to sell for

E. M. Forster in India

Ford Madox Ford

serialization in America, Lawrence refusing to make money for himself out of the Arab revolt || E. M. Forster leaves for India, where he serves for six months as Private Secretary to H. H. Sir Tukoji Rao IV, the Maharajah of Dewas State Senior: "I was delighted. My fare both ways was to be paid. I was to get three hundred rupees per month. I was not clear what I was to do, nor when I came away was I clear what I had done . . ." || Marianne Moore becomes an assistant librarian at the Hudson Park Branch of the New York Public Library || After marrying Hadley Richardson in September, Ernest Hemingway sails for Paris as foreign correspondent for the Toronto *Star Weekly,* becoming fascinated by the use of the cable to express what he had to say: "Cabelese . . . Isn't it a great language?" he asks Lincoln Steffens one day || Glenway

Wescott and Monroe Wheeler visit England, calling on Ford Madox Ford at a crucial moment: "If Mr. Wescott had not paid me a visit of some duration," Ford declared later, "I do not think that I should have taken seriously again to writing. He was himself charming, intelligent in the extreme and a delicious poet just having his first affair with the muse. That in itself was good enough. But, in addition, he gave me an idea of a great background of youth, intelligence and energy . . ."

Jane Austen, as seen by her sister Cassandra

1922

James Joyce and Sylvia Beach

Great Britain

FICTION

Jane Austen: *Love and Freindship and Other Early Works Now First Printed from the Original MS* (Preface by G. K. Chesterton)

John Galsworthy: *The Forsyte Saga (The Man of Property*, 1906; *In Chancery*, 1920; *To Let*, 1921)

David Garnett: *Lady into Fox*

Aldous Huxley: *Mortal Coils*

James Joyce: *Ulysses* (Paris)

D. H. Lawrence: *Aaron's Rod; England, My England and Other Stories*

Katherine Mansfield: *The Garden Party and Other Stories*

A. A. Milne: *The Red House Mystery*

May Sinclair: *The Life and Death of Harriet Frean*

Robert Louis Stevenson: *Works* (Vailima Edition)

Rebecca West: *The Judge*

Virginia Woolf: *Jacob's Room*

Constance Garnett: translation of Gogol's works (through 1928)

Virginia Woolf and S. S. Koteliansky: translation of Fyodor Dostoevsky's *Stavrogin's Confession*

VERSE AND DRAMA

Edmund Blunden: *The Shepherd*

Walter de la Mare: *Down-Adown-Derry*

Thomas Hardy: *Late Lyrics and Earlier*

A. E. Housman: *Last Poems*

Richard Hughes: *Gipsy Night and Other Poems*

Isaac Rosenberg: *Poems* (edited by Gordon Bottomley, with a memoir by Laurence Binyon)

Edith Sitwell: *Façade*

W. B. Yeats: *Later Poems* (Collected Edition, Vol. I); *Plays in Prose and Verse* (Vol. II); *Seven Poems and a Fragment* (Cuala Press)

NON-FICTION

Maurice Baring: *The Puppet Show of Memory*

Max Beerbohm: *Rossetti and His Circle*

Clive Bell: *Since Cézanne*

George Gordon, Lord Byron: *Letters*

E. M. Forster: *Alexandria: A History and a Guide* (1938 edition dedicated to Constantin Cavafy)

Sir James Frazer: *The Golden Bough* (one-volume edition)

Robert Graves: *On English Poetry*

W. H. Hudson: *A Hind in Richmond Park* (edited by Morley Roberts)

D. H. Lawrence: *Fantasia of the Unconscious* (U.S.)

W. Somerset Maugham: *On a Chinese Screen* (U.S.)

John Middleton Murry: *Countries of the Mind*

Lytton Strachey: *Books and Characters, French and English*

W. B. Yeats: *The Trembling of the Veil* (limited edition)

❧❧ *"Never mind—work, work. Lytton says we have still 20 years before us . . ."*
VIRGINIA WOOLF

United States

FICTION

Willa Cather: *One of Ours*

F. Scott Fitzgerald: *The Beautiful and Damned; Tales of the Jazz Age*

Sinclair Lewis: *Babbitt*

Carl Sandburg: *Rootabaga Stories*

Gertrude Stein: *Geography and Plays* (Introduction by Sherwood Anderson)

Carl Van Vechten: *Peter Whiffle*

Edith Wharton: *The Glimpses of the Moon*

T. S. Eliot

VERSE AND DRAMA

Conrad Aiken, ed.: *Modern American Poets* (G.B.)

John Peale Bishop and Edmund Wilson: *The Undertaker's Garland* (verse and stories)

e. e. cummings

T. S. Eliot: *The Waste Land* (dedicated to Ezra Pound, "*il miglior fabbro*")

Amy Lowell: *A Critical Fable* (written as a hoax and published anonymously)

Louise Pound, ed.: *American Ballads and Songs*

Carl Sandburg: *Slabs of the Sunburnt West*

NON-FICTION

Ambrose Bierce: *Letters* (edited by Bertha Clark Pope, with a memoir by George Sterling)

e.e. cummings: *The Enormous Room*

John Dewey: *Human Nature and Conduct: An Introduction to Social Psychology*

Theodore Dreiser: *A Book About Myself*

Ludwig Lewisohn: *Up Stream: An American Chronicle*

George Santayana: *Soliloquies in England and Later Soliloquies*

Ezra Pound: translation of Rémy de Gourmont's *Physique de l'amour; essai sur l'instinct sexuel* (*The Natural Philosophy of Love*)

❧ ❧ *"It is after all a grrrreat littttttterary period."*

EZRA POUND

Related Events

DEATHS

Marcel Proust: French novelist; 51; of exhaustion and chronic asthma aggravated by bronchitis; in Paris, on November 18

Other Deaths:

Wilfrid Scawen Blunt, British poet and career diplomat, age 82

Giovanni Verga, Italian novelist, age 82

W. H. Hudson, Argentina-born, English man-of-letters, age 81

Alice Meynell, British poet, age 75

Bertolt Brecht: *Baal* (his first play; produced 1923)
Jean Cocteau: *Vocabulaire; Le Secret Professionnel*
Colette: *La Maison de Claudine*
Herman Hesse: *Siddhartha*
Luigi Pirandello: *Enrico IV (Henry IV)*
Marcel Proust: *Sodome et Gomorrhe II*
Paul Valéry: *Charmes*
Stefan Zweig: *Amok*

Marcel Proust

Stage: W. Somerset Maugham: *East of Suez; Rain* (adapted by John Colton and Clemence Randolph from Maugham's story "Miss Thompson") || Eugene O'Neill: *The Hairy Ape*

Music: Charles Ives: *114 Songs with Postface* (published at Ives's own expense) || First Salzburg International Festival

Films: Robert Flaherty: *Nanook of the North* || F. W. Murnau: *Nosferatu*

Calendar: January 24: On a special amplifier named for its inventor and called a Sengerphone, Miss Edith Sitwell recites the poems of her *Façade* cycle, with instrumental accompaniment arranged by William Walton || February 11: At Castle Muzot in the Swiss Valais, Rainer Maria Rilke finishes the last of his ten *Duineser Elegien*, begun a decade before || March: Ezra Pound, Richard Aldington, and May Sinclair found *Bel Esprit*—to raise a fund of "£300 annually . . . in order that T. S. Eliot may leave his work in Lloyd's Bank and devote his whole time to literature . . ." || August: At his own expense, T. E. Lawrence has eight copies of the manuscript of *Seven Pillars of Wisdom* printed by the presses of the Oxford *Times*, and then enlists in the newly formed R.A.F. under the name of J. H. Ross, with the serial number 352087 || October 17: Attempting to find a cure for her tuberculosis, Katherine Mansfield enters the Gurdjieff-inspired Institute for the Harmonious Development of Man, at Fontainebleau, and as part of her treatment begins spending several hours a day deep-breathing on a platform suspended over a cow manger

Geography: Alexandria, Egypt: After thirty years service, Constantin Cavafy retires as a clerk in the Ministry of Irrigation || Haiti: Ronald Firbank pays a visit: "They say the President is a *Perfect Dear!*" || Taos, New Mexico: By way of Ceylon and Australia, D. H. Lawrence arrives at the ranch of Mabel Dodge Luhan || Port of New York: 500 copies of the 2nd printing of James Joyce's *Ulysses* are seized and burned by United States Post Office authorities; at Folkestone, England, 499 copies of a third printing are confiscated by British Customs

Laurels: The Pulitzer Prize for Drama to Eugene O'Neill's *Anna Christie* || The James Tait Black Prize to Walter de la Mare's *Memoirs of a Midget* and Lytton Strachey's *Queen Victoria* || The Dial Award to T. S. Eliot

Beginnings: The Fugitive, published at Nashville, Tennessee, as the voice of "The Fugitive Group": John Crowe Ransom, Allen Tate, Donald Davidson, Robert Penn Warren, Merrill Moore || *The Criterion,* edited by T. S. Eliot, makes its debut in October || Contact Editions (Paris), edited by Robert McAlmon and publishing Hemingway (1923) and Gertrude Stein (1925)

In the Wings:

For W. H. Auden, age 15,

"Crazes had come and gone in short, sharp gales.
For motor-bikes, photography, and whales.
But indecision broke off with a clean-cut end
   One afternoon in March at half-past three
When walking in a ploughed field with a
      friend;
   Kicking a little stone, he turned to me
   And said, 'Tell me, do you write poetry?'
I never had, and said so, but I knew
That very moment what I wished to do."

Bengal-born Eric Blair (George Orwell), age 19, leaves Eton after two years, and goes to Burma, taking a position with the Indian Imperial Police and not returning to England again until 1927

Vladimir Nabokov, age 23, takes an Honors Degree in Slavic and Romance Languages at Cambridge University

Working in Paris in the glue trade and harboring ambitions of a literary career, V. S. Pritchett breaks into print with a joke submitted to the New York *Herald:* "It was published. And underneath was my full name and address. I was twenty-two. Most people have written their novels by then. And as for poets—it is their old age"

A Novelists' Symposium on Ulysses:

Virginia Woolf: "I finished *Ulysses* and think it is a mis-fire. Genius it has, I think; but of the inferior water. The book is diffuse. It is brackish. It is pretentious. It is underbred, and not only in the obvious sense, but in the literary sense. A first rate writer, I mean, respects writing too much to be tricky; startling; doing stunts. I'm reminded all the time of some callow board school boy, full of wits and powers, but so self-conscious and egotistical that he loses his head, becomes extravagant, mannered, uproarious, ill at ease, makes kindly people feel sorry for him and stern ones merely annoyed; and one hopes he'll grow out of it; but as Joyce is 40 this scarcely seems likely . . ."

T. E. Lawrence

Ford Madox Ford: "I am inclined to think that Mr. Joyce is riding his method to death."

D. H. Lawrence: "My God, what a clumsy olla putrida James Joyce is! Nothing but old fags and cabbage-stumps of quotations from the Bible and the rest, stewed in the juice of deliberate, journalistic dirty-mindedness—what old and hard-worked staleness, masquerading as the all-new!"

E. M. Forster: "Joyce is horrified and fascinated by the human body; it seems to him ritually unclean and in direct contact with all the evil in the universe, and though to some of us this seems awful tosh, it certainly helps him to get some remarkable literary effects . . ."

In the Great World:

October 26: Fascista Manifesto in Italy
December 6: First Parliament of the newly created Irish Free State

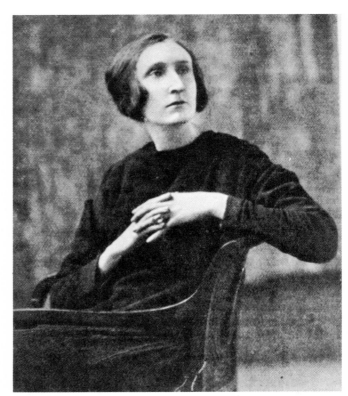

Edith Sitwell

1923

Great Britain

FICTION

Arnold Bennett: *Riceyman Steps*
Elizabeth Bowen: *Encounters*
Joseph Conrad: *The Rover; Collected Works* (Uniform Edition, 22 vols., 1923–28)
Walter de la Mare: *The Riddle and Other Stories*
Ronald Firbank: *The Flower Beneath the Foot: Being a Record of the Early Life of St. Laura de Nazianzi and the Times in Which She Lived*
Ford Madox Ford: *The Marsden Case*
Aldous Huxley: *Antic Hay*
Rudyard Kipling: *Land and Sea Tales for Scouts and Guides*
D. H. Lawrence: *Kangaroo; The Ladybird* (U.S. title: *The Captain's Doll*)

Rose Macaulay: *Told by an Idiot*
Katherine Mansfield: *The Dove's Nest and Other Stories*
Dorothy Richardson: *Revolving Lights*
Dorothy Sayers: *Whose Body?*

D. H. Lawrence: translation of Giovanni Verga's *Mastro-don Gesualdo*

VERSE AND DRAMA

Richard Aldington: *Exile and Other Poems*
Walter de la Mare, ed.: *Come Hither*
Ford Madox Ford: *Mister Bosphorus and the Muses*
Robert Graves: *The Feather Bed; Whipperginny*
D. H. Lawrence: *Birds, Beasts and Flowers*
Alice Meynell: *Last Poems*
Edith Sitwell: *Bucolic Comedies*

Thomas Hardy: *The Famous Tragedy of the Queen of Cornwall*

Rose Macaulay

Elinor Wylie

NON-FICTION

Samuel Butler: *Works* (edited by H. F. Jones and
    A. T. Bartholomew; 20 vols., 1923–26)
Norman Douglas: *Together*
Havelock Ellis: *The Dance of Life*
Ford Madox Ford: *Women and Men* (Paris)
E. M. Forster: *Pharos and Pharillon*
Frank Harris: *My Life and Loves* (Germany)
Aldous Huxley: *On the Margin: Notes and Essays*
D. H. Lawrence: *Studies in Classic American
    Literature*
Hugh MacDiarmid (C. M. Grieve): *Annals of
    the Five Senses* (essays, poems, stories)
I. A. Richards and C. K. Ogden: *The Meaning of
    Meaning*
W. B. Yeats: *Plays and Controversies* (Collected
    Edition, Vol. III); *Speeches* (Dublin)

❦ ❦ *"In other words, I wanted to write a
certain amount of pages of prose, which,
strictly speaking, is my proper business."*
               JOSEPH CONRAD

United States

FICTION

Sherwood Anderson: *Horses and Men* (dedicated
    to Theodore Dreiser); *Many Marriages*
Djuna Barnes: *A Book* (stories, plays, and verse;
    enlarged and reissued in 1929 as *A Night
    Among the Horses*)
James Branch Cabell: *The High Place*
Willa Cather: *A Lost Lady*
Ernest Hemingway: *Three Stories and Ten
    Poems* (Paris)
Edith Wharton: *A Son at the Front*
William Carlos Williams: *The Great American
    Novel* (Paris)
Elinor Wylie: *Jennifer Lorn*

Louise Bogan

VERSE AND DRAMA

Conrad Aiken: *The Pilgrimage of Festus*
Louise Bogan: *Body of This Death*
Willa Cather: *April Twilights and Other Poems*
e. e. cummings: *Tulips and Chimneys*
Robert Frost: *New Hampshire; Selected Poems*
    (dedicated in memory of Edward Thomas)
Edna St. Vincent Millay: *The Harp-Weaver and
    Other Poems*
Marianne Moore: *Marriage*
E. A. Robinson: *Roman Bartholow*
George Santayana: *Poems: Selected by the
    Author and Revised*
Wallace Stevens: *Harmonium* (revised 1931)
William Carlos Williams: *Spring and All; Go Go*
Elinor Wylie: *Black Armour*

NON-FICTION

Theodore Dreiser: *The Color of a Great City*
Ezra Pound: *Indiscretions or, Une Revue de
    Deux Mondes* (Paris)
George Santayana: *Skepticism and Animal Faith:
    Introduction to a System of Philosophy*
Mark Twain: *Europe and Elsewhere* (edited by
    Albert B. Paine)

❧ ❧ *"Always, in whatever I wrote—prose
or verse—I have had a burning desire to
be explicit . . ."*

MARIANNE MOORE

Related Events

DEATHS

Katherine Mansfield (Kathleen Mansfield
    Beauchamp): New Zealand-born short-story
    writer and diarist; age 35; of pulmonary
    tuberculosis, in Fontainebleau, France, on
    January 9. "Perhaps it does not so much matter
    what one loves in this world. But love
    something one must."

Other Deaths:

Sarah Bernhardt
Raymond Radiguet
Warren G. Harding
Kate Douglas Wiggin

IN OTHER LANGUAGES

Jean Cocteau: *Le Grand Écart; Thomas
    l'Imposteur*
Colette: *Le Blé en Herbe*
Sigmund Freud: *Das Ich und Das Es* (*The Ego
    and the Id*)
André Gide: *Dostoievsky*
Georg Groddeck: *Das Buch vom Es* (*The Book
    of the It*)

Marcel Proust: *La Prisonnière*

Raymond Radiguet: *Le Diable au Corps*

Rainer Maria Rilke: *Duineser Elegien (Duino Elegies)*; *Die Sonette an Orpheus (Sonnets to Orpheus)*

Italo Svevo (Ettore Schmitz): *La Conscienza di Zeno (Confessions of Zeno)*

IN OTHER ARTS

Stage: F. Scott Fitzgerald: *The Vegetable: or, From President to Postman* || Sean O'Casey: *The Shadow of a Gunman* || G. B. Shaw: *St. Joan* (New York)

Films: Charles Chaplin: *A Woman of Paris*

Music: Manuel de Falla: *Retablo* || Arthur Honegger: *Pacific 231*

Other: George Grosz: *Ecce Homo* || Le Corbusier: *Towards a New Architecture*

IN THE MARGIN

Laurels: Pulitzer Prizes to Willa Cather, for *One of Ours*, and to Edna St. Vincent Millay, for *The Ballad of the Harp-Weaver* and other poems || The James Tait Black and Hawthornden Prizes to David Garnett for *Lady into Fox* || The Nobel Prize for Literature to W. B. Yeats

Beginnings: Nonesuch Press founded by Francis Meynell || Albert and Charles Boni launch their publishing house || *Mannikin* (edited by Monroe Wheeler from Bonn, Germany, and New York City) publishes Marianne Moore, William Carlos Williams, and Janet Lewis || José Ortega y Gasset begins editing *Revista de Occidente* (until 1936 and the Spanish Civil War)

Willa Cather

Robert Penn Warren

Katherine Mansfield

In the Wings: William Faulkner, 26, with a file cabinet full of poems and stories, goes to New York looking for some literary connections. After clerking for a few months in a bookstore, he returns to Oxford, Mississippi, and takes a job as postmaster at the local university || Thomas Wolfe, 23, in his graduate year at Harvard's 47 Workshop for playwriting, finishes a "leviathan of a ten-scene, three-hour play," which, in spite of drastic cutting by the director, runs over four hours at its performance, with 44 characters, 31 speaking parts, and 7 changes of scene || At Eton, Henry Green, 18, observes the rules of the game: ". . . like everyone else, I began to write a novel" || At Vanderbilt University, "Fugitives" John Orley Allen Tate, 24, and Robert (Red) Penn Warren, 18, share dormitory quarters: "In order to get into bed at night we had to shovel books, trousers, shoes, hats and fruit jars onto the floor, and in the morning, to make walking-space, we heaped it all back upon the beds . . . Red had made some good black-and-white drawings in the Beardsley style. One day he applied art gum to the dingy plaster and when we came back we saw four murals, all scenes from *The Waste Land.* I remember particularly the rat creeping softly through the vegetation, and the typist putting a record on the gramophone."

Veterans:

Ford Madox Ford signs his new name to a book (*The Marsden Case*) for the first time. According to Ford's own account, it was publisher Gerald Duckworth who had suggested it, on the grounds that readers might have an easier time asking for his books if the author's name were pronounceable. "And how *should* one pronounce your beastly name? Hoo-fer? Hweffer? Hoifer? Hyoofer? It's impossible to know." (Other "mispronunciations" included Osbert Sitwell's "Freud Madox Fraud" and Ezra Pound's "Forty Mad-dogs Hoofer.") Undaunted,

Raymond Radiguet

inveterate, heroically literature-loving, Ford wrote on January 28 to a friend, Edgar Jepson, asking permission to offer him the dedication of *The Marsden Case,* and added: "I have just come across this To-Day's Great Thought in Jules Renard: '*Oui. Homme de lettres! Je le serai jusqu'à ma mort . . . Et, si par hazard, je suis éternel, je ferai, durant l'éternité, de la littérature. Et jamais je ne me fatigue d'en faire, et toujours j'en fais, et je me f . . . du reste . . .*'"

Ronald Firbank, describing his new novel (*The Flower Beneath the Foot*) in a letter to his mother, says it is "quite in the style of *Valmouth,* vulgar, cynical & 'horrid', but of course beautiful here and there for those that can see . . ."

In the Great World:

With the death of Warren G. Harding on August 2, Calvin Coolidge becomes the 30th President of the United States

November: the value of the German mark drops to four billion to the dollar. On the evening of the 8th, Adolf Hitler leads his "Beer Hall Putsch" in the Buegerbräutkeller outside Munich, and the next day, with Hermann Goering and assorted storm troopers, "marches" on the city and is arrested

1924

E. M. Forster

Great Britain

FICTION

Michael Arlen: *The Green Hat*

Joseph Conrad and Ford Madox Ford: *The Nature of a Crime*

Ronald Firbank: *Prancing Nigger* (Introduction by Carl Van Vechten; original G.B. title: *Sorrow in Sunlight*)

Ford Madox Ford: *Some Do Not*

E. M. Forster: *A Passage to India*

David Garnett: *A Man in the Zoo*

Aldous Huxley: *The Little Mexican and Other Stories* (U.S. title: *Young Archimedes*)

D. H. Lawrence and M. L. Skinner: *The Boy in the Bush*

Katherine Mansfield: *Something Childish and Other Stories* (U.S. title: *The Little Girl*)

Ralph Hale Mottram: *The Spanish Farm* (first volume of trilogy; completed 1926)

Osbert Sitwell: *Triple Fugue*

Mary Webb: *Precious Bane*

Richard Aldington: translation of Choderlos de Laclos's *Les Liaisons Dangereuses* (*Dangerous Acquaintances*)

George Moore: translation of Longus's *The Pastoral Loves of Daphnis and Chloë*

VERSE AND DRAMA

Roy Campbell: *The Flaming Terrapin*

Robert Graves: *Mock Beggar Hall* (poetry and prose)

A. A. Milne: *When We Were Very Young*

Edith Sitwell: *The Sleeping Beauty*

John Skelton: *Poems* (edited by Richard Hughes)

W. B. Yeats: *The Cat and the Moon and Certain Poems* (Cuala Press)

Richard Hughes: *The Sisters' Tragedy and Three Other Plays* (U.S. title: *A Rabbit and a Leg: Collected Plays*)

Aldous Huxley: adaptation of *The Discovery*, by
Mrs. Frances Sheridan

G. B. Shaw: *St. Joan* (produced 1923, New York)

NON-FICTION

Max Beerbohm: *Around Theatres*

R. B. Cunninghame Graham: *Inveni Portam:
Joseph Conrad* (U.S.)

Ford Madox Ford: *Joseph Conrad: A Personal
Remembrance*

Robert Graves: *The Meaning of Dreams*
(dedicated to Susan and John Buchan)

Gerald Heard: *Narcissus: An Anatomy of Clothes*

T. E. Hulme: *Speculations* (edited by Herbert
Read)

D. H. Lawrence: Introduction to the *Memoirs of
the Foreign Legion*, by M.M. (Maurice
Magnus)

George Moore: *Conversations in Ebury Street*

I. A. Richards: *Principles of Literary Criticism*

Virginia Woolf: *Mr. Bennett and Mrs. Brown*

Herman Melville

W. B. Yeats: *Essays* (Collected Edition, Vol.
IV); *The Irish Dramatic Movement: Lecture
Delivered to the Royal Academy of Sweden*
(Stockholm)

❧ ❧ *"There can be no good literature
without praise."*

W. B. YEATS

Emily Dickinson

United States

FICTION

Nancy Boyd (Edna St. Vincent Millay):
Distressing Dialogues (Preface by Miss
Millay)

James Joyce, Ezra Pound, Ford Madox Ford, John Quinn

Louis Bromfield: *The Green Bay Tree*

Kenneth Burke: *The White Oxen and Other Stories*

Edna Ferber: *So-Big*

Ernest Hemingway: *in our time: stories* (Paris)

Ring Lardner: *How to Write Short Stories (With Samples)*

Herman Melville: *Billy Budd and Other Prose Pieces* (edited by Raymond Weaver; G.B.)

Glenway Wescott: *The Apple of the Eye*

Edith Wharton: *Old New York*

VERSE AND DRAMA

H.D.: *Heliodora and Other Poems*

Donald Davidson: *An Outland Piper*

Emily Dickinson: *Complete Poems* (edited by Martha Dickinson Bianchi); *Selected Poems* (edited by Conrad Aiken; G.B.)

William Faulkner: *The Marble Faun* (Preface by Phil Stone, a Mississippi lawyer who paid for the printing)

Robinson Jeffers: *Tamar and Other Poems*

Archibald MacLeish: *The Happy Marriage and Other Poems*

Herman Melville: *Poems* (G.B.)

Marianne Moore: *Observations*

John Crowe Ransom: *Chills and Fever; Grace After Meat* (Introduction by Robert Graves; G.B.)

E. A. Robinson: *The Man Who Died Twice*

NON-FICTION

Sherwood Anderson: *A Storyteller's Story*

T. S. Eliot: *Homage to John Dryden* (G.B.)

Ezra Pound: *Anthiel: and the Treatise on Harmony* (Paris)

Mark Twain: *Autobiography* (edited by Albert B. Paine)

❧❧ "... I found the greatest difficulty, aside from knowing truly what you really felt, rather than what you were supposed to feel ... was to put down what really happened in action; what the actual things were which produced the emotion that you experienced ..."

ERNEST HEMINGWAY

Joseph Conrad

Related Events

DEATHS

Franz Kafka: Prague-born, German-language writer of religious parables ("A cage went in search of a bird ..."); age 51; of tuberculosis, in a sanatorium near Vienna, on June 3, with three of his principal works (*Der Prozess, Das Schloss, Amerika*) still in manuscript and leaving a plea to his friend Max Brod to destroy them. Brod published them instead, and a generation later (1941) W. H. Auden declared: "Had one to name the artist who comes nearest to bearing the same kind of relation to our age that Dante, Shakespeare and Goethe bore to theirs, Kafka is the first one would think of ..."

Joseph Conrad: Polish-born, English-language novelist and short-story writer; age 76; of a heart attack; at his home in Bishopsbourne, near Canterbury, on August 3.

Norman Douglas: "... He seldom explored the human heart, that wonderful tangle of motives pure and impure (as they are called) ... he never so much as glanced down into its depths lest he should discover, down in those muddy recesses, something rotten, something which had no right to be there. Can a man who lacks sympathy with erring humanity give us a convincing picture of it?"

Franz Kafka

Ernest Hemingway: "It is agreed by most of the people I know that Conrad is a bad writer, just as it is agreed that T. S. Eliot is a good writer. If I knew that by grinding Mr. Eliot into a fine dry powder and sprinkling that powder on Mr. Conrad's grave, Mr. Conrad would shortly appear, looking very annoyed at the forced return and commence writing, I would leave for London early tomorrow morning with a sausage grinder . . ."

Paul Valéry: "Conrad parlait le français avec un bon accent provençal; mais l'anglais avec un accent horrible qui m'amusait beaucoup. Être un grand écrivain dans une langue que l'on parle si mal est chose rare et éminemment originale."

André Gide: "Si grande que fût sa curiosité pour les replis ténébreux de l'âme humaine, il détestait tout ce que l'homme pouvait présenter de sournois, de louche ou de vil . . ."

Other Deaths:

Ferruccio Busoni
Eleonore Duse
Gabriel Fauré
Anatole France
Nikolai Lenin
Gene Stratton Porter
Giacomo Puccini
Woodrow Wilson

IN OTHER LANGUAGES

André Breton: *Manifeste du Surréalisme* (First Surrealist Manifesto): "SURRÉALISME, n.m. Automatisme psychique pur par lequel on se propose d'exprimer, soit verbalement, soit par écrit, soit de toute autre manière, le fonctionnement réel de la pensée . . ."
Jean Cocteau: *Poésies: 1916–1923*
André Gide: *Incidences; Corydon* (public edition)
Thomas Mann: *Der Zauberberg* (*The Magic Mountain*)
Saint-John Perse: *Anabase*
Pierre Reverdy: *Les Épaves du Ciel*

IN OTHER ARTS

Stage: Noel Coward: *The Vortex* ‖ Sean O'Casey: *Juno and the Paycock* ‖ Eugene O'Neill: *Desire Under the Elms; All God's Chillun Got Wings; Welded* ‖ Founding of Teatro d'Arte di Roma with Luigi Pirandello as director
Music: George Gershwin: *Rhapsody in Blue* ‖ Arnold Schoenberg: *Erwartung* (*Expectation*); *Die Glückliche Hand* (*The Lucky Hand*) ‖ Igor Stravinsky: *Concerto for Piano and Wind Instruments*

Robert Frost

IN THE MARGIN

Publishers: In Florence, Norman Douglas begins to print his own books in limited, signed editions for subscribers ‖ With ex-banker T. S. Eliot on its Board of Directors, the firm of Faber & Gwyer opens offices in London ‖

In New York, Lincoln MacVeagh starts the Dial Press; and Richard Simon and M. L. Schuster inaugurate their imprint with *The Cross-Word Puzzle Book*, the sale price including a Venus pencil

Magazines: *The American Mercury* (until 1933), edited by H. L. Mencken and George Jean Nathan || *transatlantic review* (until 1925), edited by Ford Madox Ford with the help of, among others, Ernest Hemingway; financed by Ford and the American lawyer and bibliophile John Quinn; and publishing Gertrude Stein's *The Making of Americans*, as well as Joyce, cummings, Pound, and Hemingway himself || *1924* (from July to December of the calendar year), edited by Edwin Seaver, and publishing William Carlos Williams, Yvor Winters, Pound, and Hart Crane || *The Saturday Review of Literature*

Laurels: The Pulitzer Prize for Poetry to Robert Frost for *New Hampshire: A Poem with Notes and Grace Notes* || James Tait Black Prize to Arnold Bennett for *Riceyman Steps*

Milestone: On January 15, the B.B.C. broadcasts Richard Hughes's specially commissioned script, *Danger*, believed by the author to be the "first radio-drama in the world." The text concerned three English visitors trapped in a Welsh coal mine, and contained what was probably the first manual on sound effects: "There must be an echo, to give the effect of a tunnel. (A good way to produce this is for each person to speak into a large bucket . . .)"

In the Wings: Recently married, Allen Tate and Caroline Gordon move to Patterson, New York, where for $10 a month they rent eight rooms and share housekeeping with Hart Crane || Vowing "never to work for anyone again!" Henry Miller quits his job as a branch employment manager for Western Union after four and a half years, a "period comparable, for me, to Dostoievsky's stay in Siberia"

In the Great World: On April 1, Adolf Hitler is found guilty of high treason and sentenced to five years in prison, where he begins writing *Mein Kampf*; thanks to a Christmas amnesty, he is released the following December 20

1925

Great Britain

FICTION

Jane Austen: *Sanditon; Lady Susan*
Ivy Compton-Burnett: *Pastors and Masters*
Joseph Conrad: *Suspense: A Napoleonic Novel; Tales of Hearsay*
Walter de la Mare: *Broomsticks and Other Tales*
Ford Madox Ford: *No More Parades*
David Garnett: *The Sailor's Return*

Virginia Woolf

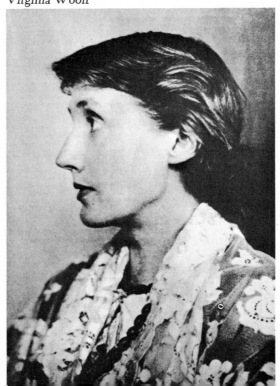

Dorothy Richardson

Robert Graves: *My Head! My Head!* (dedicated to T. E. Lawrence)
Aldous Huxley: *Those Barren Leaves*
Sebastian Knight: *The Prismatic Bezel*
D. H. Lawrence: *St. Mawr and The Princess*
W. Somerset Maugham: *The Painted Veil*
Liam O'Flaherty: *The Informer*
William Plomer: *Turbott Wolfe*
Dorothy Richardson: *The Trap*
Virginia Woolf: *Mrs. Dalloway*

D. H. Lawrence: translation of Giovanni Verga's *Novelle Rusticane* (*Little Novels of Sicily*)
Arthur Waley: translation of Lady Murasaki's *Tales of Genji*

VERSE AND DRAMA

William Blake: *Works* (edited by G. L. Keynes)
Robert Bridges: *New Verse*
Robert Graves: *Welchman's Hose; Twenty-Three Poems; John Kemp's Wager: A Ballad Opera*
Graham Greene: *Babbling April*
Thomas Hardy: *Human Shows, Far Phantasies, Songs and Trifles*
Aldous Huxley: *Selected Poems*
Edwin Muir: *First Poems*
Edith Sitwell: *Troy Park*
Algernon Charles Swinburne: *Works* (Bonchurch Edition, 20 vols., 1925–27; edited by Edmund Gosse and Thomas J. Wise)
W. B. Yeats: *Early Poems and Stories* (Collected Edition, Vol. V)

NON-FICTION

Norman Douglas: *Experiments* (dedicated to Bryher); *D. H. Lawrence and Maurice Magnus: A Plea for Better Manners* (privately printed, Florence)
Robert Graves: *Contemporary Techniques of Poetry* (dedicated to Edith Sitwell); *Poetic Unreason*
Aldous Huxley: *Along the Road: Notes and Essays of a Tourist*
W. P. Ker: *Collected Essays* (edited by Charles Whibley)
D. H. Lawrence: *Reflections on the Death of a Porcupine* (U.S.)
J. Middleton Murry: *Keats and Shakespeare*
Edith Sitwell: *Poetry and Criticism*
Virginia Woolf: *The Common Reader*
W. B. Yeats: *A Vision* (privately printed edition of an early version of the book which was published in its final form in 1937)

❧ ❧ *"Work is the best, and a certain numbness, a merciful numbness."*

D. H. LAWRENCE

Mr. and Mrs. F. Scott Fitzgerald and their daughter Frances, in Paris

United States

FICTION

Conrad Aiken: *Bring! Bring! and Other Stories*
Sherwood Anderson: *Dark Laughter*
Willa Cather: *The Professor's House*
Stephen Crane: *Works* (edited by Wilson Follett)
John Dos Passos: *Manhattan Transfer*
Theodore Dreiser: *An American Tragedy*
F. Scott Fitzgerald: *The Great Gatsby*
Ellen Glasgow: *Barren Ground*
Ernest Hemingway: *In Our Time*
Sarah Orne Jewett: *Best Stories* (edited by Willa Cather)
Sinclair Lewis: *Arrowsmith*
Anita Loos: *Gentlemen Prefer Blondes*
Gertrude Stein: *The Making of Americans* (Paris)
Elinor Wylie: *The Venetian Glass Nephew*

VERSE AND DRAMA

Léonie Adams: *Those Not Elect*
Conrad Aiken: *Priapus and the Pool and Other Poems*
Countee Cullen: *Color*
e. e. cummings: *&; XLI Poems*
H.D.: *Collected Poems*
Babette Deutsch: *Honey Out of the Rock*
T. S. Eliot: *Poems 1909–1925* (G.B.)
Robinson Jeffers: *Roan Stallion, Tamar and Other Poems*
James W. Johnson, ed.: *The Book of American Negro Spirituals*
Amy Lowell: *What's O'Clock*
Ezra Pound: *A Draft of XVI Cantos of Ezra Pound for the Beginning of a Poem of Some Length, Now First Made Into a Book* (Paris)
E. A. Robinson: *Dionysus in Doubt*
Ridgely Torrence: *Hesperides*
Glenway Wescott: *Natives of Rock: XX Poems: 1921–22*

Archibald MacLeish: *The Pot of Earth*

Theodore Dreiser

NON-FICTION

Van Wyck Brooks: *The Pilgrimage of Henry James*
Alfred Kreymborg: *Troubadour*
Amy Lowell: *John Keats*
George Santayana: *Dialogues in Limbo*
Edith Wharton: *The Writing of Fiction*
William Carlos Williams: *In the American Grain*

❧❧ *"I am writing for myself and strangers. This is the only way that I can do it."*

GERTRUDE STEIN

Related Events

DEATHS

Amy Lowell: American poet and biographer of
Keats; age 51; of a stroke, at her home in
Brookline, Massachusetts, on May 12

Erik Satie: French composer and wit; age 59; in
Paris, on July 1

IN OTHER LANGUAGES

Guillaume Apollinaire: *Il y a* (Preface by Ramón
Gómez de la Serna)

Franz Kafka: *Der Prozess*, edited by Max Brod
(*The Trial*)

José Ortega y Gasset: *La Deshumanización del
Arte* (*The Dehumanization of Art*)

Marcel Proust: *Albertine Disparue*

Jules Renard: *Journal*

IN OTHER ARTS

Films: Charles Chaplin: *The Gold Rush*

Music: Alban Berg: *Wozzeck* ‖ George
Gershwin: *Piano Concerto in F* ‖ Maurice
Ravel: *L'Enfant et les Sortilèges* (with
libretto by Colette)

Stage: Noel Coward: *Hay Fever* ‖ Eugene
O'Neill: *The Fountain*

Architecture: The Bauhaus, designed by Walter
Gropius, in Dessau, Germany (completed in
1928)

IN THE MARGIN

Laurels: The Dial Award to e. e. cummings ‖
The Pulitzer Prize for Fiction to Edna Ferber,
for *So-Big* ‖ The James Tait Black Prize to
E. M. Forster, for *A Passage to India* ‖ The
Hawthornden Prize to Sean O'Casey, for *Juno
and the Paycock* ‖ The Nobel Prize for
Literature to G. B. Shaw ‖ Paul Valéry
elected to the chair in *l'Académie française*
formerly held by Anatole France

Faits Divers:

With four children, and his wife in poor health,
Robert Graves accepts a position as Professor
of English Literature at the Royal Egyptian
University in Cairo, which he then, in spite of
the £1,400 salary, resigns the following year

The John Simon Guggenheim Memorial
Foundation gives its first fellowships

Having recently observed that those who win the
Nobel Prize are "like the modest hotels in
Baedeker—established, safe, uncontroversial,"
G. B. Shaw accepts his own award with the
provision that the money be used to establish
an Anglo-Swedish Literary Foundation, for
the purpose of encouraging "intercourse and
understanding between Sweden and the
British Isles"

Sean O'Casey

Langston Hughes

Working as a busboy in the Wardman Park Hotel in Washington, D.C., and unable to get into the hotel's "White Only" theater to hear Vachel Lindsay recite, Langston Hughes pays homage by leaving three of his own poems beside Lindsay's plate: "I looked back once and saw Mr. Lindsay reading the poems, as I picked up a tray of dirty dishes . . . and started for the dumb-waiter." That evening Lindsay began his recital by reading Hughes's poems, and the next morning Hughes arrived at work to find himself surrounded by reporters and his career launched

The New Yorker magazine, edited by Harold Ross, with Janet Flanner (Genêt) as Paris correspondent, begins publishing weekly

Hart Crane writes to banker-patron Otto Kahn, outlining his plans for *The Bridge*, offering references, and asking for a loan. Several days later, he emerges from an interview with Kahn with $1,000 in hand and the promise of another thousand to come

Progress Report on the Great American Novel:

E. M. Forster, on *The Making of Americans*, by Gertrude Stein: "There is nothing to ridicule in such an experiment as hers. It is much more important to play about like this than to re-write the Waverley Novels . . ."

James Agee (age 17½), on *An American Tragedy*, by Theodore Dreiser: "You feel you're reading a rather inadequate translation of a very great foreign novel—Russian, probably . . ."

T. S. Eliot, on *The Great Gatsby*, by F. Scott Fitzgerald: "It seems to me to be the first step that American fiction has taken since Henry James."

In the Great World: On May 9, in Dayton, Tennessee, John T. Scopes is arrested for teaching Darwin's theory of evolution in violation of a state law forbidding the dissemination in public schools of anything not conforming to "the story of the Divine creation of man as taught in the Bible." Scopes was tried in July, convicted, and fined $100.

In New York, Bennett Cerf and Donald Klopfer buy the Modern Library from Horace Liveright and begin their own Random House

En route to Europe for the first time, William Faulkner stops over in New Orleans, meets Sherwood Anderson, and lingers for six months, during which he completes his first novel, *Soldier's Pay*. A little later, reportedly in gratitude for not having been asked to read the manuscript, Anderson recommends it to his own publisher

This Quarter (edited intermittently until 1932 out of Paris, Milan and Monte Carlo) begins to publish Bryher, Kay Boyle, Ezra Pound, Valéry, Hemingway, etc.

Glenway Wescott settles in Villefranche, in the legendary Hotel Welcome, where Jean Cocteau is finishing his play *Orphée* in a room up the hall

Great Britain

FICTION

Agatha Christie: *The Murder of Roger Ackroyd*

Walter de la Mare: *The Connoisseur and Other Stories*

Ronald Firbank: *Concerning the Eccentricities of Cardinal Pirelli* (with a portrait by Augustus John)

Ford Madox Ford: *A Man Could Stand Up*

Henry Green (Henry Yorke): *Blindness*

Richard Hughes: *A Moment of Time*

Aldous Huxley: *Two or Three Graces, and Other Stories*

Rudyard Kipling: *Debits and Credits* (stories and poems)

D. H. Lawrence: *The Plumed Serpent*

W. Somerset Maugham: *The Casuarina Tree: Six Stories*

A. A. Milne: *Winnie the Pooh*

Sylvia Townsend Warner: *Lolly Willowes*

H. G. Wells: *The World of William Clissold*

VERSE AND DRAMA

W. H. Auden and Charles Plumb, eds.: *Oxford Poetry, 1926*

Wilfrid Gibson: *Collected Poems 1905–1925*

Richard Hughes: *Confessio Juvenis: Collected Poems*

Hugh MacDiarmid: *Penny Weep; A Drunk Man Looks at the Thistle*

Edwin Muir: *Chorus of the Newly Dead*

Herbert Read: *Collected Poems, 1913–1925*

Siegfried Sassoon: *Satirical Poems*

Edith Sitwell: *Elegy on Dead Fashion*

Humbert Wolfe: *News of the Devil*

D. H. Lawrence: *David*

G. B. Shaw: *Translations and Tomfooleries*

NON-FICTION

Joseph Conrad: *Last Essays*

Ford Madox Ford: *A Mirror to France* (dedicated to Gertrude Stein)

Robert Graves: *Another Future of Poetry*

Aldous Huxley: *Jesting Pilate*

T. E. Lawrence: *Seven Pillars of Wisdom* (limited edition of 128 subscription copies, sold at 30 guineas; trade edition 1935)

Wyndham Lewis: *The Art of Being Ruled*

Forrest Reid: *Apostate*

I. A. Richards: *Science and Poetry*

Sacheverell Sitwell: *All Summer in a Day: An Autobiographical Fantasia*

W. B. Yeats: *Estrangement: Being Some Fifty Thoughts from a Diary Kept in the Year 1909* (Cuala Press); *Autobiographies* (Collected Edition, Vol. VI)

❦ ❦ *"My poetry-writing has always been a painful process of continual corrections, corrections on top of corrections, and persistent dissatisfaction."*

ROBERT GRAVES

United States

FICTION

James Branch Cabell: *The Silver Stallion*

Willa Cather: *My Mortal Enemy*

Robert M. Coates: *The Eater of Darkness* (Paris)

H.D.: *Palimpsest*

William Faulkner: *Soldier's Pay*

Edna Ferber: *Show Boat*

F. Scott Fitzgerald: *All the Sad Young Men*

Janet Flanner: *The Cubical City*

Ellen Glasgow: *The Romantic Comedians*

Ernest Hemingway: *The Sun Also Rises* (G.B. title: *Fiesta*); *The Torrents of Spring*

Ring Lardner: *The Love Nest and Other Stories*

Sinclair Lewis: *Mantrap*

Elizabeth Madox Roberts: *The Time of Man*

Gertrude Stein: *A Book Concluding With As a Wife Has a Cow a Love Story* (with lithographs by Juan Gris; Paris)

D. H. Lawrence and Frieda in Mexico

Rainer Maria Rilke with Valéry's bust

Ernest Hemingway

S. S. Van Dine (Willard Huntington Wright):
    The Benson Murder Case
Carl Van Vechten: *Nigger Heaven*
Glenway Wescott: *Like a Lover* (Villefranche)
Thornton Wilder: *The Cabala*
Elinor Wylie: *The Orphan Angel* (G.B. title:
    Mortal Image)

VERSE AND DRAMA

Hart Crane: *White Buildings* (Foreword by
    Allen Tate)
e. e. cummings: *Is 5*
John Gould Fletcher: *Branches of Adam*
Langston Hughes: *The Weary Blues*
    (Introduction by Carl Van Vechten)
Vachel Lindsay: *The Candle in the Cabin: A
    Weaving Together of Script and Singing*
Amy Lowell: *East Wind*
Archibald MacLeish: *Streets in the Moon*

1926

Ezra Pound: *Personae: The Collected Poems of Ezra Pound*

Carl Sandburg: *Selected Poems* (edited by Rebecca West)

Genevieve Taggard: *Words for the Chisel*

Sara Teasdale: *Dark of the Moon*

Archibald MacLeish: *Nobodaddy*

NON-FICTION

Sherwood Anderson: *Sherwood Anderson's Notebook; Tar: A Midwest Childhood*

Will Durant: *The Story of Philosophy*

H. L. Mencken: *Notes on Democracy*

Carl Sandburg: *Abraham Lincoln: The Prairie Years*

Gertrude Stein: *Composition as Explanation* (G.B.)

Edmund Wilson: *Discordant Encounters: Plays and Dialogues*

❧❧ *"If a poet is anybody, he is somebody to whom things made matter very little— somebody who is obsessed by Making . . ."*

E. E. CUMMINGS

Related Events

DEATHS

Arthur Annesley Ronald Firbank: British novelist; 40; of pneumonia, in Rome, on May 21. Buried by mistake in the Protestant Cemetery, he was later reburied in the Catholic Cemetery of San Lorenzo. "Certainly he had wandered . . . He had been into Arcadia, even, a place where artificial temperaments so seldom get . . ."

Isaac Babel

Rainer Maria Rilke: Prague-born, German-language poet; 51; of leukemia, in Valmont, Switzerland, on December 29. "Works of art are of an infinite loneliness and nothing to be so little reached as with criticism. Only love can grasp and hold and fairly judge them."

IN OTHER LANGUAGES

Isaac Babel: *Konarmiya (Red Cavalry)*

Georges Bernanos: *Sous le Soleil de Satan*

Jean Cocteau: *Le Rappel à l'Ordre; Lettre à Jacques Maritain*

Colette: *La Fin de Chéri*

Sigmund Freud: *Hemmung, Symptom und Angst (The Problem of Anxiety)*

André Gide: *Les Faux-Monnayeurs*

Franz Kafka: *Das Schloss*, edited by Max Brod *(The Castle)*

V. Sirin (Vladimir Nabokov): *Maschenka*

IN OTHER ARTS

Stage: Sean O'Casey: *The Plough and the Stars* (with a riot at the Abbey Theatre, and Yeats mounting the stage to cry: "You have disgraced yourselves again . . . Synge first and then O'Casey . . . Dublin has once more rocked the cradle of genius!") || Eugene O'Neill: *The Great God Brown* || Eva Le Gallienne's Civic Repertory Theater opens on East 14th Street in New York

Music: Ezra Pound's opera based on François Villon's *Testament* is performed at the Salle Pleyel in Paris. ("It may well be the finest poet's music since Thomas Campion," said Virgil Thomson) || Giacomo Puccini's posthumous opera, *Turandot* || Maurice Ravel's *Chansons Madécasses* || Dmitri Shostakovich's *First Symphony*

Films: Sergei Eisenstein: *Potemkin* || V. I. Pudofkin: *Mother*

Other: The two sheets of glass on which Marcel Duchamp's *La Mariée mise à nu par ses célibataires même* (1915–23) was painted are accidentally broken: Duchamp declares that the cracks are part of his work

IN THE MARGIN

Accustomed to taking along a volume of the Encyclopedia Britannica on any short jaunt,

Sergei Eisenstein

Aldous Huxley has a special packing case made for the entire set, and in June sets out on a world cruise.

In March, **Sean O'Casey** goes to London to accept the previous year's Hawthornden Prize for *Juno and the Paycock*, and never again resumes residence in Ireland.

At the instigation of Edith Sitwell, **Gertrude Stein** crosses the Channel and delivers her lecture "Composition as Explanation" to the Ordinary Society at Oxford University. "It was very exciting. They asked all sorts of questions . . . One of the men was so moved that he confided to me as we went out that the lecture had been his greatest experience since he had read Kant's *Critique of Pure Reason*."

In May, **D. H. Lawrence** settles at the Villa Mirenda, near Florence, where he begins to write three different versions of his last novel, *Lady Chatterley's Lover*.

Mrs. Elizabeth Ames,
executive director of Yaddo

In June, the Corporation of Yaddo, established by the will of Katrina Trask, opens its doors at Saratoga Springs, New York, with Mrs. Elizabeth Ames as executive director and a first guest list including Louise Bogan and Joseph Warren Beach ___

Laurels:

The Dial Award to William Carlos Williams

The Pulitzer Prize for Poetry to Amy Lowell, for *What's O'Clock*

The Pulitzer Prize for Fiction to Sinclair Lewis—who refused it—for *Arrowsmith*

"Little Mags":

New Masses, with Michael Gold among its editors, and contributors including Eugene O'Neill, Carl Sandburg, Babette Deutsch, Kenneth Fearing, Horace Gregory, D. H. Lawrence

Voorslaag, edited in Durban, South Africa, by Roy Campbell, William Plomer, and Laurens van der Post, lasts for only a few issues because of its frontal attack on the color bar

Publishing: The Book-of-the-Month Club is founded in New York, its initial (April) selection being Sylvia Townsend Warner's novel, *Lolly Willowes*. Shortly afterward, The Literary Guild is set up along similar lines. New publishers include The Cresset Press in England, and in the United States, W. W. Norton, William Morrow, and the Vanguard Press.

In the Wings: Graham Greene, 22, is received into the Roman Catholic Church

In the Great World: The "General Strike" in Great Britain || Byrd flies over the North Pole

1927

Great Britain

FICTION

Elizabeth Bowen: *The Hotel*

Norman Douglas: *In the Beginning* (Florence)

Arthur Conan Doyle: *The Case-Book of Sherlock Holmes*

David Garnett: *Go She Must!*

Rosamond Lehmann: *Dusty Answer*

Wyndham Lewis: *The Wild Body, A Soldier of Humour, and Other Stories*

Compton Mackenzie: *Vestal Fire*

Forrest Reid: *Demophon: A Traveller's Tale*

Dorothy Richardson: *Oberland*

Virginia Woolf: *To the Lighthouse*

Wyndham Lewis

VERSE AND DRAMA

W. H. Auden and C. Day Lewis, eds.: *Oxford Poetry, 1927*

G. K. Chesterton: *Collected Poems*

Walter de la Mare: *Stuff and Nonsense*

Ford Madox Ford: *New Poems*

Robert Graves: *Poems 1914–1926*; ed., *The Less Familiar Nursery Rhymes*; ed.: *Selected Poems of John Skelton*

James Joyce: *Pomes Penyeach* (Paris)

A. A. Milne: *Now We Are Six*

Ruth Pitter: *First and Second Poems*

Edith Sitwell: *Rustic Elegies*

W. B. Yeats: *October Blast* (Cuala Press)

Norman Douglas

NON-FICTION

Joseph Conrad: *Life and Letters* (edited by G. Jean-Aubry)

Norman Douglas: *Birds and Beasts of the Greek Anthology* (Florence)

Ford Madox Ford: *New York Is Not America*

E. M. Forster: *Aspects of the Novel* (The Clark Lectures delivered at Cambridge University)

Roger Fry: *Cézanne: A Study of His Development*

Robert Graves: *Lars Porsena, or the Future of Swearing and Improper Language*; *Lawrence and the Arabs*; *The English Ballad*

Robert Graves and Laura Riding: *A Survey of Modernist Poetry*

Aldous Huxley: *Proper Studies*

D. H. Lawrence: *Mornings in Mexico*

T. E. Lawrence: *Revolt in the Desert* (abridged version of *Seven Pillars of Wisdom*)

Wyndham Lewis: *Time and Western Man*; *The Lion and the Fox: The Role of the Hero in the Plays of Shakespeare*

John Livingston Lowes: *The Road to Xanadu*

Katherine Mansfield: *Journal* (edited by J. Middleton Murry)

Harold Nicolson: *Some People*

Victoria Sackville-West: *Aphra Behn, the Incomparable Astrea*

❦❦ *"Yes—oh, dear, yes—the novel tells a story."*

E. M. FORSTER

United States

FICTION

Conrad Aiken: *Blue Voyage*

Willa Cather: *Death Comes for the Archbishop*

Theodore Dreiser: *Chains: Lesser Novels and Stories*

William Faulkner: *Mosquitoes*

Ernest Hemingway: *Men Without Women*
Sinclair Lewis: *Elmer Gantry*
Don Marquis: *Archy and Mehitabel*
Upton Sinclair: *Oil!*
Glenway Wescott: *The Grandmothers*
Edith Wharton: *Twilight Sleep*
Thornton Wilder: *The Bridge of San Luis Rey*

VERSE AND DRAMA

Sherwood Anderson: *A New Testament*
Donald Davidson: *The Tall Men*
T. S. Eliot: *Journey of the Magi* (G.B.)
Langston Hughes: *Fine Clothes to the Jew*
Robinson Jeffers: *The Women at Point Sur*
James W. Johnson: *God's Trombones: Seven Negro Sermons in Verse*
Amy Lowell: *Ballads for Sale* (edited by Mrs. Harold Russell)
John Crowe Ransom: *Two Gentlemen in Bonds*
E. A. Robinson: *Tristram; Collected Poems*
Carl Sandburg, ed.: *The American Song Bag* (folksong anthology)
Yvor Winters: *The Bare Hills*

H.D.: *Hippolytus Temporizes: A Play in Three Acts*
e. e. cummings: *him*

NON-FICTION

Charles A. and Mary R. Beard: *The Rise of American Civilization*
Van Wyck Brooks: *Emerson and Others*
T. S. Eliot: *Shakespeare and the Stoicism of Seneca* (G.B.)
Charles Lindbergh: *"We"*
Vernon L. Parrington: *Main Currents in American Thought*
George Santayana: *The Realm of Essence: Book First of Realms of Being*
Elizabeth Shepley Sergeant: *Fire Under the Andes: A Group of North American Portraits*

❧ ❧ *". . . the land that has inspired sentiment in the poet ultimately receives its sentiment from him."*

THORNTON WILDER

Glenway Wescott

Related Events

DEATHS

Brooks Adams: American political theorist and brother of Henry; on February 13
Isadora Duncan: American dance theorist and sister of Raymond; on September 14

IN OTHER LANGUAGES

Julien Benda: *La Trahison des Clercs*
Bertolt Brecht: *Die Hauspostille* (*Family Devotions*)
Jean Cocteau: *Opéra; Orphée*
Sigmund Freud: *Die Zukunft einer Illusion* (*The Future of an Illusion*)
Federico García Lorca: *Canciones* (*Songs*)

Thornton Wilder

W. H. Auden

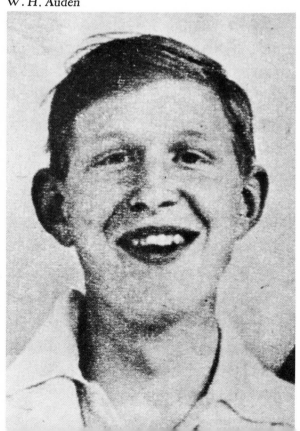

André Gide: *Voyage au Congo* (dedicated to Joseph Conrad)

Hermann Hesse: *Der Steppenwolf* (*The Steppenwolf*)

Franz Kafka: *Amerika*, edited by Max Brod (*America*)

Boris Pasternak: *Tysiacha deviat' sot piatyi god* (*This Year, 1905*)

Marcel Proust: *Le Temps Retrouvé*

IN OTHER ARTS

George Antheil's *Ballet Méchanique* performed in New York

Bertolt Brecht–Kurt Weill's opera *Mahagonny* has it première (original version) at Baden-Baden

Manuel de Falla's *Harpsichord Concerto* is played by the composer in Paris

Buckminster Fuller completes his first design for a Dymaxion House

Al Jolson stars in *The Jazz Singer*, the first feature-length talking picture

Ernst Křenek's opera *Jonny Spielt Auf* (*Johnny Plays On*)

W. Somerset Maugham's *The Constant Wife* and *The Letter*

Edna St. Vincent Millay–Deems Taylor's opera *The King's Henchman*

Jean Cocteau–Igor Stravinsky's oratorio *Oedipus Rex*

IN THE MARGIN

Names: Henri Bergson receives the Nobel Prize for Literature ‖ Theodore Dreiser visits the Soviet Union ‖ T. S. Eliot becomes a British citizen ‖ On behalf of James Joyce, 167 men-of-letters sign a protest against the pirated (and bowdlerized) version of *Ulysses* which had been appearing in an American magazine called *Two Worlds Monthly*, edited by a former bookshop proprietor named Samuel Roth ‖ Ezra Pound accepts the fifth Dial Award of $2,000

Ezra Pound, as seen by Jean Cocteau

In the Great World: Charles Lindbergh flies solo from New York to Paris in 33 hours and 30 minutes on May 21 || Nicola Sacco and Bartolomeo Vanzetti are electrocuted by the State of Massachusetts at midnight on August 22

In the Wings:

C. P. Snow, 22, after taking first class honors in chemistry, proceeds to research in infrared spectroscopy at Leicester University

Employed as an assistant night manager in a New York hotel, Nathanael West, 25, works on his first novel, and "arranges" special rates and free rooms for various friends, among them Dashiell Hammett, who finishes *The Maltese Falcon* while he is West's "house guest"

W. H. Auden, 20, has rooms on the second floor of Peckwater Quad in Christ Church, Oxford, where Christopher Isherwood, 23, visits him: "Over the writing table was a Picasso etching of two young acrobats (*'frightfully emotive!'*) [He] thrust into my hands an enormous book by Gertrude Stein ('my God, she's good!'),

Publishing: In Paris, the Black Sun Press is founded by Harry and Caresse Crosby || The first issue (there were four in all) of Ezra Pound's *Exile* appears in the spring || *The Hound and Horn* (until 1934) has Harvard undergraduates Lincoln Kirstein and R. P. Blackmur among its editors || Alfred Kreymborg, Lewis Mumford, and Paul Rosenfeld assemble the first of ten annual volumes (until 1936) of *The American Caravan* || "We are tired of the word that does not express the kinetic and the subconscious," declare Eugene Jolas and Elliot Paul, and their magazine *transition* (appearing monthly until 1933) publishes important sections of Joyce's *Work in Progress*, as well as Gertrude Stein, Franz Kafka, Hart Crane || Hilaire Belloc, 57, issues his 100th title (with 53 more to come): "The more enormous one's output, the more the publishers get to regard you as a reliable milch cow"

*Federico García Lorca
and Salvador Dali*

Jean Cocteau,
as the poet's guardian angel Heurtebise,
in his play Orphée

but I had barely opened it before I was told to 'listen to this: she's absolutely the *only* woman comedian. [He] had put a record of Sophie Tucker, singing 'After you've gone away' on to the gramophone, but I couldn't hear much of it, because he began, at the same time, to read aloud a poem by Morgenstern, despite my protests that I didn't understand a word of German . . .'

In Paris, writing book reviews and cresting his 24th birthday, Cyril Connolly makes assorted vows: "To be obtained before I am twenty-five: £1,000 a year, a book published, a Spanish mistress, some fame, more friends, a knowledge of German, and a visit to Cadiz"

Great Britain

FICTION

Jane Austen: *The Watsons: Completed in Accordance with Her Intentions by Edith* (her great grand-niece) *and Francis Brown*

Ford Madox Ford: *The Last Post; A Little Less Than Gods*

E. M. Forster: *The Eternal Moment and Other Stories* (dedicated to T. E. Lawrence)

David Garnett: *The Old Dovecote and Other Stories*

Radclyffe Hall: *The Well of Loneliness*

Aldous Huxley: *Point Counter Point*

Christopher Isherwood: *All the Conspirators*

James Joyce: *Anna Livia Plurabelle* (U.S.)

D. H. Lawrence: *The Woman Who Rode Away; Lady Chatterley's Lover* (Florence)

Wyndham Lewis: *The Childermass, Section I*

Compton Mackenzie: *Extraordinary Women*

W. Somerset Maugham: *Ashenden, or The British Agent*

A. A. Milne: *The House at Pooh Corner*

Siegfried Sassoon: *Memoirs of a Fox-Hunting Man* (first impression published anonymously)

Evelyn Waugh: *Decline and Fall, an Illustrated Novelette*

Virginia Woolf: *Orlando* (dedicated to Vita Sackville-West)

D. H. Lawrence: translation of Giovanni Verga's *Cavalleria Rusticana and Other Stories*

VERSE AND DRAMA

W. H. Auden: *Poems* (printed by Stephen Spender on an Adana press used for making chemists' labels, and dedicated to Christopher Isherwood)

Roy Campbell: *The Wayzgoose*

Norman Douglas: *Some Limericks*

Thomas Hardy: *Winter Words in Various Moods and Metres*

1928

Siegfried Sassoon

D. H. Lawrence: *Collected Poems*
Edith Sitwell: *Five Poems*
Stephen Spender: *Nine Experiments*
W. B. Yeats: *The Tower*

W. B. Yeats: *Sophocles' "King Oedipus": A Version for the Modern Stage*

NON-FICTION

Max Beerbohm: *A Variety of Things*
Joseph Conrad: *Letters from Conrad, 1895–1924* (edited by Edward Garnett)
Florence E. Hardy: *The Early Life of Thomas Hardy, 1840–91*
W. P. Ker: *Form and Style in Poetry* (edited by R. W. Chambers)
Edwin Muir: *The Structure of the Novel*
V. S. Pritchett: *Marching Spain*
Forrest Reid: *Illustrators of the Sixties*
G. B. Shaw: *The Intelligent Woman's Guide to Socialism and Capitalism*

Lytton Strachey: *Elizabeth and Essex: A Tragic History*
Evelyn Waugh: *Rossetti, His Life and Work*
Rebecca West: *The Strange Necessity*
W. B. Yeats: *The Death of Synge, and Other Passages from an Old Diary* (Cuala Press)

W. A. Craigie and C. T. Onions (editorial supervisors): *The Oxford Dictionary on Historical Principles* (final volume, completing 15,487 pages; "A–Ant" published in 1884)

❧ ❧ *"Sheashell ebb music wayriver she flows."*

JAMES JOYCE

United States

FICTION

Conrad Aiken: *Costumes by Eros*
Djuna Barnes: *Ryder*
H.D.: *Hedylus* (G.B.)
Sinclair Lewis: *The Man Who Knew Coolidge*
Glenway Wescott: *Good-Bye, Wisconsin*

W. B. Yeats

Edith Wharton: *The Children*
William Carlos Williams: *A Voyage to Pagany*
(dedicated "to the first of us all: my old friend
Ezra Pound . . .")
Elinor Wylie: *Mr. Hodge and Mr. Hazard*

VERSE AND DRAMA

Stephen Vincent Benét: *John Brown's Body*
T. S. Eliot: *A Song for Simeon* (G.B.)
John Gould Fletcher: *The Black Rock*
Robert Frost: *West-Running Brook*
Rolfe Humphries: *Europa and Other Poems and
Sonnets*
Robinson Jeffers: *Cawdor and Other Poems*
Vachel Lindsay: *Johnny Appleseed and Other
Poems*
Amy Lowell: *Selected Poems* (edited by John
Livingston Lowes)
Archibald MacLeish: *The Hamlet of A.
MacLeish*
Edna St. Vincent Millay: *The Buck in the Snow
and Other Poems*
Ezra Pound: *A Draft of Cantos XVII to XXVII,
Selected Poems* (Introduction by T. S. Eliot;
G.B.)
E. A. Robinson: *Sonnets 1889–1927*
Carl Sandburg: *Good Morning, America*
Genevieve Taggard: *Travelling Standing Still:
Poems, 1918–1928*
Allen Tate: *Mr. Pope and Other Poems*

Allen Tate

Djuna Barnes

Elinor Wylie: *Trivial Breath*

Thornton Wilder: *The Angel That Troubled the
Waters and Other Plays*

Eugene O'Neill

NON-FICTION

Djuna Barnes: *Ladies Almanac, showing their signs and their tides; their moons and their changes; their seasons as it is with them; their eclipses and equinoxes; as well as a full record of diurnal and nocturnal distempers* (published anonymously as by "A Lady of Fashion"; Paris)

Theodore Dreiser: *Dreiser Looks at Russia*

T. S. Eliot: *For Lancelot Andrewes: Essays on Style and Order* (G.B.)

Zona Gale: *Portage, Wisconsin, and Other Essays*

Laura Riding: *Contemporaries and Snobs*

Gertrude Stein: *Useful Knowledge*

Allen Tate: *Stonewall Jackson: The Good Soldier*

❧ ❧ *"What we call the creative spirit really does not create anything. It evokes and recollects and relates."*

GLENWAY WESCOTT

Related Events

DEATHS

Thomas Hardy, British poet and novelist; 88; of heart failure, at his home, Max Gate, near Dorchester, on January 11. His ashes were interred in the Poets' Corner of Westminster Abbey (the pallbearers including Prime Minister Stanley Baldwin, G. B. Shaw, Rudyard Kipling, A. E. Housman), and a casket containing his heart was buried beside the grave of his first wife under a yew tree in the churchyard of Stinsford, Dorset, where Hardy had been baptized and attended services as a boy.

Charlotte Mew, British poet; 58; of suicide (by swallowing disinfectant), in London, on March 24. As one of her staunchest admirers, Thomas Hardy once copied her poem "Fin de Fête" on the back of a Reading Room slip in the British Museum, and in 1923, he helped secure her a Civil List Pension of £75 a year, calling her "the least pretentious but undoubtedly the best woman poet of our day."

Other Deaths:

Edmund Gosse, British man-of-letters and critic, May 26

Elinor Wylie, American poet and novelist, December 16

IN OTHER LANGUAGES

Rafael Alberti: *Sobre los Ángeles* (*About the Angels*)

André Breton: *Nadja*

Colette: *La Naissance du Jour*

Stefan George: *Das Neue Reich* (*The New Reich*)

André Gide: *Le Retour du Tchad*

Federico García Lorca: *Romancero Gitano* (*Gypsy Ballads*)

V. Sirin (Vladimir Nabokov); *Korol, Dama, Walet* (*King, Queen, Knave*)

Jakob Wassermann: *Der Fall Maurizius* (*The Maurizius Case*)

IN OTHER ARTS

Music: Igor Stravinsky's *Apollon Musagètes* (April 27, Washington, D.C.) ‖ Kurt Weill's *Dreigroschenoper* (with libretto by Bertolt Brecht, based on John Gay's *Threepenny Opera*; August 31, Berlin) ‖ Maurice Ravel's *Boléro* (November 22, Paris) ‖ George Gershwin's *An American in Paris* (December 13, New York)

Theater: e. e. cummings' *him* produced by the Provincetown Playhouse, with 105 characters played by a cast of 30, and 21 scene changes ‖ W. Somerset Maugham's *The Sacred Flame* ‖ Sean O'Casey's *The Silver Tassie* ‖ Eugene O'Neill's *Marco Millions*; *Lazarus Laughed* (Pasadena); *Strange Interlude*

Films: Charles Chaplin: *The Circus* ‖ Carl Dreyer: *La Passion de Jeanne d'Arc* ‖ Sergei Eisenstein: *October (Ten Days That Shook the World)*

IN THE MARGIN

Laurels: Pulitzer Prizes: for the Novel, to Thornton Wilder, for *The Bridge of San Luis Rey*; for Drama, to Eugene O'Neill, for *Strange Interlude*; for Poetry, to E. A. Robinson, for *Tristram*; for History, to Vernon L. Parrington, for *Main Currents in American Thought* ‖ The Nobel Prize for Literature to Sigrid Undset, of Norway

From Lady Chatterley's Mailbag:

Aldous Huxley, in a letter to Victoria Ocampo: "C'est un livre sur lequel on pourrait faire une étude très intéressante. Ce fait si curieux, par example, que Lawrence ne dit rien sur les sentiments et les sensations de Mellors—qu'il parle seulement de la femme . . . J'admire énormement les livres de Lawrence et je l'ai beaucoup aimé personnellement—mais je souffre souvent en le lisant d'une espèce de claustrophobie . . ."

W. B. Yeats, in a letter to Olivia Shakespear: ". . . the language is sometimes that of cabmen and yet the book is all fire. Those two lovers, the gamekeeper and his employer's wife, each separated from their class by their love, and by fate, are poignant in their loneliness, and the coarse language of the one, accepted by both, becomes a forlorn poetry uniting their solitudes, something ancient, humble and terrible . . ."

Thomas Hardy with the Prince of Wales

At Law: In November, Radclyffe Hall's novel about Lesbian love, *The Well of Loneliness*, is put on trial in London. Declining to hear some forty witnesses, the presiding magistrate declares that the book's gravest offense is its failure to suggest "that anyone with the horrible tendencies described is in the least degree blameworthy. All the characters are presented as attractive people and put forward with admiration." Speaking from a less sheltered point of view, Rebecca West nevertheless felt strained: "Everybody who knows Miss Radclyffe Hall wants to stand by her. But they are finding it far from easy to stand by *The*

Well of Loneliness, for the simple reason that it is, in a way which is particularly inconvenient in the present circumstances, not a very good book . . ." *The Well of Loneliness* was not republished in Great Britain until 1949. At the American trial in New York in 1929, the judge rendered much the same opinion as his English colleague, but his verdict was unanimously reversed by a higher court, marking the end of successful prosecutions of subject matter per se.

In the Wings:

In Vienna, after attending the Oktoberfest, Thomas Wolfe receives a letter from Scribner's Maxwell Perkins, expressing interest in the manuscript of *Look Homeward, Angel,* as well as concern over the book's length. Wolfe's reply was frankly forewarning: ". . . although I am able to criticize wordiness and overabundance in others, I am not able practically to criticize it in myself. The business of selection and of revision is simply hell for me—my efforts to cut out 50,000 words may sometimes result in my adding 75,000."

In Berlin, W. H. Auden discovers Tolstoy during Christmas week: "I had spent my month's allowance and the friends from whom I might have borrowed were all out of town, so that I could not afford to leave the house and passed the days with my feet up on the very inadequate tiled stove, reading *War and Peace* for the first time, cold, hungry and very happy . . ."

In Liverpool, after leaving Oxford, Henry Green goes to work as an iron molder for the family firm of H. Pontifex & Sons, Ltd., manufacturers of distillery equipment

In Connecticut, Richard Hughes spends the winter alone in a rundown, stoveless farmhouse—writing *A High Wind in Jamaica*

In the Great World: Herbert Hoover elected 31st President of the United States

Richard Hughes

Great Britain

FICTION

Richard Aldington: *Death of a Hero*
Elizabeth Bowen: *The Last September*
Ivy Compton-Burnett: *Brothers and Sisters*
Norman Douglas: *Nerinda* (originally published in *Unprofessional Tales,* 1901)
Ronald Firbank: *Collected Works* (Rainbow Edition in 8 volumes, with an Introduction by Arthur Waley and a Biographical Memoir by Osbert Sitwell)

Ford Madox Ford: *No Enemy* (U.S.)

John Galsworthy: *A Modern Comedy* (includes *The White Monkey*, 1924; *The Silver Spoon*, 1926; *Swan Song*, 1928)

Henry Green: *Living*

Graham Greene: *The Man Within*

Richard Hughes: *A High Wind in Jamaica* (U.S. title: *The Innocent Voyage*)

James Joyce: *Tales Told of Shem and Shaun* (Paris)

D. H. Lawrence: *The Escaped Cock* (Paris; reprinted in 1931 as *The Man Who Died*)

J. C. Powys: *Wolf Solent*

J. B. Priestley: *The Good Companions*

Rebecca West: *Harriet Hume: A London Fantasy*

VERSE AND DRAMA

Edmund Blunden: *Near and Far*

Robert Bridges: *The Testament of Beauty*

Robert Graves: *Poems*

Robert Graves

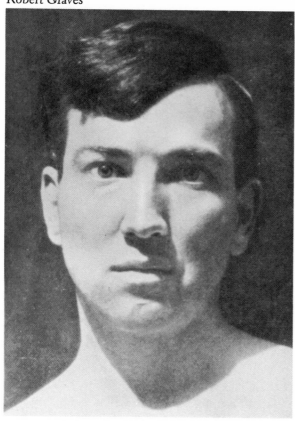

Aldous Huxley: *Arabia Infelix and Other Poems*

D. H. Lawrence: *Pansies*

C. Day Lewis: *Transitional Poem*

Louis MacNeice: *Blind Fireworks*

Charlotte Mew: *The Rambling Sailor*

Edith Sitwell: *Gold Coast Customs*

Stephen Spender and Louis MacNeice, eds.: *Oxford Poetry, 1929*

W. B. Yeats: *The Winding Stair* (N.Y.; trade edition, enlarged, in 1933)

NON-FICTION

Samuel Beckett *et al.*: *Our Exagmination Round His Factification for Incamination of Work in Progress* (Paris)

David Cecil: *The Stricken Deer; or, The Life of Cowper*

Joseph Conrad: *Lettres françaises* (edited by G. Jean-Aubry; Paris)

Bonamy Dobrée: *The Lamp and the Lute: Studies in Six Modern Authors*

Norman Douglas: *One Day; How About Europe?*

Ford Madox Ford: *The English Novel*

Robert Graves: *Goodbye to All That* (dedicated to Laura Riding)

Aldous Huxley: *Do What You Will*

D. H. Lawrence: *Pornography and Obscenity; Paintings* (privately printed)

Katherine Mansfield: *Letters* (edited by J. Middleton Murry)

Forrest Reid: *Walter de la Mare: A Critical Study*

I. A. Richards: *Practical Criticism*

Sacheverell Sitwell: *The Gothick North: A Study of Mediaeval Life, Art, and Thought* (3 vols. through 1930)

Virginia Woolf: *A Room of One's Own*

W. B. Yeats: *A Packet for Ezra Pound* (Cuala Press)

❧ ❧ *" 'Formlessness' is a relative term (i.e., no form is form till it is repeated) . . ."*

RICHARD HUGHES

Thomas Wolfe

Edith Wharton

United States

FICTION

Djuna Barnes: *A Night Among the Horses*
Theodore Dreiser: *A Gallery of Women*
William Faulkner: *Sartoris; The Sound and the
     Fury*
Ellen Glasgow: *They Stooped to Folly*
Ernest Hemingway: *A Farewell to Arms*
Oliver La Farge: *Laughing Boy*
Ring Lardner: *Round Up*
Sinclair Lewis: *Dodsworth*
John Steinbeck: *The Cup of Gold*
Edith Wharton: *Hudson River Bracketed*
Edmund Wilson: *I Thought Of Daisy*
Thomas Wolfe: *Look Homeward, Angel: A Story
     of the Buried Life*

Malcolm Cowley: translation of Raymond
     Radiguet's *Le bal du Comte d'Orgel* (*The
     Count's Ball*)
Janet Flanner: translation of Colette's *Chéri*

VERSE AND DRAMA

Léonie Adams: *High Falcon and Other Poems*
Conrad Aiken: *Selected Poems*; ed.: *American
     Poetry 1671–1928: A Comprehensive
     Anthology*
Louise Bogan: *Dark Summer*
Malcolm Cowley: *Blue Juniata*
H.D.: *Red Roses for Bronze*
Emily Dickinson: *Further Poems: Withheld
     from Publication by Her Sister Lavinia*
     (edited by Martha Dickinson Bianchi and
     Alfred L. Hampson)
T. S. Eliot: *Animula* (G.B.)
Kenneth Fearing: *Angel Arms*
Robinson Jeffers: *Dear Judas and Other Poems*

Malcolm Cowley and Robert Penn Warren

Vachel Lindsay: *Every Soul Is a Circus*
Archibald MacLeish: *Einstein* (Paris)
Merrill Moore: *The Noise That Time Makes*
    (Foreword by John Crowe Ransom)
E. A. Robinson: *Cavender's House*
Edmund Wilson: *Poets, Farewell!*
Elinor Wylie: *Angels and Earthly Creatures*

Witter Bynner: translation of *The Jade
    Mountain: A Chinese Anthology of T'ang
    Dynasty Poems:* A.D. 618–906

NON-FICTION

Sherwood Anderson: *Hello Towns!*
John Dewey: *The Quest for Certainty*
T. S. Eliot: *Dante* (G.B.)
Alfred Kreymborg: *Our Singing Strength: An
    Outline of American Poetry* (1620–1930)
Joseph Wood Krutch: *The Modern Temper: A
    Study and a Confession*

Ludwig Lewisohn: *Mid-Channel: An American
    Chronicle*
Carl Sandburg: *Steichen, the Photographer*
Allen Tate: *Jefferson Davis: His Rise and Fall*
James Thurber and E. B. White: *Is Sex
    Necessary? or Why You Feel the Way You Do*
Robert Penn Warren: *John Brown: The Making
    of a Martyr*

❧❧ "*. . . the writer has not got time to
say 'Now, I'm going to teach you a lesson.'
The writer is saying 'I'm going to tell you
a story that is funny or tragic.'*"

WILLIAM FAULKNER

The marriage of Henry Green

Related Events

DEATHS

Bliss Carman, Canadian poet

Harry Crosby, American publisher and cultural emblem

Sergei Pavlovich Diaghilev, Russian lover of the arts, bibliophile, and ballet impresario

Hugo von Hofmannsthal, Austrian dramatist, poet, man-of-letters, and librettist for Richard Strauss

IN OTHER LANGUAGES

Paul Claudel: *Le Soulier de Satin*

Jean Cocteau: *Les Enfants Terribles*

Colette: *La Seconde*

André Gide: *L'École des Femmes*

Alberto Moravia (Alberto Pincherle): *Gli Indifferenti (The Indifferent Ones)*

French translation of James Joyce's *Ulysses*, by Auguste Morel, with the assistance of Stuart Gilbert, Valéry Larbaud, and the author

IN OTHER ARTS

Theater: The First G. B. Shaw Festival at Malvern, with *The Apple Cart* || Eugene O'Neill's *Dynamo* || Noel Coward's *Bitter-Sweet* || Sean O'Casey's *The Silver Tassie*

Films: Luis Buñuel—Salvador Dali's *Un Chien Andalou* || Walt Disney's *Skeleton Dance*

Music: Igor Stravinsky's *Capriccio for Piano and Orchestra*

Other: Museum of Modern Art founded in New York

IN THE MARGIN

Laurels: Pulitzer Prize for Poetry to Stephen Vincent Benét, for *John Brown's Body* || Nobel Prize for Literature to Thomas Mann || James Tait Black Prize to Siegfried Sassoon, for *Memoirs of a Fox-Hunting Man* || Rhodes Scholarship to Robert Penn Warren

Faits Divers:

Following his return to America after five years' residence in France, Archibald MacLeish sets out by pack mule to retrace Cortez's route through Mexico, gathering impressions for his poem-to-be, *Conquistador*

Henry Green's marriage to Mary Adelaide provides his future reading public with one of the few front-view photographs of himself he has ever permitted

Visiting Ireland, Robinson Jeffers makes a special trip to see Yeats's Tour Ballylee and compare it with his own bastion on the Carmel coast in California

Thirteen paintings by D. H. Lawrence are confiscated by the police at Dorothy Warren's gallery in London; in addition, his publisher, in fear of prosecution, omits fourteen poems from *Pansies*; and imported copies of the Florence edition of *Lady Chatterley's Lover* are regularly seized and destroyed by order of the Home Secretary

In America's Deep South, William Faulkner begins "to think of books in terms of possible money . . . I took a little time out, and speculated what a person in Mississippi would believe to be current trends, chose what I thought was the right answer and invented the most horrific tale I could imagine and wrote it in about three weeks . . ." The result: *Sanctuary*

John Farrar and Stanley Rinehart start their own publishing house

Nancy Cunard inaugurates her Hours Press in Paris

Boston Posts Its Bans: Among the thirty current books being suppressed in the "Hub" of America are Upton Sinclair's *Oil*, Bertrand Russell's *What I Believe*, Sinclair Lewis's *Elmer Gantry*, H. G. Wells's *The World of William Clissold*, and Ernest Hemingway's *The Sun Also Rises*

In the Great World: First Five Year Plan in the U.S.S.R. ‖ The New York Stock Market Crash (October 29) precipitates a decade of economic depression in the U.S. and Western Europe

Evelyn Waugh

1930

Great Britain

FICTION

John Collier: *His Monkey Wife*
Walter de la Mare: *On the Edge*
John Galsworthy: *On Forsyte Change*
Graham Greene: *The Name of Action*
Aldous Huxley: *Brief Candles*
James Joyce: *Haveth Childers Everywhere* (U.S.)

Rudyard Kipling: *Thy Servant a Dog: Told by Boots; edited by Rudyard Kipling*
D. H. Lawrence: *The Virgin and the Gypsy; Love Among the Haystacks* (with a Reminiscence by David Garnett)
Wyndham Lewis: *The Apes of God*
Frederick Manning: *Her Privates We, by Private 19022* (originally published in 1929, in Paris, as *The Middle Parts of Fortune*)
Katherine Mansfield: *The Aloe* (original version of *Prelude*)
W. Somerset Maugham: *Cakes and Ale: or the Skeleton in the Cupboard*
George Moore: *Aphrodite in Aulis*
J. B. Priestley: *Angel Pavement*
Victoria Sackville-West: *The Edwardians*
Siegfried Sassoon: *Memoirs of an Infantry Officer*
G. B. Shaw: *Immaturity* (written in 1879)
Evelyn Waugh: *Vile Bodies*
Charles Williams: *War in Heaven*

Willa and Edwin Muir: translation of Franz Kafka's *Das Schloss* (*The Castle*)

VERSE AND DRAMA

Richard Aldington: *A Dream in the Luxembourg*
W. H. Auden: *Poems*
Samuel Beckett: *Whoroscope* (Paris)

W. Somerset Maugham

Hilaire Belloc: *New Cautionary Tales*
Edmund Blunden: *Poems 1914–30*
Roy Campbell: *Adamastor; Poems* (Paris)
Elizabeth Daryush: *Verses*
Walter de la Mare, ed.: *Desert Islands*
Robert Graves: *Ten Poems More* (Paris)
Gerard Manley Hopkins: *Poems* (enlarged
    edition, edited by Charles Williams)
D. H. Lawrence: *Nettles*
Hugh MacDiarmid: *To Circumjack Cencrastus,
    or the Curly Snake*
Edith Sitwell: *Collected Poems*
Stephen Spender: *Twenty Poems*
Humbert Wolfe: *The Uncelestial City*

G. B. Shaw: *The Apple Cart* (produced 1929);
    Collected Works

NON-FICTION

Norman Douglas: *Capri: Materials for a
    Description of the Island* (Florence); *Paneros*
    (Florence)
William Empson: *Seven Types of Ambiguity*
Robert Graves: *But It Still Goes On: An
    Accumulation*
Florence E. Hardy: *The Later Years of Thomas
    Hardy, 1892–1928*
Aldous Huxley: *Vulgarity in Literature*
D. H. Lawrence: *Assorted Articles; A Propos of
    Lady Chatterley's Lover*
Katherine Mansfield: *Novels and Novelists*
W. Somerset Maugham: *The Gentleman in the
    Parlor: A Record of a Journey from Rangoon
    to Haiphong*
G. B. Shaw and Ellen Terry: *A Correspondence*
Edith Sitwell: *Alexander Pope*
Queen Victoria: *Letters, 1886–1901*
Evelyn Waugh: *Labels, a Mediterranean Journal*
Rebecca West: *D. H. Lawrence*
Charles Williams: *Poetry at Present*

Christopher Isherwood: translation of Charles
    Baudelaire's *Journaux Intimes* (*Intimate
    Journals*), with an Introduction by T. S. Eliot

❧ ❧ *"I always say, my motto is 'Art for my
sake.'"*

               D. H. LAWRENCE

United States

FICTION

Edward Dahlberg: *Bottom Dogs* (Preface
    by D. H. Lawrence)
John Dos Passos: *The 42nd Parallel*
William Faulkner: *As I Lay Dying*
Dashiell Hammett: *The Maltese Falcon*
Langston Hughes: *Not Without Laughter*
Katherine Anne Porter: *Flowering Judas*
    (enlarged 1935)
Elizabeth Madox Roberts: *The Great Meadow*
Gertrude Stein: *Lucy Church Amiably: A Novel
    of Romantic Beauty and Nature Which Looks
    Like an Engraving* (Plain Edition)
Glenway Wescott: *The Babe's Bed* (Paris)
Edith Wharton: *Certain People*
Thornton Wilder: *The Woman of Andros*

John Dos Passos

Katherine Anne Porter

NON-FICTION

Henry Adams: *Letters* (edited by Chauncey Ford; Vol. II in 1938)

Michael Gold: *Jews Without Money*

Amy Lowell: *Poetry and Poets: Essays* (edited by Ferris Greenslet)

H. L. Mencken: *Treatise on the Gods*

Ezra Pound: *Imaginary Letters* (Paris)

John Crowe Ransom: *God Without Thunder;* ed.: *I'll Take My Stand* (a symposium of Southern agrarians, with contributions by Andrew Lytle, Robert Penn Warren, etc.)

George Santayana: *The Realm of Matter: Book Second of Realms of Being*

Genevieve Taggard: *The Life and Mind of Emily Dickinson*

VERSE AND DRAMA

Conrad Aiken: *John Deth: A Metaphysical Legend and Other Poems*

Hart Crane: *The Bridge* (photographs by Walker Evans)

Stephen Crane: *Collected Poems* (edited by Wilson Follett)

e. e. cummings: ―――― [no title]

Babette Deutsch: *Fire for the Night*

T. S. Eliot: *Ash Wednesday; Marina* (G.B.)

Robert Frost: *Collected Poems*

Horace Gregory: *Chelsea Rooming House*

Archibald MacLeish: *New Found Land*

Ezra Pound: *A Draft for XXX Cantos* (Paris; trade edition 1933)

E. A. Robinson: *The Glory of the Nightingales*

Allen Tate: *Ode to the Confederate Dead, Message from Abroad, and The Cross*

T. S. Eliot: translation of Saint-John Perse's *Anabase (Anabasis)*

D. H. Lawrence

1930

❦❦ *"All the things I write of I have first known, and they are real to me."*

KATHERINE ANNE PORTER

Related Events

DEATHS

D. H. Lawrence, British poet, novelist, essayist, translator, and prophet of sexual emancipation ("Serve the Holy Ghost; never serve mankind"); age 45; of consumption, on March 2, in Vence, Alps Maritimes, France. In a letter to *The Nation and the Athenaeum*, dated March 29, E. M. Forster wrote: "Now he is dead, and the low-brows whom he scandalized have united with the high-brows whom he bored to ignore his greatness . . . All that we can do . . . is to say straight out that he was the greatest imaginative novelist of our generation." The following week, T. S. Eliot challenged Forster to define his terms, and had a reply dated April 12: "Mr. T. S. Eliot duly entangles me in his web. He asks exactly what I mean by 'greatest', 'imaginative', and 'novelist', and I cannot say. Worse still, I cannot even say what 'exactly' means—only that there are occasions when I would rather feel like a fly than a spider, and that the death of D. H. Lawrence is one of these."

Other Deaths:

Robert Bridges, British Poet Laureate and editor of Gerard Manley Hopkins, age 86
Arthur Conan Doyle, British novelist and creator of Sherlock Holmes, age 71

IN OTHER LANGUAGES

André Breton: *Second Manifeste du Surréalisme*
Jean Cocteau: *Opium*
Colette: *Sido*

Sigmund Freud: *Das Unbehagen in der Kultur* (Civilization and Its Discontents)
Thomas Mann: *Mario und Der Zauberer* (Mario and the Magician)
Robert Musil: *Der Mann Ohne Eigenschaften* (The Man Without Qualities)
V. Sirin (Vladimir Nabokov): *Saschtschita Luschina* (The Defense)
José Ortega y Gasset: *La Rebelión de las Masas* (The Revolt of the Masses)
Luigi Pirandello: *Questa Sera Si Recita a Soggetto* (Tonight We Improvise); *Come Tu Mi Vuoi* (As You Desire Me)
Ignazio Silone (Secondo Tranqilli): *Fontamara* (Zurich)

IN OTHER ARTS

Brussels: Igor Stravinsky: *Symphonie des Psaumes*
Leipzig: Kurt Weill's expanded version of *Aufstieg und Fall der Stadt Mahagonny*, with Bertolt Brecht's libretto

Sinclair Lewis receiving the Nobel Prize for Literature in Stockholm

London: Noel Coward: *Private Lives* || W. Somerset Maugham: *The Breadwinner*

Los Angeles: Sergei Eisenstein contracts with Mrs. Upton Sinclair to make a film based on Jack London's "The Mexican," specifying that in return for a capital of $25,000, Mrs. Sinclair "may market the material in any manner . . . she desires, and shall be the sole owner of all the world rights." In December, Eisenstein and his camera crew leave for Mexico City to begin work on *Que Viva Mexico!*

New York: Aaron Copland: *Piano Variations* (dedicated to Gerald Sykes)

LAURELS

England: John Masefield appointed Poet Laureate to succeed Robert Bridges

United States: Pulitzer Prize for Poetry to Conrad Aiken, for *Selected Poems*

Sweden: Nobel Prize for Literature to Sinclair Lewis, who delivered his acceptance speech on December 12: "There are young Americans to-day who are doing such passionate and authentic work that it makes me sick to see that I am a little too old to be one of them. There is Ernest Hemingway, a bitter youth, educated by the most intense experience, disciplined by his own high standards, an authentic artist whose home is the whole of life: there is Thomas Wolfe, a child of, I believe, thirty or younger, whose one and only novel, *Look Homeward, Angel*, is worthy to be compared with the best in our literary production, a Gargantuan creature with great gusto of life . . ."

IN THE MARGIN

Gertrude Stein sells a painting, Picasso's "Girl with a Fan," and with the money, finances the "Plain Edition," managed by Alice B. Toklas, for the purpose of publishing her own writings. The first volume, *Lucy Church Amiably*, is ready for subscription sale at the end of the year.

At the Grand Hotel at Aix-les-Bains, **Willa Cather** encounters a gracious old lady, Madame Grout, who turns out to be Flaubert's niece:

Willa Cather

"Some moments went by. There was no word with which one could greet such a revelation. I took one of her lovely hands and kissed it, in homage to a great period . . ."

Barbara Harrison and **Monroe Wheeler** launch their fine-editions press, Harrison of Paris.

Elk-hunting near Cooke, Montana, **Ernest Hemingway** and **John Dos Passos** drive their Ford into a ditch; Hemingway incurs a fractured arm.

In Zurich, on May 15, Professor Alfred Vogt performs the ninth operation for tertiary cataract on **James Joyce**'s left eye.

Aged 21, and a junior at Harvard University, **James Agee** writes to Father James Harold Flye, and dreams of his future: "I'd do anything on earth to become a really great writer. That's as sincere a thing as I've ever said . . . I should like to parallel, foolish as it sounds, what Shakespeare did. That is—in general—to write primarily about people, giving their emotions and dramas the expression that, because of its beauty and power, will be most likely to last. But—worse than that: I'd like, in a sense, to combine what Chekhov did with what Shakespeare did—that is, to move from the dim, rather eventless beauty of C. to huge geometric plots such as *Lear* . . ."

Aged 27, **Evelyn Waugh** is received into the Roman Catholic Church, and goes to Abyssinia to report on the coronation of Emperor Haile Selassie.

Federico García Lorca is in New York; **Henry Miller** settles in Paris, remaining resident until 1939; and at the University of Chicago, **Thornton Wilder** inaugurates a class in Creative Writing, which he offers for a part of each year until 1936.

"Little Mags" of the year include *Pagany* (until 1933), which publishes William Carlos Williams, John Dos Passos, Edward Dahlberg, Kenneth Rexroth and Gertrude Stein; and *Symposium* (until 1934), edited by James Burnham and Philip Wheelwright, which publishes Louis Zukofsky, I. A. Richards, Harold Rosenberg, and Herbert Read.

Ford Madox Ford: *When the Wicked Man*
Graham Greene: *Rumour at Nightfall*
W. Somerset Maugham: *Six Stories Written in the First Person Singular*
Anthony Powell: *Afternoon Men*
Forrest Reid: *Uncle Stephen*
Dorothy Richardson: *Dawn's Left Hand*
Victoria Sackville-West: *All Passion Spent*
Charles Williams: *Many Dimensions; The Place of the Lion*
Virginia Woolf: *The Waves*
W. B. Yeats: *Stories of Michael Robartes and His Friends* (Cuala Press)

VERSE AND DRAMA

John Betjeman: *Mount Zion, or In Touch with the Infinite*
Laurence Binyon: *Collected Poems*
Roy Campbell: *The Georgiad: A Satirical Fantasy in Verse*

1931

Great Britain

FICTION

Stella Benson: *Tobit Transplanted* (U.S. title: *The Far-Away Bride*)
Elizabeth Bowen: *Friends and Relations*
Ivy Compton-Burnett: *Men and Wives*

C. Day Lewis

Robert Graves: *Poems: 1926–1930; To Whom Else?* (Majorca)
Aldous Huxley: *The Cicadas and Other Poems*
C. Day Lewis: *From Feathers to Iron*
Hugh MacDiarmid: *First Hymn to Lenin* (Preface by Æ)
Wilfred Owen: *Poems* (edited by Edmund Blunden)
Edith Sitwell: *Epithalamium; In Spring; Jane Barston*
Osbert Sitwell: *Collected Satires and Poems*
Humbert Wolfe: *Snow*

NON-FICTION

Maurice Baring: *In My End Is My Beginning*
Samuel Beckett: *Proust*
Edmund Blunden: *Votive Tablets*
Norman Douglas: *Summer Islands*
Ford Madox Ford: *Return to Yesterday*
Lady Gregory: *Coole* (Cuala Press)
Aldous Huxey: *Music at Night and Other Essays*
D. H. Lawrence: *Apocalypse* (Florence)
Wyndham Lewis: *Hitler*
Desmond MacCarthy: *Portraits*
John Middleton Murry: *Son of Woman: The Story of D. H. Lawrence*
G. B. Shaw: *Pen Portraits and Reviews; Our Theatres in the Nineties* (3 vols.); *Music in London* (3 vols.)
Lytton Strachey: *Portraits in Miniature*
Evelyn Waugh: *Remote People*
Rebecca West: *Ending in Earnest: A Literary Log*
Virginia Woolf: "Introductory Letter" to *Life As We Have Known It,* by Co-Operative Working Women (edited by Margaret Llewelyn Davies)

❧ ❧ *"I—I—I—how we have lost the secret of saying that!"*

VIRGINIA WOOLF

Edith Sitwell

United States

FICTION

Kay Boyle: *Plagued By the Nightingale*
Pearl Buck: *The Good Earth*
Willa Cather: *Shadows on the Rock*
William Faulkner: *Sanctuary; These Thirteen*
Caroline Gordon: *Penhally*
Damon Runyon: *Guys and Dolls*
James Thurber: *The Owl in the Attic and Other Perplexities*
Nathanael West (Nathan Weinstein): *The Dream Life of Balso Snell* (privately printed)

Wallace Stevens

VERSE AND DRAMA

Conrad Aiken: *Preludes for Memnon; The Coming Forth by Day of Osiris Jones*

e. e. cummings: *W*

Babette Deutsch: *Epistle to Prometheus*

T. S. Eliot: *Triumphal March* (G.B.)

Robinson Jeffers: *Descent to the Dead*

Edna St. Vincent Millay: *Fatal Interview*

Ogden Nash: *Free Wheeling*

Howard Phelps Putnam: *The Five Seasons*

E. A. Robinson: *Matthias At the Door*

Gertrude Stein: *Before the Flowers of Friendship Faded Friendship Faded* (Plain Edition)

Wallace Stevens: *Harmonium* (revised edition)

Horace Gregory: translation of *Poems of Catullus*

Thornton Wilder: *The Long Christmas Dinner and Other Plays*

NON-FICTION

Sherwood Anderson: *Perhaps Women*

Kenneth Burke: *Counter-Statement*

e. e. cummings: *CIOPW* (Charcoal, Ink, Oil, Pencil, Watercolor)

Theodore Dreiser: *Dawn*

Max Eastman: *The Literary Mind: Its Place in an Age of Science*

T. S. Eliot: *Thoughts After Lambeth* (G.B.); *Charles Whibley: A Memoir* (G.B.)

Andrew Lytle: *Bedford Forrest and His Critter Company*

Ezra Pound: *How to Read* (G.B.)

Constance M. Rourke: *American Humor: A Study of the National Character*

George Santayana: *The Genteel Tradition at Bay*

Lincoln Steffens: *Autobiography*

Gertrude Stein: *How to Write* (Plain Edition)

Edmund Wilson

Dilly Tante (Stanley J. Kunitz), ed.: *Living Authors: A Book of Biographies*

Edmund Wilson: *Axel's Castle: A Study in the Imaginative Literature of 1870–1930*

❦❦ *". . . writing about literature, for me, has always meant narrative and drama as well as the discussion of comparative values."*

EDMUND WILSON

Related Events

DEATHS

Arnold Bennett: British novelist, short-story writer, and playwright; age 64; of typhoid fever

Arnold Bennett

Vachel Lindsay

contracted after drinking water from a carafe in a Paris hotel to demonstrate that the local water was perfectly safe; on March 27: "I have written between seventy and eighty books. But also I have written only four: *The Old Wives' Tale, The Card, Clayhanger,* and *Riceyman Steps.*"

Vachel Lindsay: American poet and elocutionist; age 52; of suicide by drinking a bottle of Lysol; in Springfield, Illinois (his birthplace), on December 5: ". . . my best years . . . simply used up in shouting."

Other Deaths:

David Belasco, American playwright (*The Girl of the Golden West*)

Anna Pavlova, Russian prima ballerina assoluta

O. E. Rölvaag, American regional novelist (*Giants of the Earth*)

G. B. Shaw and Konstantin Stanislavsky

IN OTHER LANGUAGES

Hermann Broch: *Die Schlafwandler* (*The Sleepwalkers*)

Boris Pasternak: *Okhrannia gramota: Vospominaniia* (1900–1930) (*Safe Conduct*)

Antoine de Saint-Exupéry: *Vol de Nuit* (Preface by André Gide)

IN OTHER ARTS

Theater: George and Ira Gershwin: *Of Thee I Sing* ‖ Eugene O'Neill: *Mourning Becomes Electra* ‖ Harold Clurman's Group Theatre (New York)

Films: Charles Chaplin: *City Lights* ‖ René Clair: *À Nous la Liberté*

IN THE MARGIN

Final Drafts: On February 7, after 18 months of work, Virginia Woolf completes her novel *The Waves:* "I wrote the words O Death fifteen minutes ago, having reeled across the last ten pages with some moments of such intensity and intoxication that I seemed only to stumble after my own voice . . . Anyhow, it is done; and I have been sitting these 15 minutes in a state of glory, and calm, and some tears . . ." ‖ In April, Forrest Reid finishes *Uncle Stephen,* the first novel of his Tom Barber trilogy: "During the two years spent on it, Tom grew to be extraordinarily real to me . . . real, I think, in a way none of my other characters has ever been, so that sometimes for a few minutes I would stop writing because he seemed to be actually there in the room. I knew the tones of his voice, I caught glimpses of him in the street, and one evening, after finishing a chapter, I put down my work to go out for a walk with him . . ."

Change of Pace: Sworn off the pen and supporting his family in Provençal by bull wrestling, taking bribes to lose in local jousting matches, spear-fishing, and diving for relics (earning, in addition to his keep, five broken ribs, a shattered collarbone, a close call with a German sea mine, and a near-fatal encounter with an octopus), Roy Campbell suffers a sudden spell of *taedium vitae,* and settles down to do nothing but read and write

Travels: William Empson to Tokyo, as a Professor of English Literature (until 1934) || Mr. and Mrs. G. B. Shaw to Russia, where they are received by Stalin || Hart Crane to Mexico (on a Guggenheim Fellowship), where he settles next door to Katherine Anne Porter and plans an epic poem on the Spanish Conquest || e. e. cummings to Russia, keeping "an old-fashioned diary," which becomes *Eimi* || Theodore Dreiser to Kentucky to attract national attention to injustices in the mining industry makes headlines of another kind when he is indicted there for adultery. (Observing a woman enter Dreiser's hotel room one evening, local officials propped toothpicks against the door—and finding them still in place the next morning, filed charges.) Back in New York, Dreiser defended himself in a press release, citing his age (60) and announcing: ". . . you may lock me in the most luxurious boudoir with the most attractive woman in the world, and be convinced that we are discussing nothing more than books or art . . ." Since Dreiser could not be extradited for a misdemeanor, there was no possibility of his claim being contradicted in court

Publishing: *Story* magazine, edited by Whit Burnett and Martha Foley, makes its debut in April || In Buenos Aires, Victoria Ocampo publishes the first issue of her international review, *SUR* || In London, Hamish Hamilton inaugurates his own imprint || In Paris, the Obelisk Press is founded by Jack Kahane || Robert Frost's *Collected Poems* receives the Pulitzer Prize for Poetry

In the Great World: Japan invades Manchuria || Birth of the Spanish Republic

Great Britain

FICTION

Elizabeth Bowen: *To the North*
Joyce Cary: *Aissa Saved*
Stella Gibbons: *Cold Comfort Farm*
Graham Greene: *Stamboul Train* (U.S. title: *Orient Express*)
Aldous Huxley: *Brave New World*
Christopher Isherwood: *The Memorial*
Rudyard Kipling: *Limits and Renewals* (stories and poems)
Wyndham Lewis: *Snooty Baronet*
W. Somerset Maugham: *The Narrow Corner*
Charles Morgan: *The Fountain*

Aldous Huxley

Sean O'Faolain: *Midsummer Night Madness*
William Plomer: *The Case Is Altered*
Anthony Powell: *Venusberg*
G. B. Shaw: *The Adventures of the Black Girl in Her Search for God*
Evelyn Waugh: *Black Mischief*
H. G. Wells: *The Bulpington of Blup*
Charles Williams: *The Greater Trumps*

Edwin and Willa Muir: translation of Hermann Broch's *Die Schlafwandler* (*The Sleepwalkers*)
T. E. Shaw (T. E. Lawrence): translation of Homer's *Odyssey*

VERSE AND DRAMA

Richard Aldington: *Movietones* (privately printed)
W. H. Auden: *The Orators* (dedicated to Stephen Spender)
Edmund Blunden: *Halfway House*
D. H. Lawrence: *Last Poems* (edited by Richard Aldington and Pino Orioli; Florence)
Hugh MacDiarmid: *Scots Unbound and Other Poems*
Clere Parsons: *Poems*
Michael Roberts, ed.: *New Signatures*
W. B. Yeats: *Words for Music Perhaps* (Cuala Press)

Frank O'Connor (Michael O'Donovan): *The Wild Bird's Nest: Poems Translated from the Irish* (Preface by Æ; Cuala Press)
Helen Rootham: translation of *Prose Poems from "Les Illuminations" of Arthur Rimbaud* (Introduction by Edith Sitwell)

NON-FICTION

Arnold Bennett: *Journals, 1896–1931* (edited by Newman Flower)
Aldous Huxley, ed.: *Texts and Pretexts* (anthology with commentary)
D. H. Lawrence: *Etruscan Places; Letters* (edited by Aldous Huxley)
F. R. Leavis: *New Bearings in English Poetry*
Herbert Read: *Form in Modern Poetry*

Hugh MacDiarmid and family

William Faulkner

Edith Sitwell: *Bath*
Sacheverell Sitwell: *Mozart*
Charles Williams: *The English Poetic Mind*
Virginia Woolf: *The Common Reader: Second Series; A Letter to a Young Poet* (to John Lehmann)

❧ ❧ *"As the influence of religion declines, the social importance of art increases. We must beware of exchanging good religion for bad art."*

ALDOUS HUXLEY

United States

FICTION

Sherwood Anderson: *Beyond Desire*
Erskine Caldwell: *Tobacco Road*
Willa Cather: *Obscure Destinies*
John Dos Passos: *1919*
Leonard Ehrlich: *God's Angry Man*
James T. Farrell: *Young Lonigan: A Boyhood in Chicago Streets*
William Faulkner: *Light in August*
Ellen Glasgow: *The Sheltered Life*
Charles Nordhoff and James Hall: *Mutiny on the Bounty*
Elizabeth Madox Roberts: *The Haunted Mirror*
John Steinbeck: *The Pastures of Heaven*
Edith Wharton: *The Gods Arrive*
William Carlos Williams: *A Novelette and Other Prose* (Toulon); *The Knife of the Times and Other Stories*

Kay Boyle: translation of Raymond Radiguet's *Le Diable au Corps* (*The Devil in the Flesh*) with an Introduction by Aldous Huxley

VERSE AND DRAMA

Robinson Jeffers: *Thurso's Landing and Other Poems*

Archibald MacLeish: *Conquistador*
Edwin Markham: *New Poems: Eighty Songs at Eighty*
Ezra Pound, ed.: *Profile: An Anthology* (Milan)
E. A. Robinson: *Nicodemus*
Allen Tate: *Poems: 1928–1931*
William Carlos Williams: *The Cod Head* (privately printed)
Elinor Wylie: *Collected Poems* (edited by William Rose Benét)
Louis Zukofsky, ed.: *An "Objectivists" Anthology* (Paris)

T. S. Eliot: *Sweeney Agonistes: Fragments of an Aristophanic Melodrama* (G.B.)
Gertrude Stein: *Operas and Plays* (including the text of *Four Saints in Three Acts;* Plain Edition)

Robinson Jeffers

NON-FICTION

Van Wyck Brooks: *The Life of Emerson*
Theodore Dreiser: *Tragic America*
T. S. Eliot: *Selected Essays: 1917–1932;* *John Dryden*
William Faulkner: *Salamagundi* (essays and poems)
Ernest Hemingway: *Death in the Afternoon*
Ludwig Lewisohn: *Expression in America*
Mabel Dodge Luhan: *Lorenzo in Taos*
H. L. Mencken: *Making a President: A Footnote to the Saga of Democracy*
Anaïs Nin: *D. H. Lawrence: An Unprofessional Study* (Paris)
Upton Sinclair: *American Outpost: A Book of Reminiscences*
James Thurber: *The Seal in the Bedroom and Other Predicaments*
Mark Twain: *Mark Twain the Letter Writer* (compiled by Cyril Clemens)
Glenway Wescott: *A Calendar of Saints for Unbelievers; Fear and Trembling*
Edmund Wilson: *The American Jitters, A Year of the Slump* (G.B. title: *Devil Take the Hindmost*)

T. S. Eliot

❧ ❧ *"In anything funny you write that isn't close to serious you've missed something . . ."*

JAMES THURBER

Related Events

DEATHS

Hart Crane, American poet; 33; of suicide, by leaping into the Caribbean Sea from the stern of the S.S. Orizaba while en route to New York, on April 26. ". . . drunk, he would weep and shout, shaking his fist, 'I am Baudelaire, I am Christopher Marlowe, I am Christ,' but never once did I hear him say he was Hart Crane." —Katherine Anne Porter

Other Deaths:

Lady Augusta Gregory, Irish playwright and co-founder, with Yeats, of the Abbey Theatre
Harold Monro, British poet

IN OTHER LANGUAGES

Louis-Ferdinand Céline: *Voyage au Bout de la Nuit*
Jean Cocteau: *Essai de Critique Indirecte*
Colette: *Ces Plaisirs* . . .
Boris Pasternak: *Spektorskii* (Spectorsky)
V. Sirien (Vladimir Nabokov): *Podwig* (*The Exploit*); *Kamera Obskura* (*Laughter in the Dark*)

Cesare Pavese: Italian translation of Herman Melville's *Moby Dick* and Sherwood Anderson's *Dark Laughter*

IN OTHER ARTS

Theater: W. Somerset Maugham: *For Services Rendered*

Films: Jean Cocteau: *Le Sang d'un Poète* || Marx Brothers: *Animal Crackers*

Music: Maurice Ravel: *Piano Concerto in G* and *Piano Concerto for the Left Hand* || Arnold Schoenberg: *Moses und Aron* (Acts I and II completed) || Carl Ruggles: *Sun-Treader*

IN THE MARGIN

In the Limelight: The Nobel Prize for Literature to John Galsworthy || The Pulitzer Prize for Fiction to Pearl Buck, for *The Good Earth* || The Pulitzer Prize for Drama to *Of Thee I Sing* by George S. Kaufman, Morrie

Ryskind, and Ira Gershwin || At the urging of Yeats, an Irish Academy of Letters is established September 12

Poet's Progress: William Faulkner goes to Hollywood for the first time, under contract to M.G.M. || W. H. Auden is teaching at Downs School, near Malvern, in Hereford || At Harvard, T. S. Eliot delivers the Charles Eliot Norton Lectures || In December, Edna St. Vincent Millay begins a series of readings of her own poetry on a nation-wide radio network || Thomas Wolfe is injured jumping from a train as it pulls out of Grand Central Station—he having suddenly decided that instead of spending the weekend in Connecticut with Maxwell Perkins, he should be back in Brooklyn writing || Upon graduating in June, James Agee takes a position as staff writer on *Fortune* magazine

In the Outside World: Franklin Delano Roosevelt, 50, is elected 32nd President of the United States || On the night of March 1, the infant son of Charles A. Lindbergh is kidnapped

Hart Crane

1933

Great Britain

FICTION

Joyce Cary: *An American Visitor*
Ivy Compton-Burnett: *More Women Than Men*
Walter de la Mare: *The Lord Fish and Other Stories*
Ford Madox Ford: *The Rash Act*
David Gascoyne: *Opening Day*
Robert Graves: *The Real David Copperfield*
James Hilton: *Lost Horizon*

W. B. Yeats

D. H. Lawrence: *The Lovely Lady*
Malcolm Lowry: *Ultramarine*
W. Somerset Maugham: *Ah King*
Sean O'Faolain: *A Nest of Simple Folk*
Anthony Powell: *From a View to a Death*
C. P. Snow: *New Lives for Old* (published
  anonymously)

VERSE AND DRAMA

George Barker: *Thirty Preliminary Poems*
Roy Campbell: *Flowering Reeds*
Walter de la Mare: *The Fleeting and Other
  Poems*
Robert Graves: *Poems 1930–1933*
C. Day Lewis: *The Magnetic Mountain*
  (dedicated to W. H. Auden)
Wyndham Lewis: *One Way Song*
Harold Monro: *Collected Poems* (edited by Alida
  Monro)
Michael Roberts, ed.: *New Country*
Edith Sitwell: *Five Variations on a Theme*
Stephen Spender: *Poems*
Helen Waddell, ed.: *Medieval Lyrics*
W. B. Yeats: *Collected Poems; The Winding
  Stair and Other Poems* (trade edition)

Laurence Binyon: translation of Dante's *Divina
  Commedia* (*Divine Comedy*); completed 1943

W. H. Auden: *The Dance of Death* (produced
  1935)
D. H. Lawrence: *Plays*

NON-FICTION

John Betjeman: *Ghastly Good Taste, or A
  Depressing Story of the Rise and Fall of
  English Architecture*
Norman Douglas: *Looking Back*
Ford Madox Ford: *It Was the Nightingale*
A. E. Housman: *The Name and Nature of
  Poetry* (Leslie Stephen Lecture)
George Moore: *A Communication to My Friends*
John Middleton Murry: *Reminiscences of D. H.
  Lawrence*
George Orwell: *Down and Out in Paris and
  London*
Herbert Read: *The Innocent Eye*

Gertrude Stein

Edith Sitwell: *The English Eccentrics* (book
jacket designed by Pavel Tchelitchev)
Lytton Strachey: *Characters and Commentaries*
H. G. Wells: *The Shape of Things to Come*
Rebecca West: *A Letter to a Grandfather*
Charles Williams: *Reason and Beauty in the
Poetic Mind*
Virginia Woolf: *Flush*

❦ ❦ *"To feel strange, to retain throughout
life the sense of being a voyager on the
earth come from another sphere, to whom
everything remains wonderful, horrifying,
and new is, I suppose, to be an artist."*
STEPHEN SPENDER

Stephen Spender

United States

FICTION

Conrad Aiken: *Great Circle*
Hervey Allen: *Anthony Adverse*
Sherwood Anderson: *Death in the Woods and
Other Stories*
Kay Boyle: *Gentlemen, I Address You Privately*
Erskine Caldwell: *God's Little Acre*
Ernest Hemingway: *Winner Take Nothing*
Ring Lardner: *Lose with a Smile*
Sinclair Lewis: *Ann Vickers*
Dorothy Parker: *After Such Pleasures . . .*
John Steinbeck: *To a God Unknown*
Nathanael West: *Miss Lonelyhearts*
Edith Wharton: *Human Nature*

VERSE AND DRAMA

Léonie Adams: *This Measure*
John Peale Bishop: *Now with His Love*
Hart Crane: *Collected Poems* (edited by Waldo
Frank)
William Faulkner: *A Green Bough*
Robinson Jeffers: *Give Your Heart to the Hawks
and Other Poems*
Archibald MacLeish: *Frescos for Mr.
Rockefeller's City; Poems, 1924–1933*
Ezra Pound, ed.: *Active Anthology* (G.B.)
E. A. Robinson: *Talifer*
Sara Teasdale: *Strange Victory*

e. e. cummings: translation of Louis Aragon's *Le
Front Rouge* (*The Red Front*)
Katherine Anne Porter: translation, *Katherine
Anne Porter's French Song Book* (Paris)

NON-FICTION

e. e. cummings: *Eimi*
T. S. Eliot: *The Use of Poetry and the Use of
Criticism* (Charles Eliot Norton Lectures)
Horace Gregory: *Pilgrim of the Apocalypse: A
Critical Study of D. H. Lawrence*
Granville Hicks: *The Great Tradition: An
Interpretation of American Literature Since
the Civil War*
Ezra Pound: *A B C of Economics* (G.B.)

Archibald MacLeish

Colette: *La Chatte*
Sigmund Freud: *Neue Folge der Vorlesungen zur
    Einführung in die Psychoanalyse* (*New
    Introductory Lectures on Psychoanalysis*)
Federico García Lorca: *Oda a Walt Whitman*
André Malraux: *La Condition Humaine*
Thomas Mann: *Joseph und Seine Brüder*
    (*Joseph and His Brothers*; 4 volumes through
    1943)
Boris Pasternak: *Vozdushnye puti* (*Ariel Ways*)

Gertrude Stein: *The Autobiography of Alice B.
    Toklas; Matisse, Picasso and Gertrude Stein*
    (Plain Edition)
James Thurber: *My Life and Hard Times*

❧❧ *"God DAMN this constant nostalgia
for something always new."*

HART CRANE

Constantin Cavafy

Related Events

Theater: Noel Coward: *Design For Living* ‖
    Federico García Lorca: *Bodas de Sangre*
    (*Blood Wedding*) ‖ Eugene O'Neill: *Ah,
    Wilderness!* ‖ W. Somerset Maugham:
    Sheppey

DEATHS

Irving Babbitt, American critic
Constantin Cavafy, Greek poet
John Galsworthy, British novelist
Stefan George, German poet
Ring Lardner, American short-story writer
George Moore, Irish novelist
Sara Teasdale, American poet

Music: Première (June 7, Paris) of the Kurt Weill–Bertolt Brecht–George Balanchine–Boris Kochno ballet, *Die Sieben Todsunden* (*The Seven Deadly Sins*) ‖ Arnold Schoenberg arrives in the United States on October 31, in self-exile from Nazi Germany

Films: Jean Vigo: *Zéro de Conduite* ‖ Sergei Eisenstein: *Thunder Over Mexico* (released by Upton Sinclair and edited without Eisenstein's participation or consent from part of the original footage for *Que Viva Mexico!*)

IN THE MARGIN

In November, Ernest Hemingway makes his first trip to Africa, in the course of which he contracts amoebic dysentery and is flown from his Serengetti Plain encampment to Nairobi over Mt. Kilimanjaro

Under the pen name "Samuel Jeake, Jr.," Conrad Aiken serves as London correspondent for *The*

H.D.

New Yorker magazine. (The pseudonym was taken from the ghost and original owner of Aiken's Rye house, who had unsuccessfully tried to fly an "airplane" off the town walls in 1620)

In March, in Vienna, H.D. begins her psychoanalysis with Sigmund Freud, age 77, who observes during one session: "The trouble is—I am an old man—*you do not think it worth your while to love me*"

In the course of a world cruise, G. B. Shaw visits the United States for the only time

The first issue of *New Verse*, edited by Geoffrey Grigson, and publishing Auden, Empson, Spender, Day Lewis, MacNeice, appears in January (through May, 1939)

Nathanael West goes to Hollywood with a contract as a scriptwriter for $350 a week

Laurels: The Nobel Prize for Literature to Russian novelist and short-story writer Ivan Bunin ‖ The Pulitzer Prize for Poetry to Archibald MacLeish, for *Conquistador*

André Malraux

Mary McCarthy

at Archer's Bookshop with other literary hopefuls including David Gascoyne, John Cornford, and Dylan Thomas, "with a dirty wool scarf wound around himself like an old love affair, looking [like] a runaway schoolboy . . . I do not know how many juvenile revolutionaries were temporarily harboured on the top floor of this bookshop, but they came and went like a rotation of furious tiger-moths, always at night. Mothers arrived, weeping, in taxicabs"

In the Great World: January 30: Adolf Hitler becomes Chancellor of the German Republic || February 27: the Reichstag fire in Berlin || Albert Einstein is among the first of the decade's refugees from the Nazi regime to arrive in the United States

German poet and dramatist Bertolt Brecht settles in Svendborg, Denmark, in the first stage of a decade's exile

On December 6, U. S. District Judge John M. Woolsey interprets the law of the land: ". . . my considered opinion, after long reflection, is that whilst in many places the effect of *Ulysses* on the reader undoubtedly is somewhat emetic, no where does it tend to be an aphrodisiac. *Ulysses* may, therefore, be admitted to the United States"

In the Wings: Eudora Welty working as a junior publicity agent for the W.P.A. in Mississippi || Mary McCarthy graduates from Vassar College in Poughkeepsie, New York || George Barker, living in an attic and finishing his first collection of poems, takes up his stand

1934

Great Britain

FICTION

Samuel Beckett: *More Pricks than Kicks*
Elizabeth Bowen: *The Cat Jumps*
John Collier: *Defy the Foul Fiend*
Baron Corvo: *The Desire and Pursuit of the Whole*
Ronald Firbank: *The Artificial Princess*
Ford Madox Ford: *Henry for Hugh* (U.S.)
John Galsworthy: *End of the Chapter* (includes *Maid in Waiting*, 1931; *Flowering Wilderness*, 1932; and *Over the River*, 1933)
Robert Graves: *I, Claudius; Claudius the God and His Wife Messalina*
Graham Greene: *It's a Battlefield*
Thomas Hardy: *An Indiscretion in the Life of an Heiress* (privately printed)
James Hilton: *Goodbye, Mr. Chips*

James Joyce: *The Mime of Mick, Nick and the Maggies* (The Hague)

D. H. Lawrence: *A Modern Lover; The Tales*

George Orwell: *Burmese Days* (U.S.)

Forrest Reid: *Brian Westby*

Dorothy Sayers: *The Nine Tailors*

C. P. Snow: *The Search*

Evelyn Waugh: *A Handful of Dust*

VERSE AND DRAMA

Edwin Muir: *Variations on a Time Theme*

Ruth Pitter: *A Mad Lady's Garland*

Stephen Spender: *Vienna*

Dylan Thomas: *18 Poems*

W. B. Yeats: *The King of the Great Clock Tower: Commentaries and Poems*

D. H. Lawrence: *A Collier's Friday Night* (Introduction by Edward Garnett)

G. B. Shaw: *Too True to Be Good* (produced 1932); *On the Rocks* (produced 1933); *Village Wooing* (produced 1934, Dallas)

W. B. Yeats: *The Words Upon the Window Pane: A Play in One Act* (Cuala Press); *Collected Plays; Wheels and Butterflies*

Evelyn Waugh and John Betjeman

NON-FICTION

Roy Campbell: *Broken Record*

David Cecil: *Early Victorian Novelists*

E. M. Forster: *Goldsworthy Lowes Dickinson*

Graham Greene, ed.: *The Old School: Essays by Divers Hands*

Rayner Heppenstall: *Middleton Murry: A Study in Excellent Normality*

Aldous Huxley: *Beyond the Mexique Bay*

Frieda Lawrence: *"Not I, But the Wind"*

C. Day Lewis: *A Hope for Poetry*

Wyndham Lewis: *Men without Art*

Edith Sitwell: *Aspects of Modern Poetry*

Frank Swinnerton: *The Georgian Scene: A Literary Panorama*

Arnold Toynbee: *A Study of History* (first of 12 volumes)

Evelyn Waugh: *Ninety-two Days*

H. G. Wells: *Experiment in Autobiography*

Charles Williams: *James I*

Virginia Woolf: *Walter Sickert: A Conversation*

W. B. Yeats: *Letters to the New Island*

❦ ❦ *"It may well happen that there are lean years ahead in which our posterity will look back hungrily to this period, when there was so much will and so much ability to please."*

EVELYN WAUGH

United States

FICTION

Conrad Aiken: *Among the Lost People*

James T. Farrell: *The Young Manhood of Studs Lonigan; Calico Shoes and Other Stories*

William Faulkner: *Dr. Martino and Other Stories*

F. Scott Fitzgerald: *Tender Is the Night*

Caroline Gordon: *Aleck Maury, Sportsman*

Langston Hughes: *The Ways of White Folks*

1934

Dylan Thomas

Sinclair Lewis: *Work of Art*
Henry Miller: *The Tropic of Cancer* (Preface by
  Anaïs Nin; Paris)
Katherine Anne Porter: *Hacienda* (Paris)
William Saroyan: *The Daring Young Man on
  the Flying Trapeze and Other Stories*
Gertrude Stein: *The Making of Americans*
  (abridged by the author)
Nathanael West: *A Cool Million*
Thornton Wilder: *Heaven's My Destination*

VERSE AND DRAMA

James Agee: *Permit Me Voyage* (Foreword by
  Archibald MacLeish)
Conrad Aiken: *Landscape West of Eden* (G.B.)
John A. and Alan Lomax, eds.: *American Ballads
  and Folksongs*
Phyllis McGinley: *On the Contrary*
Edna St. Vincent Millay: *Wine from
  These Grapes*

Ezra Pound: *Eleven New Cantos: XXXI–XLI;
  Homage to Sextus Propertius* (G.B.)
E. A. Robinson: *Amaranth*
Jesse Stuart: *Man with a Bull-Tongue Plow*
William Carlos Williams: *Collected Poems,
  1921–1931* (Preface by Wallace Stevens)

T. S. Eliot: *The Rock: A Pageant Play* (produced
  1934)

NON-FICTION

Sherwood Anderson: *No Swank*
Van Wyck Brooks: *Three Essays on America*
Malcolm Cowley: *Exile's Return: A Narrative of
  Ideas*
John Dewey: *Art as Experience*
Isak Dinesen (Karen Blixen): *Seven Gothic Tales*
T. S. Eliot: *After Strange Gods: A Primer of
  Modern Heresy; Elizabethan Essays* (G.B.)
Henry James: *The Art of the Novel: Critical
  Prefaces* (Introduction by R. P. Blackmur)
H. L. Mencken: *Treatise on Right and Wrong*
Ezra Pound: *A B C of Reading* (G.B.); *Make It
  New* (G.B.)
Gertrude Stein: *Portraits and Prayers* (reprinting
  "An Elucidation," 1927, with what was to
  become the author's most celebrated line:
  ". . . a rose is a rose is a rose is a rose")
Edith Wharton: *A Backward Glance*
Alexander Woollcott: *While Rome Burns*

❧ ❧ *"But my God! it was my material, and
it was all I had to deal with . . ."*
                    F. SCOTT FITZGERALD

Related Events

DEATHS

Frederick Delius, British composer
Edward Elgar, British composer
Roger Fry
Arthur Wing Pinero, British playwright

Robert Graves

William Saroyan

IN OTHER LANGUAGES

René Char: *Le Marteau sans Maître*

Jean Cocteau: *La Machine Infernale*

Colette: *Duo*

Sigmund Freud: *Selbstdarstellung (An Autobiographical Study)*

Rainer Maria Rilke: *Späte Gedichte (Late Poems)*

Cesare Pavese: Italian translation of James Joyce's *Portrait of the Artist as a Young Man*

IN OTHER ARTS

Music: Moscow, January 22: Dmitri Shostakovich's opera *Lady Macbeth of Mzensk* ‖ Hartford, Connecticut, February 8: Virgil Thomson's opera *Four Saints in Three Acts*, with libretto by Gertrude Stein ‖ Paris, April 30: Igor Stravinsky's *Perséphone*, with text by André Gide

Theater: Eugene O'Neill: *Days without End* ‖ Federico García Lorca: *Yerma* ‖ Sean O'Casey: *Within the Gates*

Films: Jean Vigo: *l'Atalante* ‖ Robert Flaherty: *Man of Aran*

IN THE MARGIN

On October 24, Gertrude Stein and Alice B. Toklas arrive in New York for a lecture tour, and in November, speaking on "Poetry and Grammar" before an audience of 500 students at the University of Chicago, Miss Stein declares: "I really do not know that anything has ever been more exciting than diagraming sentences."

In February, the first issue of *Partisan Review*, with Edward Dahlberg and Philip Rahv on its editorial board; Dwight Macdonald, F. W. Dupee, and Delmore Schwartz among its editors

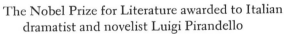
James T. Farrell

Henry Miller

The Nobel Prize for Literature awarded to Italian dramatist and novelist Luigi Pirandello

C. Day Lewis has a change in fortune when a gossip column reports that Winston Churchill has recently been tipped off by T. E. Lawrence to Day Lewis's hot prospects as a poet: "Hardly had the newspaper come out when the telephone bell started ringing in the office of the Hogarth Press. Leonard and Virginia Woolf, having sold the usual small number of each of my three books of verse they had so far published, had covered the stack of unsold copies with chintz . . . and were using it as a settee. The orders now pouring in for these books caused Leonard and Virginia to subside until, within a few hours, they were sitting on the floor."

Sometime in the spring, W. B. Yeats undergoes the Steinach glandular operation, and later, in Rapallo, shows the manuscript of *The King of the Great Clock Tower* to Ezra Pound, who says, "Putrid."

In the Wings: Jobless in Paris and embarked on his first attempt at a novel, Hungarian-born Arthur Koestler, 29, earns his keep by writing *The Encyclopedia of Sexual Knowledge* under the name of "Dr. A. Costler." Based on a dozen reference books and on Koestler's brief experience in 1932 as an observer at Dr. Magnus Hirshfeld's *Sexualwischenschaftliches Institut*, the *Encyclopedia* became an international best seller, but Koestler's fee of 3,000 francs included the sale of the copyright and the good "Dr. C." was never to receive any royalties.

In the Great World: August 2: President von Hindenburg of Germany dies: the office of president is abolished and Adolf Hitler assumes absolute dictatorship, becoming Führer as well as Reich's Chancellor

Luigi Pirandello

*Four Saints in Three Acts, by
Gertrude Stein and Virgil Thomson*

Great Britain

FICTION

Elizabeth Bowen: *The House in Paris*
Ivy Compton-Burnett: *A House and Its Head*
Lawrence Durrell: *Pied Piper of Lovers*
Graham Greene: *England Made Me; The
    Basement Room and Other Stories*
Christopher Isherwood: *Mr. Norris Changes
    Trains* (dedicated to W. H. Auden)
Vladimir Nabokov: *Camera Obscura* (first
    English translation of Nabokov's work; U. S.
    edition, 1938, revised and translated by the
    author, published as *Laughter in the Dark*)
George Orwell: *A Clergyman's Daughter*
V. S. Pritchett: *Nothing Like Leather*
Herbert Read: *The Green Child*
Dorothy Richardson: *Clear Horizon*
Dorothy Sayers: *Gaudy Night*
Rebecca West: *The Harsh Voice*

VERSE AND DRAMA

W. H. Auden and John Garrett, eds.: *The Poet's
    Tongue*
George Barker: *Poems*
Walter de la Mare, ed.: *Early One Morning in
    Spring*
William Empson: *Poems*
Rayner Heppenstall: *First Poems*
C. Day Lewis: *A Time to Dance; Collected
    Poems 1929–1933*
Louis MacNeice: *Poems*
Siegfried Sassoon: *Vigils*
W. B. Yeats: *A Full Moon in March*

W. H. Auden and Christopher Isherwood: *The
    Dog Beneath the Skin, or Where Is Francis?*
    (produced 1936)

NON-FICTION

Richard Aldington: *Artifex: Sketches and Ideas*
William Empson: *Some Versions of Pastoral*

Elizabeth Bowen

Louis MacNeice

Ford Madox Ford: *Provence* (dedicated to
    Caroline Gordon and Allen Tate)
David Gascoyne: *A Short Survey of Surrealism*
Gerard Manley Hopkins: *Letters to Robert
    Bridges* (edited by Claude Abbott)
T. E. Lawrence: *Seven Pillars of Wisdom* (trade
    edition)
W. Somerset Maugham: *Don Fernando; or
    Variations on Some Spanish Themes*
John Middleton Murry: *Between Two Worlds*
Peter Quennell: *Byron: The Years of Fame*
Stephen Spender: *The Destructive Element: A
    Study of Modern Writers and Beliefs*
Evelyn Waugh: *Edmund Campion: Jesuit and
    Martyr*

❦❦ ". . . *don't you see*, what I know is
what I am? *And I can't tell you that. You
have to find it out for yourself. I'm like a
book you have to read. A book can't read
itself to you. It doesn't even know what
it's about* . . ."

CHRISTOPHER ISHERWOOD

United States

FICTION

Conrad Aiken: *King Coffin*
Nelson Algren: *Somebody in Boots*
Erskine Caldwell: *Kneel to the Rising Sun and
    Other Stories*
Willa Cather: *Lucy Gayheart*
James T. Farrell: *Judgment Day; Guillotine
    Party and Other Stories*
William Faulkner: *Pylon*
F. Scott Fitzgerald: *Taps at Reveille*
Ellen Glasgow: *Vein of Iron*
Sinclair Lewis: *It Can't Happen Here*
John O'Hara: *Butterfield 8*
Frederic Prokosch: *The Asiatics*
Laura Riding: *Progress of Stories*

William Empson

William Carlos Williams

Elizabeth Madox Roberts: *He Sent Forth a
　Raven*
John Steinbeck: *Tortilla Flat*
James Thurber: *The Middle-Aged Man on the
　Flying Trapeze*
Thomas Wolfe: *From Death to Morning; Of
　Time and the River: A Legend of Man's
　Hunger in His Youth* (dedicated to Maxwell
　Perkins)

VERSE AND DRAMA

e. e. cummings: *No Thanks* (dedicated to
　fourteen publishers who had rejected the
　manuscript, and to the author's mother, who
　paid the printing bill)
T. S. Eliot: *Words for Music* (Bryn Mawr)
Kenneth Fearing: *Poems*
Horace Gregory: *Chorus for Survival*
Robinson Jeffers: *Solstice and Other Poems*
Marianne Moore: *Selected Poems* (Introduction
　by T. S. Eliot)

E. A. Robinson: *King Jasper* (Introduction by
　Robert Frost)
Muriel Rukeyser: *Theory of Flight*
Karl Shapiro: *Poems* (privately printed)
Robert Penn Warren: *XXXVI Poems*
William Carlos Williams: *An Early Martyr and
　Other Poems*

e. e. cummings: *Tom: A Ballet*
T. S. Eliot: *Murder in the Cathedral* (produced
　1935)

NON-FICTION

Sherwood Anderson: *Puzzled America*
R. P. Blackmur: *The Double Agent: Essays in
　Craft and Elucidation*
Kenneth Burke: *Permanence and Change: An
　Anatomy of Purpose*
Babette Deutsch: *This Modern Poetry*
Ernest Hemingway: *The Green Hills of Africa*

Edgar Lee Masters: *Vachel Lindsay: A Poet in America*

Herman Melville: *Journal Up the Straits, October 11, 1856–May 5, 1857* (edited by Raymond Weaver)

Henry Miller: *Aller Retour New York* (Paris)

Ezra Pound: *Jefferson and/or Mussolini* (G.B.); *Social Credit: An Impact* (G.B.)

Gertrude Stein: *Lectures in America; Narration* (Introduction by Thornton Wilder)

❧ ❧ *"To work was the only thing, it was the one thing that always made you feel good . . ."*

ERNEST HEMINGWAY

Related Events

DEATHS

T. E. Lawrence, British self-chronicler and legend, variously known as "Lawrence of Arabia," T. E. Shaw, J. H. Ross, A/C2 No. 352087, and "Private Meek," hero of G. B. Shaw's *Too Good To Be True*; aged 46; of brain injuries incurred in an accident while swerving his motorcycle (a gift of Mr. and Mrs. G. B. Shaw) to avoid hitting two boys on bicycles; in Dorsetshire, on May 19

Other Deaths:

Æ (George William Russell), Irish poet and agrarian reformer

Alban Berg, Austrian composer (*Wozzeck*)

René Crevel, French surrealist poet, whose suicide note said *"Je suis dégouté de tout"*

Edwin Arlington Robinson, American poet

Marianne Moore

e. e. cummings

T. E. Lawrence

E. M. Forster

IN OTHER LANGUAGES

Jean Cocteau: *Portraits Souvenirs*

Federico García Lorca: *Llanto por Ignacio Sánchez Mejías* (*Lament for the Death of a Bullfighter*)

André Gide: *Les Nouvelles Nourritures*

Franz Kafka: *Gesammelte Schriften* (the novels, as well as stories, parables, journals, aphorisms; edited by Max Brod)

Igor Stravinsky: *Chroniques de Ma Vie*

IN OTHER ARTS

Theater and Music: W. H. Auden's *The Dance of Death* (with Death's mask designed by Henry Moore) and T. S. Eliot's *Sweeney Agonistes* share a double bill || Noel Coward's *To-Night at 8:30* || Clifford Odets's *Waiting for Lefty* || George Gershwin's opera, *Porgy and Bess*

Cinema: Cavalcanti's documentary *Coalface*, with text by W. H. Auden and music by Benjamin Britten || Alfred Hitchcock's *The Thirty-Nine Steps* || John Ford's *The Informer*

Art: Henri Matisse illustrates James Joyce's *Ulysses* for the Limited Editions Club of New York || In an interview in *Cahiers d'Art*, Pablo Picasso speaks: "A picture is not thought out and settled beforehand. While it is being done, it changes as one's thoughts change. And when it is finished, it still goes on changing, according to the state of mind of whoever is looking at it . . ."

IN THE MARGIN

In Paris, the First International Congress of Writers for the Defence of Culture meets in June. Among the speakers is **E. M. Forster**: "One must behave as if one is immortal, and as if civilization is eternal. Both statements are false—I shall not survive, no more will the great globe itself—but both of them must be assumed to be true if we are to go on eating and working and travelling, and keep open a few breathing holes for the human spirit . . ." Among the listeners, was **Katherine Anne Porter**: "[Mr. Forster] paid no attention to the microphone, but wove back and forth, from side to side, gently, and every time his face passed the mouthpiece I caught a high-voiced syllable or two, never a whole word, only a thin recurring sound like the wind down a chimney as Mr. Forster's pleasant good countenance advanced and retreated and returned. Then, surprisingly, once he came to a moment's pause before the instrument and there sounded into the hall clearly but wistfully a complete sentence: 'I DO believe in liberty!' "

In June, **W. H. Auden** is married by proxy to Thomas Mann's eldest daughter, Erika

In Vienna, **Thornton Wilder** visits Sigmund Freud, who is in a matchmaking mood: "My daughter Anna will be sorry to have missed you. You can come again? She is older than you—you do not have to be afraid. She is a sensible reasonable girl. You are not afraid of women? She is a sensible—no nonsense about her. Are you married, may I ask?"

The cremated remains of **D. H. Lawrence** are transferred from Vence, in the South of France, to their final resting place at the Kiowa ranch in the Sangre de Cristo mountains, New Mexico

The Hawthornden Prize awarded to **Robert Graves** for *I, Claudius*

Graham Greene begins contributing weekly film reviews to *The Spectator*

Allen Lane begins issuing Penguin paperbacks at 6*d.* a copy

"Little Mags": *American Prefaces,* successively edited by Paul Engle, Jean Garrigue, and others until 1943 || *Southern Review,* edited by Robert Penn Warren, Cleanth Brooks, and others until 1942

In the Wings: **Carson McCullers**, 18 and studying creative writing at Columbia University, is fired from her part-time job as a real-estate clerk for reading Proust on company time

1936

Great Britain

FICTION

Joyce Cary: *The African Witch*
Cyril Connolly: *The Rock Pool* (Paris)
Robert Graves: *Antigua Penny Puce* (U.S. title: *The Antigua Stamp*)
Graham Greene: *A Gun for Sale* (U.S. title: *This Gun for Hire*)

E. M. Forster and Forrest Reid

W. H. Auden, Christopher Isherwood,
Stephen Spender

George Santayana

Aldous Huxley: *Eyeless in Gaza*
Christopher Isherwood: *The Nowaks* (in *New
Writing*)
W. Somerset Maugham: *Cosmopolitans:
Twenty-Nine Very Short Stories*
George Orwell: *Keep the Aspidistra Flying*
Anthony Powell: *Agents and Patients*
Forrest Reid: *The Retreat; or, The Machinations
of Henry*
Stephen Spender: *The Burning Cactus*
Evelyn Waugh: *Mr. Loveday's Little Outing and
Other Sad Stories*
Rebecca West: *The Thinking Reed*

VERSE AND DRAMA

W. H. Auden: *Look, Stranger!* (U.S. title: *On
This Island*)
Roy Campbell: *Mithraic Emblems*
Ford Madox Ford: *Collected Poems* (U.S.)
David Gascoyne: *Man's Life Is This Meat*
A. E. Housman: *More Poems* (edited by
Laurence Housman)
James Joyce: *Collected Poems* (U.S., limited
edition; trade edition 1937)

Ruth Pitter: *A Trophy of Arms: Poems
1926–1935*
Michael Roberts, ed.: *The Faber Book of Modern
Verse*
Edith Sitwell: *Selected Poems. With an Essay on
Her Own Poetry*
Sacheverell Sitwell: *Collected Poems. With a
Long Introductory Essay by Edith Sitwell*
Dylan Thomas: *Twenty-Five Poems*
W. B. Yeats, ed.: *The Oxford Book of Modern
Verse*

W. H. Auden and Christopher Isherwood: *The
Ascent of F-6* (produced 1937)
Louis MacNeice: translation of *The Agamemnon
of Aeschylus*
G. B. Shaw: *The Simpleton of the Unexpected
Isles* (produced 1935); *The Six of Calais*
(produced 1934); *The Millionairess* (produced
1936, Vienna)

NON-FICTION

G. K. Chesterton: *Autobiography*
E. M. Forster: *Abinger Harvest*

Graham Greene: *Journey without Maps: A Travel Book*

Rayner Heppenstall: *Apology for Dancing*

Aldous Huxley: *The Olive Tree*

D. H. Lawrence: *Phoenix* (edited by E. D. MacDonald)

T. E. Lawrence: *The Mint* (limited edition, U.S.)

C. S. Lewis: *The Allegory of Love*

Edith Sitwell: *Victoria of England*

Evelyn Waugh: *Waugh in Abyssinia*

W. B. Yeats: *Dramatis Personae* (trade edition)

❧❧ *"What is written should seem a happy accident."*

W. SOMERSET MAUGHAM

United States

FICTION

Sherwood Anderson: *Kit Brandon: A Portrait*

Djuna Barnes: *Nightwood* (G.B.; Introduction by T. S. Eliot in U. S. edition, 1937)

Kay Boyle: *The White Horses of Vienna and Other Stories; Death of a Man*

John Dos Passos: *The Big Money*

James T. Farrell: *A World I Never Made*

William Faulkner: *Absalom! Absalom!*

Andrew Lytle: *The Long Night*

Henry Miller: *Black Spring* (dedicated to Anaïs Nin; Paris)

Margaret Mitchell: *Gone With the Wind*

Anaïs Nin: *House of Incest* (Paris)

John O'Hara: *Appointment in Samarra*

George Santayana: *The Last Puritan: A Memoir in the Form of a Novel*

William Saroyan: *Inhale and Exhale; Three Times Three*

John Steinbeck: *In Dubious Battle*

VERSE AND DRAMA

Conrad Aiken: *Time in the Rock: Preludes to Definition*

e. e. cummings: *1/20* (G.B.)

Richard Eberhart: *Reading the Spirit*

T. S. Eliot: *Collected Poems: 1909–1935*

Robert Frost: *A Further Range; From Snow to Snow; Selected Poems* (with introductory essays by W. H. Auden, C. Day Lewis, Paul Engle, and Edwin Muir; G.B.)

Archibald MacLeish: *Public Speech*

Marianne Moore: *The Pangolin and Other Verse* (G.B.)

Dorothy Parker: *Not So Deep as a Well*

Carl Sandburg: *The People, Yes*

Wallace Stevens: *Owl's Clover; Ideas of Order*

Allen Tate: *The Mediterranean and Other Poems*

William Carlos Williams: *Adam & Eve and the City*

Dudley Fitts and Robert Fitzgerald: *The Alcestis of Euripides*

Edna St. Vincent Millay and George Dillon: translation of Charles Baudelaire's *Les Fleurs du Mal* (*Flowers of Evil*)

Djuna Barnes

The Dog Beneath the Skin, or, Where Is Francis?
by W. H. Auden and Christopher Isherwood

George Santayana: *Obiter Scripta: Lectures, Essays and Reviews*

Gertrude Stein: *The Geographical History of America* (Introduction by Thornton Wilder)

Allen Tate: *Reactionary Essays on Poetry and Ideas*

Edmund Wilson: *Travels in Two Democracies*

Thomas Wolfe: *The Story of a Novel*

❦ ❦ *"C'est à grands pas et en sueur
Que vous suivrez à peine ma piste."*
T. S. ELIOT

André Gide, speaking at the Moscow
funeral of Maxim Gorky

NON-FICTION

Van Wyck Brooks: *The Flowering of New England, 1815–1865*

Willa Cather: *Not Under Forty*

Max Eastman: *Enjoyment of Laughter*

T. S. Eliot: *Essays Ancient and Modern*

James T. Farrell: *A Note on Literary Criticism*

Edgar Lee Masters: *Across Spoon River: An Autobiography*

Related Events

DEATHS

Federico García Lorca, Spanish poet and dramatist; 37; by a Falangist firing squad near Viznar, Granada, in Andalusia; on August 19

Maxim Gorky (Alexei Peshkov): Russian novelist, playwright, autobiographer and culture hero; age 68; of tuberculosis; in Moscow, on June 18. At his state funeral, André Gide, who had arrived in Russia three days before, stood before the tomb of Lenin and declared: *"Le sort de la culture est lié dans nos esprits au destin même de l'U.R.S.S. . . ."*

A. E. Housman, British poet and classical scholar ("I am not a poet by trade; I am a professor of Latin"); age 77; of a heart attack; in Cambridge, on April 30

Rudyard Kipling, Bombay-born short-story writer, novelist, and poet; age 71; of a hemorrhage; on January 18. His ashes lie in the Poet's Corner of Westminster Abbey

Other Deaths:

G. K. Chesterton

Maxim Gorky

A. E. Housman

John Cornford
Finley Peter Dunne (creator of Mr. Dooley)
Luigi Pirandello
R. B. Cunninghame Graham
Oswald Spengler

IN OTHER LANGUAGES

Georges Bernanos: *Journal d'un Curé de
    Campagne*
Colette: *Mes Apprentissages*
André Gide: *Retour de l'U.R.S.S.*
Henri de Montherlant: *Les Jeunes Filles*
Ignazio Silone: *Pane e Vino* (*Bread and Wine*)
    (the Italian original was actually published in
    1937, and the English translation in 1936)
V. Sirin (Vladimir Nabokov): *Otschajanije*
    (*Despair*)

IN OTHER ARTS

W. H. Auden and Christopher Isherwood: *The
    Dog Beneath the Skin, or, Where Is Francis?*
Charles Chaplin: *Modern Times*
Federico García Lorca: *La Casa de Bernarda Alba*
    (*The House of Bernarda Alba*)
Pare Lorentz: *The Plough That Broke the Plains,*
    with music by Virgil Thomson
Sergei Prokofiev: *Peter and the Wolf*

IN THE MARGIN

Laurels: The Nobel Prize for Literature to
    Eugene O'Neill ‖ The James Tait Black
    Prize to Robert Graves, for *I, Claudius* and
    Claudius the God ‖ The Hawthornden
    Prize to Evelyn Waugh, for *Edmund Campion*

Federico García Lorca

Rudyard Kipling

Writers in Action: With photographer Walker Evans, James Agee goes to Alabama to do a series of articles on sharecropper life for *Fortune* magazine and, instead, five years later produces a *sui generis* book, *Let Us Now Praise Famous Men* ‖ W. H. Auden and Louis MacNeice go to Iceland for the summer, with a commission from their publishers to do a travel book ‖ André Gide arrives in Moscow in mid-June as an official guest of the Soviet government. He returns to France in early September, *"consterné par l'abandon des premières directives et le fléchissement de l'idéal révolutionnaire . . . et l'étranglement des libertés"* ‖ On a walking tour through Liberia, Graham Greene notes "a seediness about the place you couldn't get to the same extent elsewhere, and seediness has a very deep appeal . . ." ‖ On an hour's notice, Robert Graves leaves Majorca in the general evacuation of British residents (following the outbreak of the Spanish Civil War); and with a single suitcase, containing "manuscripts, underclothes, and a Londonish suit," begins ten years of wandering: "Reader, never become a refugee, if you can possibly avoid it . . . Stay exactly where you are, kiss the rod and, if very hungry, eat grass or bark off the tree"

Publishers: In England, Martin Secker and Frederic T. Warburg combine operations; Left Book Club launched by Victor Gollancz; and John Lehmann begins editing *New Writing* ‖ In America, James Laughlin IV founds New Directions in a converted stable in Norfolk, Connecticut

In the Great World: January 20: Death of George V; accession of Edward VIII || March 7: In violation of the Versailles and Locarno Treaties, Hitler's army marches into the demilitarized zone of the Rhineland without opposition || July 17: Civil War in Spain || August: The first of the Moscow Purge Trials (others followed in January and June 1937 and March 1938) || November: Franklin D. Roosevelt reelected || December 11: Abdication of Edward VIII; accession of George VI

J. R. R. Tolkien: *The Hobbit*
Rex Warner: *The Wild Goose Chase: An Allegory*
Charles Williams: *Descent into Hell*
Virginia Woolf: *The Years*

Edwin and Willa Muir: translation of Franz Kafka's *Der Prozess* (*The Trial*)

VERSE AND DRAMA

W. H. Auden: *Spain*
George Barker: *Calamiterror*
John Betjeman: *Continual Dew: A Little Book of Bourgeois Verse*
Rayner Heppenstall: *Sebastian*
Isaac Rosenberg: *Collected Works* (edited by G. Bottomley and D. Harding)
Rex Warner: *Poems* (revised in 1945 as *Poems and Contradictions*; dedicated to C. Day Lewis)

Louis MacNeice: *Out of the Picture*

1937

Great Britain

FICTION

Elizabeth Bowen, ed.: *The Faber Book of Modern Stories*
Ivy Compton-Burnett: *Daughters and Sons*
Christopher Isherwood: *Sally Bowles*
David Jones: *In Parenthesis*
James Joyce: *Storiella As She Is Syung*
Wyndham Lewis: *The Revenge for Love*
Compton Mackenzie: *The Four Winds of Love* (4 vols. through 1945)
W. Somerset Maugham: *Theatre*
Charles Norden (Lawrence Durrell): *Panic Spring*
V. S. Pritchett: *Dead Man Leading*
Forrest Reid: *Peter Waring* (revised version of *Following Darkness*, 1912; dedicated to E. M. Forster)
Dorothy Sayers: *Busman's Honeymoon*
Edith Sitwell: *I Live Under a Black Sun*

Charles Williams

NON-FICTION

W. H. Auden and Louis MacNeice: *Letters from Iceland*

Christopher Caudwell (Christopher St. John Sprigg): *Illusion and Reality*

Winston S. Churchill: *Great Contemporaries*

Noel Coward: *Present Indicative*

Ford Madox Ford: *The Great Trade Route; Portraits From Life* (G.B. title: *Mightier Than the Sword*)

Gerald Heard: *The Third Morality*

Gerard Manley Hopkins: *Note-Books and Papers* (edited by Humphry House); *Further Letters* (edited by C. C. Abbott)

Laurence Housman: *AEH: Some Poems, Some Letters and a Personal Memoir*

Aldous Huxley: *Ends and Means;* ed.: *An Encyclopedia of Pacifism*

Rudyard Kipling: *Something of Myself: For My Friends, Known and Unknown*

Wyndham Lewis: *Blasting and Bombardiering*

Sean O'Casey: *The Flying Wasp*

George Orwell: *The Road to Wigan Pier*

J. B. Priestley: *Midnight on the Desert: A Chapter of Autobiography*

Victoria Sackville-West: *Pepita*

G. B. Shaw: *London Music in 1888–89 as Heard by Corno di Bassetto*

Stephen Spender: *Forward from Liberalism*

W. B. Yeats: *A Vision; Essays: 1931–1936* (Cuala Press)

W. B. Yeats and Shree Purohit Swami: translation of *The Ten Principal Upanishads*

❧❧ "*. . . the artist . . . must keep hidden*
His passion for his shop."
W. H. AUDEN

United States

FICTION

James T. Farrell: *Can All This Grandeur Perish? and Other Stories*

Caroline Gordon: *None Shall Look Back; The Garden of Adonis*

Ernest Hemingway: *To Have and Have Not*

Sarah Orne Jewett: *The Only Rose and Other Tales* (Introduction by Rebecca West)

J. P. Marquand: *The Late George Apley*

William Maxwell: *They Came Like Swallows*

Frederic Prokosch: *The Seven Who Fled*

Conrad Richter: *The Sea of Grass*

Kenneth Roberts: *Northwest Passage*

John Steinbeck: *Of Mice and Men*

Edith Wharton: *Ghosts*

William Carlos Williams: *White Mule*

VERSE AND DRAMA

R. P. Blackmur: *From Jordan's Delight*

Louise Bogan: *The Sleeping Fury*

Noel Coward

Robinson Jeffers: *Such Counsels You Gave Me*
Phyllis McGinley: *One More Manhattan*
Edna St. Vincent Millay: *Conversation at Midnight*
Ezra Pound: *The Fifth Decad of Cantos*
Wallace Stevens: *The Man with the Blue Guitar and Other Poems*
Allen Tate: *Selected Poems*
Sara Teasdale: *Collected Poems*
Marya Zaturenska: *Cold Morning Sky*

H.D.: translation of *The Ion of Euripides*

Archibald MacLeish: *The Fall of the City* (radio drama)
Edmund Wilson: *This Room and This Gin and These Sandwiches*

NON-FICTION

Kenneth Burke: *Attitudes Toward History*
John Gould Fletcher: *Life Is My Song*
Philip Horton: *Hart Crane: The Life of an American Poet*
Ezra Pound: *Polite Essays* (G.B.)
George Santayana: *The Realm of Truth; Book Third of Realms of Being*
Gertrude Stein: *Everybody's Autobiography*
Yvor Winters: *Primitivism and Decadence: A Study of American Experimental Poetry*

Ezra Pound: translation of Confucius's *Digest of the Analects* (Milan)

❦ ❦ *"New life can come into an art only when that art becomes more casual in tone."*

LOUISE BOGAN

Edna St. Vincent Millay

Related Events

DEATHS

George Gershwin, American composer; age 39; following an operation for a brain tumor; in Hollywood, California, on July 11
Maurice Ravel, French composer; age 62; following an operation for a brain tumor; in Paris, on December 28

Other Deaths:

Sir James Barrie, British dramatist and creator of Peter Pan
Christopher Caudwell (Christopher St. John Sprigg), British author of *Illusion and Reality*
Paul Elmer More, American critic and author of the *Shelburne Essays*
Edith Wharton, American novelist, expatriate, and friend of Henry James

Dylan and Caitlin Thomas

IN OTHER LANGUAGES

Jean Cocteau: *Les Chevaliers de la Table Ronde*
Colette: *Bella-Vista*
André Gide: *Retouches à mon "Retour de l'U.R.S.S."*
André Malraux: *L'Espoir*
Pablo Picasso: *Sueño y Mentira de Franco* (*Dream and Lie of Franco*)

Marguerite Yourcenar: translation into French of Virginia Woolf's *The Waves* (*Les Vagues*)

IN OTHER ARTS

Paris: Picasso paints his *Guernica* mural (May) || Jean Renoir's film, *La Grande Illusion*

Moscow: Production is halted on the Sergei Eisenstein–Isaac Babel adaptation of Turgenev's *Bezhin-Meadow* (March 17), and Eisenstein is charged with making "harmful formalistic exercises"

Zurich: Première of Alban Berg's posthumous opera, *Lulu*

London: W. H. Auden's radio documentary for the B.B.C., *Hadrian's Wall* (November 25)

New York: Clifford Odets's *Golden Boy* || Marc Blitzstein's opera *The Cradle Will Rock* (June 16) || Pare Lorentz's film *The River*, with music by Virgil Thomson || Ernest Hemingway's documentary, *The Spanish Earth*

IN THE MARGIN

Laurels: To Robert Frost, 62, the Pulitzer Prize for Poetry, for *A Further Range* || To Roger Martin du Gard, 56, the Nobel Prize for Literature || To W. H. Auden, 30, the King's Medal for Poetry

Contretemps: August 11: In between trips to the Spanish front, Ernest Hemingway throws punches at Max Eastman in Scribner's offices,

Frederic Prokosch

the provocation being Eastman's article "Bull in the Afternoon," which speculated that "some circumstance seems to have laid upon Hemingway a continual sense of obligation to put forth evidences of red-blooded masculinity" || September: Thomas Wolfe formally breaks with Scribner's and moves to Harper's, who become, as it turns out, his posthumous publishers || November: Graham Greene, who had already found film starlet Shirley Temple's "oddly precocious body . . . as voluptuous in gray flannel trousers as Miss Dietrich's," now suggests that Miss Temple's senior male fans are titillated by more than her acting talents. A prompt law suit yields Miss Temple and her American studio damages of $9,800.

Spain: W. H. Auden volunteers as an ambulance stretcher bearer, but returns home after two months || Langston Hughes covering the war for the *Baltimore Afro-American* || Gathering propaganda material for the Paris Communist AGITPROP, with assignments from the Liberal *London News Chronicle* and a press card from the Rightist Hungarian *Pester Lloyd* as alternate covers, Arthur Koestler is arrested by Franco forces in Malaga on February 9 and condemned to death as a spy. Unknown to Koestler, who was in solitary confinement for nearly four months awaiting his execution, sufficient protest was raised in England to postpone the sentence, and on May 14 he was released in exchange for the wife of one of Franco's air aces || Fighting with the militia of P.O.U.M. (Partido Obrero de Unificación Marxista) and armed with a rusty German Mauser rifle dated 1896, George Orwell is wounded in the neck by a Fascist sniper, and then, following the Communist suppression of the P.O.U.M. as a Franco "Fifth Column," is forced to escape to France || Ignoring the British ban on visas, Stephen Spender attends the Communist-organized International Writers' Conference at Madrid, traveling under the name of Ramos Ramos and with a forged passport obtained for him by André Malraux

Elsewhere: Paris: The better to let Henry Miller "go haywire," Alfred Perlès takes over *The Booster* (formerly the house organ of the American Country Club in France) and makes moderate "Little Mag" history, with a staff including Lawrence Durrell and William Saroyan as literary editors, Anaïs Nin as society editor, and Miller himself as fashion editor ||

Tennessee: Ford Madox Ford, "an old man mad about writing," is staying with Allen Tate and Caroline Gordon and working on his last book, *The March of Literature: From Confucius' Day to Our Own* || California: Aldous Huxley and Gerald Heard arrive from England and take up permanent residence || China: William Empson begins a two-year teaching stint in the Department of English Literature at the University of Peking || Cornwall: Dylan Thomas marries Caitlin Macnamara on July 11—"with no money, no prospect of money, no attendant friends or relatives, and in complete happiness" || Wisconsin: Working for his M.A. in anthropology, Saul Bellow, 22, feels his vocation stirring: "Every time I worked on my thesis, it turned out to be a story. I disappeared for the Christmas holidays and I never came back"

In the Great World: In April, at Cayoacán, Mexico, an International Commission, headed by John Dewey, begins its investigation "into the charges against Leon Trotsky in the Moscow Trials," and establishes Trotsky's innocence || On April 28, the Basque town of Guernica is destroyed by Nazi bombers flying in the service of General Franco || On June 3, the Duke of Windsor is married to Mrs. Wallis Warfield Simpson, of Baltimore, Maryland || On May 12, George VI is crowned in Westminster Abbey

Ernest Hemingway

Lawrence Durrell

Rex Warner

Great Britain

FICTION

Samuel Beckett: *Murphy*
Elizabeth Bowen: *The Death of the Heart*
Joyce Cary: *Castle Corner*
Lawrence Durrell: *The Black Book* (Paris)
Robert Graves: *Count Belisarius*
Graham Greene: *Brighton Rock*
Richard Hughes: *In Hazard*
C. S. Lewis: *Out of the Silent Planet*
V. S. Pritchett: *You Make Your Own Life*
Dorothy Richardson: *Dimple Hill*
Rex Warner: *The Professor: A Forecast*
Evelyn Waugh: *Scoop, a Novel about Journalists*

Christopher Isherwood and Desmond Vesy: translation of Bertolt Brecht's *Der Dreigroshenoper* (*A Penny for the Poor*)
Edwin and Willa Muir: translation of Franz Kafka's *Amerika* (*America*)

VERSE AND DRAMA

W. H. Auden, ed.: *The Oxford Book of Light Verse*
Walter de la Mare: *Memory and Other Poems*
Robert Graves: *Collected Poems*
C. Day Lewis: *Overtures to Death* (dedicated to E. M. Forster)
Louis MacNeice: *The Earth Compels*
Ruth Pitter: *The Spirit Watches*
F. T. Prince: *Poems*
Charles Williams: *Taliessin Through Logres*
W. B. Yeats: *New Poems* (Cuala Press)

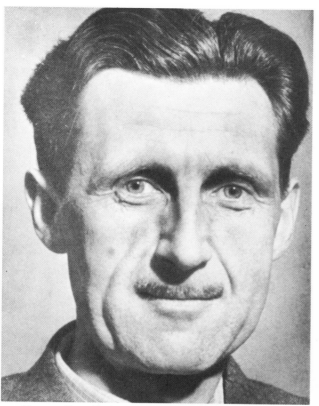

George Orwell

Delmore Schwartz

W. H. Auden and Christopher Isherwood: *On the Frontier* (produced 1938)

Stephen Spender: *Trial of a Judge: A Tragedy in Five Acts*

W. B. Yeats: *The Herne's Egg*

NON-FICTION

Christopher Caudwell: *Studies in a Dying Culture*

Cyril Connolly: *Enemies of Promise*

Ford Madox Ford: *The March of Literature: From Confucius' Day to Our Own*

David Gascoyne: *Hölderlin's Madness* (essay, translations, and poems)

Robert Graves, ed.: *T. E. Lawrence to His Biographer*

Arthur Koestler: *Spanish Testament* (including *Dialogue with Death*, published separately in U.S., 1942)

T. E. Lawrence: *Letters* (edited by David Garnett)

Louis MacNeice: *I Crossed the Minch; Zoo; Modern Poetry*

W. Somerset Maugham: *The Summing Up*

George Orwell: *Homage to Catalonia*

Herbert Read: *Collected Essays in Literary Criticism*

Osbert, Edith and Sacheverell Sitwell: *Trio: Dissertations on Some Aspects of National Genius*

Charles Williams: *He Came Down from Heaven*

Virginia Woolf: *Three Guineas*

❧❧ *"Every creative writer worth our consideration is a victim: a man given over to an obsession."*

GRAHAM GREENE

United States

FICTION

Dorothy Baker: *Young Man with a Horn*
Kay Boyle: *Monday Night*
James T. Farrell: *No Star Is Lost*
William Faulkner: *The Unvanquished*
Ernest Hemingway: *The Fifth Column and the First Forty-Nine Stories*
Sinclair Lewis: *The Prodigal Parents*
Henry Miller: *Max and the White Phagocytes* (Paris)
Elizabeth Madox Roberts: *Black Is My Truelove's Hair*
William Saroyan: *Love, Here Is My Hat*
Delmore Schwartz: *In Dreams Begin Responsibilities*
John Steinbeck: *The Long Valley*
Allen Tate: *The Fathers*
William Carlos Williams: *Life Along the Passaic River*
Richard Wright: *Uncle Tom's Children: Four Novellas*

VERSE AND DRAMA

e. e. cummings: *Collected Poems*
Donald Davidson: *Lee in the Mountains and Other Poems*
Kenneth Fearing: *Dead Reckoning*
John Gould Fletcher: *Selected Poems*
Archibald MacLeish: *Land of the Free: U.S.A.*
Merrill Moore: *M*
Ogden Nash: *I'm a Stranger Here Myself*
Laura Riding: *Collected Poems*
Muriel Rukeyser: *U.S. 1*
Genevieve Taggard: *Collected Poems, 1918–1938*
William Carlos Williams: *The Complete Collected Poems, 1906–1938*

Archibald MacLeish: *Air Raid* (radio drama)
Thornton Wilder: *Our Town* (produced 1938)

Isak Dinesen, Baroness Blixen

NON-FICTION

Rear Admiral Richard E. Byrd: *Alone*
Isak Dinesen: *Out of Africa*
Ernest Hemingway: *The Spanish Earth*
Harriet Monroe: *A Poet's Life: Seventy Years in a Changing World*
Ezra Pound: *Guide to Kulchur* (G.B.)
John Crowe Ransom: *The World's Body*
Logan Pearsall Smith: *Unforgotten Years*
Gertrude Stein: *Picasso*
Robert Penn Warren and Cleanth Brooks, eds.: *Understanding Poetry*
Edmund Wilson: *The Triple Thinkers: Ten Essays on Literature*
Yvor Winters: *Maule's Curse: Seven Studies in the History of American Obscurantism*

❧❧ *"An American is insubmissive, lonely, self-educated, and polite."*
THORNTON WILDER

Related Events

DEATHS

Thomas Wolfe, American novelist; 38; of
tuberculosis of the brain; in Baltimore, Maryland,
on September 15; buried in Riverside Cemetery,
Asheville, North Carolina. "I shall probably always
have to do essentially about as I do now—that is,
pour it out, boil it out, flood it out . . . Perhaps
there are better ways but that is my way." —Letter
to Sherwood Anderson

Other Deaths:

Karel Čapek, Czech playwright
Gabriele D'Annunzio, Italian playwright and
    friend of Eleonora Duse
Constantin Stanislavsky, Russian stage director
Owen Wister, American novelist (*The Virginian*)

IN OTHER LANGUAGES

Antonin Artaud: *Le Théâtre et Son Double*
Georges Bernanos: *Les Grands Cimetières sous la
    Lune*
Albert Camus: *Noces*
Jean Cocteau: *Les Parents Terribles*
Federico García Lorca: *Obras Completas* (edited
    by Guillermo de Torre, in Argentina)
    (*Complete Works*)
Marcel Jouhandeau: *Chroniques Maritales*
Jean-Paul Sartre: *La Nausée*
V. Sirin (Vladimir Nabokov): *Priglaschenije na
    kasnj* (*Invitation to a Beheading*)

Cesare Pavese: translation into Italian of
    Gertrude Stein's *The Autobiography of
    Alice B. Toklas*

Edmund Wilson and Mary McCarthy

Allen Tate

IN OTHER ARTS

Films: Sergei Eisenstein: *Alexander Nevsky,*
with music by Sergei Prokofiev
Theater: Thornton Wilder: *Our Town* ||
Emlyn Williams: *The Corn Is Green*
Music: Aaron Copland: *Billy the Kid*
Architecture: Construction begins on Frank
Lloyd Wright's house-school-office complex of
Taliesin West in Arizona

IN THE MARGIN

Laurels: The Nobel Prize for Literature to Pearl
Buck || The Pulitzer Prize for Drama to
Thornton Wilder (*Our Town*); for Fiction to
J. P. Marquand (*The Late George Apley*);
for Poetry to Marya Zaturenska (*Cold
Morning Sky*)

"Little Mags": *Twice a Year:* "a journal of
literature, the arts and civil liberties," edited
by Dorothy Norman || *Rocky Mountain
Review,* with an editorial board including Alan
Swallow, Weldon Kees, and Wallace Stegner

Names: After visiting China, W. H. Auden and
Christopher Isherwood return by way of the
United States to their last six months as
British residents. At a party in October,
Virginia Woolf notes that Isherwood "is a slip
of a wild boy: with quicksilver eyes: nipped,
jockeylike," and quotes Somerset Maugham:
"That young man 'holds the future of the
English novel in his hands'" || Paul Bowles
and Jane Auer are married in February ||
Sigmund Freud, 82 and a refugee from Nazi
Austria, arrives in London || Suffering from
pernicious anemia, G. B. Shaw becomes a
carnivore after half a century of vegetarianism
|| Edmund Wilson, man-of-letters and
literary editor of the *New Republic,* is married
to Mary McCarthy

In the Great World: September 30: British
Prime Minister Neville Chamberlain meets
German Führer Adolf Hitler at Munich and
they sign an agreement "symbolic of the desire
of our two peoples never to go to war with
one another again"

Thomas Wolfe

1939

Great Britain

FICTION

Eric Ambler: *The Mask of Dimitrios*
Joyce Cary: *Mister Johnson*
Ivy Compton-Burnett: *A Family and a Fortune*
Henry Green: *Party-Going*
Graham Greene: *The Confidential Agent*
Rayner Heppenstall: *The Blaze of Noon*
Aldous Huxley: *After Many a Summer*
Christopher Isherwood: *Goodbye to Berlin*
James Joyce: *Finnegans Wake*
Arthur Koestler: *The Gladiators*
W. Somerset Maugham: *Christmas Holiday*
George Orwell: *Coming Up for Air*
Anthony Powell: *What's Become of Waring*

VERSE AND DRAMA

Roy Campbell: *Flowering Rifle: A Poem from the Battlefield of Spain*

Walter de la Mare, ed.: *Behold, This Dreamer*

A. E. Housman: *Collected Poems*

Louis MacNeice: *Autumn Journal*

Siegfried Sassoon: *Rhymed Ruminations* (trade edition 1940)

Christopher Smart: *Rejoice in the Lamb: A Song from Bedlam* (edited by W. Force Stead)

Stephen Spender: *The Still Centre*

Stephen Spender and John Lehmann, eds.: *Poems for Spain*

Dylan Thomas: *The Map of Love; The World I Breathe* (U.S.)

W. B. Yeats: *Last Poems and Two Plays* (Cuala Press; trade edition 1940)

Stephen Spender and J. L. Gili: translation of Federico García Lorca's *Poems*

Stephen Spender and J. B. Leishman: translation of Rainer Maria Rilke's *Duineser elegien* (*Duino Elegies*)

Christopher Isherwood

Roy Campbell

Christopher Fry: *The Boy with a Cart*

G. B. Shaw: *In Good King Charles's Golden Days* (produced 1939); *Geneva* (produced 1938)

NON-FICTION

W. H. Auden and Christopher Isherwood: *Journey to a War* (dedicated to E. M. Forster)

John Betjeman: *Antiquarian Prejudice*

Joyce Cary: *Power in Men*

David Daiches: *The Novel and the Modern World*

E. M. Forster: *What I Believe*

Roger Fry: *Last Lectures* (Introduction by Kenneth Clark)

Graham Greene: *The Lawless Roads* (U.S. title: *Another Mexico*)

Gerald Heard: *Pain, Sex and Time: A New Hypothesis of Evolution*

Katherine Mansfield: *The Scrapbook* (edited by John Middleton Murry)

Sean O'Casey: *I Knock at the Door*

J. B. Priestley: *Rain Upon Godshill: A Further Chapter of Autobiography*

Evelyn Waugh: *Robbery Under Law, the Mexican Object-Lesson*

Charles Williams: *The Descent of the Dove*

Virginia Woolf: *Reviewing*

W. B. Yeats: *On the Boiler* (Cuala Press)

❧ ❧ *"It is a virtue in a novelist that his point be able to be missed."*

LOUIS MACNEICE

Paul Engle: *Corn*

Robert Frost: *Collected Poems*

Archibald MacLeish: *America Was Promises*

Edna St. Vincent Millay: *Huntsman, What Quarry?*

Kenneth Patchen: *First Will and Testament*

Muriel Rukeyser: *A Turning Wind*

Mark Van Doren: *Collected Poems, 1922–1938*

Dudley Fitts and Robert Fitzgerald: translation of *The Antigone of Sophocles*

Delmore Schwartz: translation of Arthur Rimbaud's *Un Saison en Enfer* (*A Season in Hell*)

T. S. Eliot: *The Family Reunion: A Play* (produced 1939)

Thornton Wilder: *The Merchant of Yonkers* (produced 1939)

United States

FICTION

Conrad Aiken: *A Heart for the Gods of Mexico* (G.B.)

Raymond Chandler: *The Big Sleep*

John Dos Passos: *Adventures of a Young Man*

William Faulkner: *The Wild Palms*

H. P. Lovecraft: *The Outsider and Others*

J. P. Marquand: *Wickford Point*

Henry Miller: *The Tropic of Capricorn* (Paris); *The Cosmological Eye*

Anaïs Nin: *Winter of Artifice* (Paris)

Dorothy Parker: *Here Lies: Collected Stories*

Katherine Anne Porter: *Pale Horse, Pale Rider*

William Saroyan: *Peace, It's Wonderful*

Gertrude Stein: *The World Is Round*

John Steinbeck: *The Grapes of Wrath*

Robert Penn Warren: *Night Rider*

Nathanael West: *The Day of the Locust*

Thomas Wolfe: *The Web and the Rock*

VERSE AND DRAMA

Babette Deutsch: *One Part Love*

T. S. Eliot: *Old Possum's Book of Practical Cats*

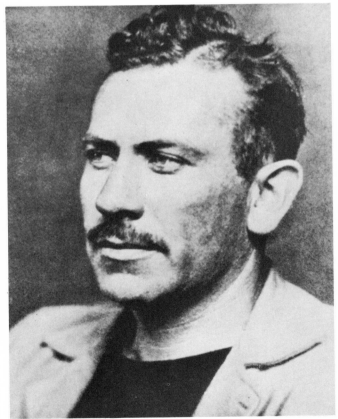

John Steinbeck

NON-FICTION

Cleanth Brooks: *Modern Poetry and the Tradition*

Aaron Copland: *What to Listen for in Music*

T. S. Eliot: *The Idea of a Christian Society*

Edna Ferber: *A Peculiar Treasure*

Henry Miller and Michael Fraenkel: *Hamlet* (Vol. II 1941; complete Vol. I 1943)

Ezra Pound: *What Is Money For?* (G.B.)

Carl Sandburg: *Abraham Lincoln: The War Years*

Virgil Thomson: *The State of Music*

Mark Van Doren: *Shakespeare*

❧❧ *". . . the artist has the only true critical intelligence."*

THOMAS WOLFE

Anaïs Nin

W. B. Yeats

Related Events

DEATHS

William Butler Yeats: Dublin-born poet, dramatist, autobiographer, and Senator of the Irish Free State; age 74; of heart failure; at the Hotel Idéal Sejour, Cap Martin, on the French Riviera, on January 28. He was first buried in the cemetery at Roquebrune, near Nice, but after the war, his body was transferred to the Drumcliffe Churchyard in County Sligo, where his great grandfather had once been rector and where he himself had lived as a child. "You were silly like us: your gift survived it all." —W. H. Auden

Ford Madox Ford: British novelist, man-of-letters, editor, and tireless counselor to three generations of the literary young; age 66; of heart failure; in Deauville, France, on July 26. "I don't suppose failure disturbed him much: he had never really believed in human happiness, his middle life had been made miserable by passion, and he had come through—with his humor intact, his stock of unreliable anecdotes, the kind of enemies a man ought to have, and a half-belief in a posterity which would care for good writing."
—Graham Greene

Sigmund Freud: Austrian poet and founder of the psychoanalytic movement; age 83; of cancer of the mouth; in Hampstead, England, on September 23: "Really, a beautiful old man . . ."
—Thornton Wilder, in a letter to Gertrude Stein

Other Deaths:
Havelock Ellis
Zane Grey
Ernst Töller

IN OTHER LANGUAGES

Bertolt Brecht: *Svendborger Gedichte (Svendborg Poems)*
Sigmund Freud: *Der Mann Moses und die Monotheistische Religion (Moses and Monotheism)*
André Gide: *Journal 1889–1939*
Ernst Jünger: *Auf den Marmorklippen (On the Marble Cliffs)*
Thomas Mann: *Lotte in Weimar (The Beloved Returns)*
Antoine de Saint-Exupéry: *Terre des Hommes*
Jean-Paul Sartre: *Le Mur*

IN OTHER ARTS

Jean Renoir: *La Regle du Jeu*
William Saroyan: *The Time of Your Life*
Igor Stravinsky arrives in the United States on September 30, to deliver the Charles Eliot Norton lectures (in French) at Harvard

Cyril Connolly

Ford Madox Ford

Sigmund Freud

IN THE MARGIN

"Little Mags": Last issue of *The Criterion* in
January: ". . . perhaps for a long way ahead,"
wrote T. S. Eliot, in his valedictory comment,
"the continuity of culture may have to be
maintained by a very small number of people
indeed—and these not necessarily the best
equipped with worldly advantages. It will not
be the large organs of opinion, or the old
periodicals; it must be the small and obscure
papers and reviews, those which hardly are
read by anyone but their own contributors,
that will keep critical thought alive, and
encourage authors of original talent . . ."
‖ First issues of *Furioso* (edited by Reed
Whittemore), *Kenyon Review* (edited by
John Crowe Ransom), and *Horizon* (edited
by Cyril Connolly) followed during the year

Faits Divers: On January 18, W. H. Auden and
Christopher Isherwood sail for the United
States, a move Cyril Connolly presently calls
"the most important literary event since the
outbreak of the Spanish War" ‖ On
February 2, James Joyce proudly displays the
first bound copy of *Finnegans Wake*, over 16
years in the making, to his friends ‖ The
same month, F. Scott Fitzgerald and Budd
Schulberg attend the Dartmouth College
Winter Carnival to gather background
material for a film script they are collaborating
on ‖ On April 21, Ezra Pound arrives in
New York after thirty years abroad, and
accepts an honorary degree from his alma
mater, Hamilton College ‖ In May, John
Gould Fletcher is awarded the Pulitzer Prize
for his *Selected Poems* ‖ In August, Henry
Miller visits Lawrence Durrell in Greece ‖
In October, William Empson returns to
England after two years in China ‖ By the
end of the year, Henry Green has joined the
Mayfair unit of the National Fire Brigade
and is having the experience he drew upon in
Caught

In the Great World: March 28: Fall of Madrid
to General Franco and the end of civil war
and the Spanish Republic ‖ June: King
George VI and Queen Elizabeth visit Canada
and the United States, eating hot dogs with
President and Mrs. Franklin Roosevelt at Hyde
Park ‖ August 23: Hitler and Stalin sign a
non-aggression pact ‖ September 1:
Hitler's Army invades Poland ‖ September
2: Great Britain declares war on the
Third Reich

1940

Arthur Koestler

Graham Greene

Great Britain

FICTION

Nicholas Blake (C. Day Lewis): *Malice in Wonderland* (one of nine Nicholas Blake mysteries, 1935–50)

Joyce Cary: *Charley Is My Darling*

Robert Graves: *Sergeant Lamb of the Ninth*

Graham Greene: *The Power and the Glory* (U.S. title: *The Labyrinthine Ways*)

Arthur Koestler: *Darkness at Noon*

W. Somerset Maugham: *The Mixture as Before*

Nancy Mitford: *Pigeon Pie*

C. P. Snow: *Strangers and Brothers*

Stephen Spender: *The Backward Son*

Dylan Thomas: *Portrait of the Artist as a Young Dog*

H. G. Wells: *Babes in the Darkling Wood*

VERSE AND DRAMA

W. H. Auden: *Another Time* (dedicated to Chester Kallman)

George Barker: *Lament and Triumph*

John Betjeman: *Old Lights for New Chancels, Verses Topographical and Amatory*

Edmund Blunden: *Poems 1930–1940*

William Empson: *The Gathering Storm*

Robert Graves: *No More Ghosts: Selected Poems*

Rayner Heppenstall: *Blind Men's Flowers Are Green*

Rudyard Kipling: *Verse, Definitive Edition*

D. H. Lawrence: *Fire and Other Poems* (Foreword by Robinson Jeffers; San Francisco)

Louis MacNeice: *The Last Ditch* (Dublin); *Selected Poems*

Edith Sitwell: *Poems New and Old*

Henry Treece: *38 Poems*

George Barker

Herbert Read

C. Day Lewis: translation of Virgil's *Georgics*

E. M. Forster: *England's Pleasant Land: A Pageant Play*

NON-FICTION

John Buchan: *Memory Hold-the-Door*
Walter de la Mare: *Pleasures and Speculations*
Havelock Ellis: *My Life*
Robert Graves and Alan Hodge: *The Long Weekend: A Social History of Great Britain, 1918–1939*
Henry Green: *Pack My Bag*
W. Somerset Maugham: *Books and You*
George Orwell: *Inside the Whale*
Herbert Read: *Annals of Innocence and Experience*
Forrest Reid: *Private Road*

Sacheverell Sitwell: *Poltergeists: An Introduction and Examination Followed by Chosen Instances*
Virginia Woolf: *Roger Fry: A Biography*
W. B. Yeats: *Letters on Poetry* (to Dorothy Wellesley)

❧ ❧ *"The waste remains, the waste remains and kills."*

WILLIAM EMPSON

United States

FICTION

Kay Boyle: *The Crazy Hunter*
Willa Cather: *Sapphira and the Slave Girl*
James T. Farrell: *Father and Son*
William Faulkner: *The Hamlet*
Ernest Hemingway: *For Whom the Bell Tolls*
Sinclair Lewis: *Bethel Merriday*
Carson McCullers: *The Heart Is a Lonely Hunter*
Conrad Richter: *The Trees*
William Saroyan: *My Name Is Aram*
James Thurber: *Fables for Our Time and Famous Poems Illustrated*
Glenway Wescott: *The Pilgrim Hawk*
William Carlos Williams: *In the Money: White Mule, Part II*
Thomas Wolfe: *You Can't Go Home Again*
Richard Wright: *Native Son*

VERSE AND DRAMA

Conrad Aiken: *And in the Human Heart*
John Berryman: *Twenty Poems* (in *Five Young American Poets*)
e. e. cummings: *50 Poems*
T. S. Eliot: *East Coker* (G.B.)
Kenneth Fearing: *Collected Poems*
Randall Jarrell: *The Rage for the Lost Penny* (in *Five Young American Poets*)
Phyllis McGinley: *A Pocketful of Wry*
Edna St. Vincent Millay: *Make Bright the Arrows*
Ogden Nash: *The Face Is Familiar*
Ezra Pound: *Cantos LII–LXXI*
Kenneth Rexroth: *In What Hour*
Yvor Winters: *Poems*

Rolfe Humphries: translation of Federico García Lorca's *Poeta en Nueva York* (*The Poet in New York*)

Janet Flanner (Genêt)

Glenway Wescott

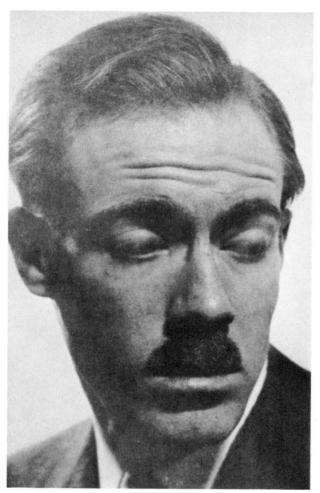

John Berryman

NON-FICTION

R. P. Blackmur: *The Expense of Greatness*
Van Wyck Brooks: *New England: Indian
    Summer, 1865–1915*
Janet Flanner: *An American in Paris*
Langston Hughes: *The Big Sea*
H. L. Mencken: *Happy Days, 1880–1892*
Henry Miller: *The World of Sex* (privately
    printed)
E. A. Robinson: *Selected Letters* (edited by
    Ridgely Torrence)
George Santayana: *The Realm of Spirit; Book
    Fourth of Realms of Being*
Gertrude Stein: *What Are Masterpieces; Paris
    France*

Edmund Wilson: *To the Finland Station: A
    Study in the Writing and Acting of History*

❧❧ "*. . . and for clarity's sake, let us
often use, and sanction the use of, words
of one syllable. The shortest and most
potent is the personal pronoun: I.*"
                              GLENWAY WESCOTT

Related Events

DEATHS

Leon Trotsky, Russian historian and revolutionary;
    age 63; by assassination at the hands of a
    G.P.U. agent, at his home in Cayoacán,
    Mexico; on August 20
Walter Benjamin, German literary critic and
    historian (descended on his father's side from
    U. S. President Martin Van Buren); age 48; of
    suicide (15 tablets of morphine compound),
    while trying to escape the Gestapo near the
    Spanish border of France, on September 27
Francis Scott Fitzgerald, American novelist,
    short-story writer, and "in the twenties, his
    heyday . . . a kind of king of our American
    youth" (Glenway Wescott); age 44; of a heart
    attack, in Hollywood, California, on December
    21
Nathanael West, American novelist, age 38; in an
    automobile accident (along with his
    seven-months bride, Eileen McKenney West);
    near El Centro, California, on December 22

Other Deaths:

John Buchan (Lord Tweedsmuir)
W. H. Davies
Hamlin Garland
Edwin Markham
John B. Wheelwright
Humbert Wolfe

André Breton: *L'Anthologie de l'Humour Noir*
Jean Cocteau: *Les Monstres Sacrés*
Colette: *Chambre d'Hôtel*
Thomas Mann: *Die Vertauschten Köpfe* (*The Transposed Heads*)
Jean-Paul Sartre: *L'Imaginaire*

Sean O'Casey: *The Star Turns Red* (London)
Tennessee Williams: *Battle of Angels* (Boston)
Igor Stravinsky: *Symphony in C* (Chicago)
Charles Chaplin: *The Great Dictator* (New York)

Laurels: James Tait Black Prize to Aldous Huxley for *After Many a Summer* ‖ The William Dean Howells Medal to Ellen Glasgow ‖ Pulitzer Prizes for Poetry to Mark Van Doren's *Collected Poems*; for Fiction to John Steinbeck's *The Grapes of Wrath*; for Drama (refused) to William Saroyan's *The Time of Your Life*; for History to Carl Sandburg's *Abraham Lincoln: The War Years* ‖ No Nobel Prize awarded until 1944

"Little Mags": Accent (Illinois), edited by Kerker Quinn and Charles Shattuck ‖ View: *"through the eyes of poets"* (New York), edited by Charles Henri Ford

Behind Bars: Having escaped from France, where he had been arrested in his bath at 7:30 one morning and interned as an undesirable alien, Arthur Koestler arrives in England and is soon installed in the Pentonville Prison for having entered the country without a visa. "If I should write a Baedeker of prisons of Europe," he reflects, "I would mark Pentonville with three stars. It is the most decent gaol I have been in, though the plumbing leaves much to be desired."

Nathanael West

Listen, Germany: Self-exiled in Santa Monica, California, Thomas Mann records a series of antiwar broadcasts to the German people, which are then flown to Great Britain and aired over the B.B.C.

"February House": Sometime in the autumn, at 7 Middaugh Street, in Brooklyn Heights, a unique Poets' Hostel is set up by Carson McCullers, W. H. Auden, and George Davis, literary editor of *Harper's Bazaar*. As described by Louis MacNeice, it was "without much furniture or carpets, but a warren of the arts, Auden writing in one room, a girl novelist writing—with a china cup of sherry—in another, a composer composing and a singer hitting a high note and holding it, and Gypsy Rose Lee, the strip-tease queen, coming round for meals like a whirlwind of laughter and

F. Scott Fitzgerald

Randall Jarrell

sex . . ." Because so many of the guests were born under the astrological sign of Pisces, Anaïs Nin named the premises "February House." Auden kept the books, and among those who paid about $25 a week were Benjamin Britten, Peter Pears, Chester Kallman, Richard Wright, and Paul and Jane Bowles.

Arrivals in America: W. Somerset Maugham, by way of England, from his Villa Mauresque on Cap Ferrat in the South of France || Henry Miller, by way of Greece, after nearly a decade's expatriation in Paris || Vladimir Nabokov (V. Sirin), by way of England, Germany, and France, after 22 years of chosen exile from his native Russia || George Barker, by way of Japan, after serving for six months as Professor of Literature at the Imperial University of Sendai, Tokyo

In the Wings: Robert Traill Spence Lowell, 23, graduates from Kenyon College, joins the Roman Catholic Church, and is married to Jean Stafford

In the Great World: May 10: Winston Churchill becomes Prime Minister of Great Britain || May 30: Evacuation of British forces at Dunkirk || June 14: Fall of Paris || July 10: French National Assembly annuls the Third Republic || August 24: The "blitz" begins with the first German bombing of London || November: Franklin D. Roosevelt elected to a third term as President of the U.S.

W. H. Auden

Great Britain

FICTION

Elizabeth Bowen: *Look at All Those Roses*
Joyce Cary: *Herself Surprised; A House of Children*
John Collier: *Presenting Moonshine*
Ivy Compton-Burnett: *Parents and Children*
Robert Graves: *Proceed, Sergeant Lamb*
H. F. (Gerald) Heard: *A Taste for Honey*
Wyndham Lewis: *The Vulgar Streak*
W. Somerset Maugham: *Up at the Villa*
Osbert Sitwell: *Open the Door!*
Rex Warner: *The Aerodrome: A Love Story*
Virginia Woolf: *Between the Acts*

VERSE AND DRAMA

W. H. Auden: *The Double Man* (G.B. Title: *New Year Letter*)

Laurence Binyon: *The North Star and Other Poems*
Walter de la Mare: *Bells and Grass*
Ralph Hodgson: *Silver Wedding and Other Poems*
Rudyard Kipling: *A Choice of Kipling's Verse* (edited by T. S. Eliot)
Louis MacNeice: *Plant and Phantom*
Vernon Watkins: *The Ballad of the Mari Lwyd*

NON-FICTION

Richard Aldington: *Life for Life's Sake*
Joyce Cary: *The Case for African Freedom*
Norman Douglas: *An Almanac* (privately printed, Lisbon; trade edition 1945)
Aldous Huxley: *Grey Eminence*
Arthur Koestler: *Scum of the Earth* (the author's first book written in English)
Louis MacNeice: *The Poetry of W. B. Yeats*
W. Somerset Maugham: *Strictly Personal*
George Orwell: *The Lion and the Unicorn: Socialism and the English Genius*
Peter Quennell: *Byron in Italy*
Forrest Reid: *Retrospective Adventures*
Rebecca West: *Black Lamb and Grey Falcon: A Journey Through Yugoslavia*
Charles Williams: *Witchcraft*

❦❦ *". . . if only I had a glass door in my heart, like the new ovens, to see what was really there . . ."*

JOYCE CARY

United States

FICTION

James T. Farrell: *Ellen Rogers*
F. Scott Fitzgerald: *The Last Tycoon: An Unfinished Novel* (edited by Edmund Wilson)

Ellen Glasgow: *In This Our Life*
Caroline Gordon: *Green Centuries*
Andrew Lytle: *At the Moon's Inn*
Carson McCullers: *Reflections in a Golden Eye*
Vladimir Nabokov: *The Real Life of Sebastian Knight*
Kenneth Patchen: *The Journal of Albion Moonlight*
Elizabeth Madox Roberts: *Not By Strange Gods*
Gertrude Stein: *Ida*
Eudora Welty: *A Curtain of Green and Other Stories* (Introduction by Katherine Anne Porter)
Thomas Wolfe: *The Hills Beyond*

VERSE AND DRAMA

Howard Baker: *A Letter from the Country and Other Poems*
John Peale Bishop: *Selected Poems*
Louise Bogan: *Poems and New Poems*
Malcolm Cowley: *The Dry Season*

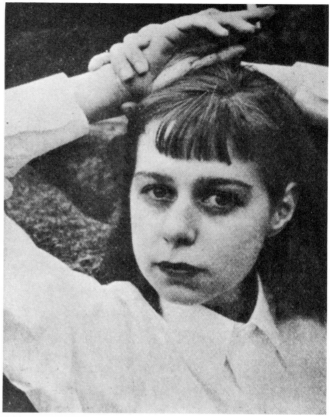

Carson McCullers

T. S. Eliot: *Burnt Norton* (G.B.); *The Dry Salvages* (G.B.)
Paul Engle: *West of Midnight*
John Gould Fletcher: *South Star*
Horace Gregory: *Poems: 1930–1940*
Robinson Jeffers: *Be Angry at the Sun*
Phyllis McGinley: *Husbands Are Difficult*
Edna St. Vincent Millay: *Collected Sonnets*
Marianne Moore: *What Are Years*
Selden Rodman, ed.: *The Poetry of Flight*
Theodore Roethke: *Open House*
Delmore Schwartz: *Shenandoah*
Allen Tate: *Sonnets at Christmas*
Ridgely Torrence: *Poems*
John Brooks Wheelwright: *Selected Poems*
William Carlos Williams: *The Broken Span*
Marya Zaturenska: *The Listening Landscape*

Rebecca West

James Agee

NON-FICTION

James Agee: *Let Us Now Praise Famous Men*
    (with photographs by Walker Evans)
Van Wyck Brooks: *The Opinions of Oliver
    Allston; On Literature Today*
Kenneth Burke: *The Philosophy of Literary
    Form: Studies in Symbolic Action*
Aaron Copland: *Our New Music*
John Dos Passos: *The Ground We Stand On*
Theodore Dreiser: *America Is Worth Saving*
Oliver Wendell Holmes and Sir Frederick
    Pollock: *The Holmes-Pollock Letters,
    1874–1932* (edited by M. A. De Wolfe Howe)
Archibald MacLeish: *A Time to Speak*
F. O. Matthiessen: *American Renaissance*

H. L. Mencken: *Newspaper Days, 1899–1906*
Henry Miller: *The Colossus of Maroussi; The
    Wisdom of the Heart*
John Crowe Ransom: *The New Criticism*
Allen Tate: *Reason in Madness: Critical Essays*
Edmund Wilson: *The Wound and the Bow:
    Seven Studies in Literature; The Boys in the
    Back Room: Notes on California Novelists*

 *"Against time and the damages of the brain
    Sharpen and calibrate."*

JAMES AGEE

Isaac Babel

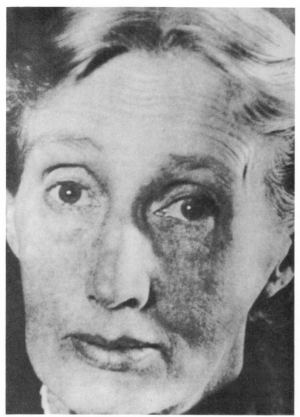

Virginia Woolf

James Joyce

Related Events

DEATHS

James Joyce, Irish poet, novelist, and wordsmith; age 59; after an operation for a perforated duodenal ulcer; in Zurich, on January 13. "The artist, like the God of the creation, remains within or behind or beyond or above his handiwork, invisible, refined out of existence, indifferent, paring his fingernails."

Sherwood Anderson, American novelist and short-story writer; age 65; of peritonitis, in the course of a South American tour; at Colon, Panama Canal Zone, March 8. "Behold in me the American man striving to become an artist, to become conscious of himself, filled with wonder concerning himself and others . . ."

Isaac Babel, Russian lyric narrative writer; age 47; manner of death unknown, possibly murder by Soviet police at some time after his arrest on May 15, 1939. He was last seen by friends at the Lubyanka Prison in Moscow shortly after, when he said: "I was not given time to finish—" In 1954, the Supreme Court of the U.S.S.R. issued a paper confirming that "a sentence of the Military College dated 26 January 1940 concerning Babel, I. E., is revoked . . . and the case against him is terminated in the absence of elements of a crime." His death certificate (also issued in 1954) only specifies that he died on March 17, 1941. "No iron can stab the heart with such force as a period put just at the right place."

Sherwood Anderson

Virginia Woolf, British novelist and lady-of-letters; age 59; by drowning (suicide), in the neighborhood of her home, Monk's House, at Rodmell, near Lewes, in Sussex, on March 28. ". . . surely nothing survives except the perfection of prose . . . *la douleur passera et la page excellente reste.*"

Other Deaths:

Sir James George Frazer
Edward J. O'Brien
Elizabeth Madox Roberts
Hugh Walpole

IN OTHER LANGUAGES

Louis Aragon: *Le Crève-Coeur*
Jean Cocteau: *La Machine à Ecrire*
Colette: *Journal à Rebours; Julie de Carneilhan*
Jean Paulhan: *Les Fleurs de Tarbes*
Franz Werfel: *Das Lied von Bernadette* (*The Song of Bernadette*)

Cesare Pavese: translation into Italian of Gertrude Stein's *Three Lives* and Herman Melville's *Benito Cereno*

IN OTHER ARTS

Bertolt Brecht: *Mutter Courage und ihre Kinder* (*Mother Courage and Her Children*)
Aaron Copland: *Piano Sonata* (commissioned by Clifford Odets)
Noel Coward: *Blithe Spirit*
Orson Welles: *Citizen Kane*

July 4: Recent applicant for American citizenship Igor Stravinsky finishes his arrangement of *The Star-Spangled Banner*
October 11: Virgil Thomson begins his 14-year stint as music critic for the New York *Herald Tribune*

IN THE MARGIN

Rewards: The Hawthornden Prize to Graham Greene for *The Power and the Glory* || Archibald MacLeish, Congressional Librarian since 1939, is appointed Director of the Office of Facts and Figures, where he is shortly, and briefly, assisted by Malcolm Cowley

Whereabouts: André Breton and Bertolt Brecht arrive in the United States respectively by way of the ports of New York and San Francisco || In Manhattan, Thomas Mann's eldest son, Klaus, begins editing *Decision, a Review of Free Culture*, assisted by Muriel Rukeyser || With a family of seven, Kay Boyle returns home after twenty years of residence in Europe || By December, Graham Greene is with a convoy en route to South Africa for the Ministry of Information, and "in spite of nausea and watches," writing 500 words a day || Gertrude Stein continues to wait out the war in the Zone Libre of France, and in New York, Bennett Cerf publishes her novel, *Ida*, writing the blurb himself: ". . . here it is, presented faithfully to you by a publisher who rarely has the faintest idea of what Miss Stein is talking about, but who admires her from the bottom of his heart for her courage and for her abounding love of humanity and freedom"

In the Wings: William Sansom, a member of the National Fire Service barracked in the "basement boot-room of Hampstead High School for Girls" takes a vow: "Such were the dock and oil fires, we all thought that it would be a question of weeks if not days before we were wiped out . . . And for the first time I said to myself: I must write down something absolutely true" ‖ J. D. Salinger, employed as an entertainer aboard the Swedish line M.S. *Kungsholm*, sells his first Holden Caulfield story to *The New Yorker*, and begins a five-year wait for its publication

In the Great World: June: after nearly a year, the German bombing of London abates. On the 22nd, Hitler invades the U.S.S.R. ‖ On December 7, the Japanese attack the U. S. fleet at Pearl Harbor, in Hawaii, and Manila, in the Philippine Islands. On December 8, the U.S. declares war on Japan, and on December 11, Germany and Italy declare war on the U.S.

Joyce Cary

Great Britain

FICTION

Joyce Cary: *To Be a Pilgrim*
James Joyce: *Introducing James Joyce* (edited by T. S. Eliot)

C. S. Lewis

W. Somerset Maugham: *The Hour Before the Dawn* (U.S.)
Evelyn Waugh: *Put Out More Flags; Work Suspended*

VERSE AND DRAMA

Alex Comfort: *A Wreath for the Living*
Walter de la Mare: *Collected Poems*
Sidney Keyes: *The Iron Laurel*
Alun Lewis: *Raider's Dawn*
Anne Ridler, ed.: *A Little Book of Modern Verse* (Preface by T. S. Eliot)
Edith Sitwell: *Street Songs*

Stephen Spender: *Ruins and Visions*
Ruthven Todd: *Until Now*
Henry Treece: *Invitation and Warning*

Norman Cameron: translation of Arthur
    Rimbaud's *Selected Verse*

NON-FICTION

Elizabeth Bowen: *Bowen's Court; Seven Winters*
    (Cuala Press)
David Daiches: *Virginia Woolf*
E. M. Forster: *Virginia Woolf* (The Rede
    Lecture)
Graham Greene: *British Dramatists*
Aldous Huxley: *The Art of Seeing*
C. S. Lewis: *The Screwtape Letters*
Sean O'Casey: *Pictures in the Hallway*
V. S. Pritchett: *In My Good Books*
Forrest Reid: *Notes and Impressions*
Siegfried Sassoon: *The Weald of Youth*
Edith Sitwell: *English Women*

Charles Williams: *The Forgiveness of Sins*
Virginia Woolf: *The Death of the Moth and
    Other Essays*

❧❧ *"The pen always finds life difficult to
record; left to itself, it records the pen."*
                                E. M. FORSTER

Thornton Wilder

United States

FICTION

Isak Dinesen: *Winter Tales*
James T. Farrell: *$1,000 a Week and Other
    Stories*
William Faulkner: *Go Down, Moses, and Other
    Stories*
Ernest Hemingway, ed.: *Men at War*

Alfred Kazin

Stephen Spender

Mary McCarthy: *The Company She Keeps*
Wright Morris: *My Uncle Dudley*
Dawn Powell: *A Time to Be Born*
John Steinbeck: *The Moon Is Down*
Allen Tate and John Peale Bishop, eds.: *American Harvest: Twenty Years of Creative Writing in the United States* (stories, poems, essays)
James Thurber: *My World—and Welcome to It*
Eudora Welty: *The Robber Bridegroom*

Katherine Anne Porter: translation of José Joaquín Fernández de Lizardi's *El Periquillo Sarniento* (*The Itching Parrot*)

VERSE AND DRAMA

Conrad Aiken: *Brownstone Eclogues and Other Poems*
John Berryman: *Poems*
T. S. Eliot: *Little Gidding* (G.B.)
Robert Frost: *A Witness Tree*
Langston Hughes: *Shakespeare in Harlem*

Rolfe Humphries: *Out of the Jewel*
Randall Jarrell: *Blood for a Stranger*
Edna St. Vincent Millay: *The Murder of Lidice*
Karl Shapiro: *Person, Place and Thing; The Place of Love* ("incantational prose poems"; Australia)
Wallace Stevens: *Parts of a World; Notes Toward a Supreme Fiction*
Genevieve Taggard: *Long View*
Robert Penn Warren: *Eleven Poems on the Same Theme*
Edmund Wilson: *Note-Books of Night* (verse and prose)

Thornton Wilder: *The Skin of Our Teeth* (produced 1942)

NON-FICTION

Sherwood Anderson: *Memoirs*
T. S. Eliot: *The Music of Poetry* (Glasgow; W. P. Ker Memorial Lecture); *The Classics and the Man of Letters*
Alfred Kazin: *On Native Grounds: An Interpretation of Modern American Prose Literature*
Stanley J. Kunitz and Howard Haycraft: *Twentieth Century Authors*
A. J. Liebling: *The Telephone Booth Indian*
H. L. Mencken, ed.: *A New Dictionary of Quotations on Historical Principles from Ancient and Modern Sources*
Constance Rourke: *The Roots of American Culture* (edited by Van Wyck Brooks)
Muriel Rukeyser: *Willard Gibbs*
E. B. White: *One Man's Meat*

❧ ❧ *"Even when it is most serious, the novel's characteristic tone is one of gossip and tittletattle."*

MARY MCCARTHY

Related Events

DEATHS

Robert Musil, Austrian novelist (self-exiled in
  Geneva)
Stefan Zweig, Austrian novelist (self-exiled in
  Brazil: suicide)

IN OTHER LANGUAGES

Louis Aragon: *Les Yeux d'Elsa*
Albert Camus: *L'Étranger; Le Mythe de Sisyphe*
Ernst Jünger: *Gärten und Strassen* (*Gardens and
  Roads*)
Antoine de Saint-Exupéry: *Pilote de Guerre*
Saint-John Perse: *Exil*
Igor Stravinsky: *Poétique Musicale: sous forme de
  six leçons* (U.S.)

Cesare Pavese: translation into Italian of William
  Faulkner's *The Hamlet*

IN OTHER ARTS

Films: David Lean–Noel Coward: *In Which
  We Serve* || Orson Welles–Booth
  Tarkington: *The Magnificent Ambersons* ||
  John Houston–Dashiell Hammett: *The
  Maltese Falcon*

IN THE MARGIN

Laurels: The James Tait Black Prize to Joyce
  Cary for *A House of Children* || The
  Pulitzer Prize for Fiction to Ellen Glasgow for
  In This Our Life

In Hollywood: I. A. Richards is busy paring the
  language down for his book on basic English,
  proposing that with a vocabulary of exactly
  850 words (600 nouns, 150 adjectives, 100
  verbs) "it is possible to say . . . anything
  needed . . . in all the arts of living, in all the
  exchanges of knowledge, desires, beliefs,
  opinions, and news which are the chief work
  of a language." At the same time, Mr. Richards
  is writing film scripts for Walt Disney "shorts"

|| William Faulkner receives screen credit for
film scripts based on Ernest Hemingway's *To
Have and Have Not* and Raymond Chandler's
The Big Sleep || Tennessee Williams is
engaged by M.G.M. at $250 a week to write
film scripts for Lana Turner and Margaret
O'Brien. Both scripts are rejected

Richard Eberhart

In Print: The exiled French Surrealists in New
  York publish a new review—VVV—edited by
  sculptor David Hare, with an advisory board
  made up of André Breton, Max Ernst, and
  Marcel Duchamp || Virginia-born French
  novelist Julian Green writes his first book in
  English, *Memories of Happy Days*, and with
  his sister Anne, edits a volume of selections
  from Charles Péguy: *Basic Verities* || Kurt
  Wolff (publisher, in Germany, of Franz
  Kafka's first book, *Betrachtung* in 1913)

inaugurates Pantheon Books in New York ‖ *The Chimera: A Rough Beast,* edited in New York by Frederick Morgan and William Arrowsmith ‖ On December 26, poet James Agee begins his weekly film commentary in *The Nation* (through September 4, 1948)

In Uniform: Thornton Wilder accepts a commission as captain in the U. S. Army Air Force ‖ Stephen Spender joins the Cricklewood, London, Branch of the National Fire Service ‖ Richard Eberhart enters the U. S. Naval Reserve, and Randall Jarrell the U. S. Army Air Force

In Dutch: Broadcasting over the Rome Radio on January 29, Ezra Pound declares that "the United States has been for months illegally at war through what I consider to be the criminal acts of a President whose mental condition was not, so far as I could see, all that could or should be desired . . ."

In the Wings: Truman Capote, 19, is working as an errand boy in the Art Department of *The New Yorker* magazine ‖ At the trial of Jean Genet, 33, in Occupied Paris, Jean Cocteau tells the Tribunal that he regards Genet, as yet unpublished, "*comme le grand écrivain de France*"

1943

Great Britain

FICTION

Walter de la Mare: *The Magic Jacket and Other Stories*
Robert Graves: *The Story of Marie Powell, Wife to Mr. Milton*

Henry Green: *Caught*
Graham Greene: *The Ministry of Fear*
James Hanley: *No Directions*
Rayner Heppenstall: *Saturnine*
Arthur Koestler: *Arrival and Departure*
C. S. Lewis: *Perelandra*
Philip Toynbee: *The Barricades*
Rex Warner: *Why Was I Killed?: A Dramatic Dialogue* (U.S. title: *Return of the Travell*

VERSE AND DRAMA

Walter de la Mare, ed.: *Love*
Lawrence Durrell: *A Private Country*
David Gascoyne: *Poems 1937–42*
Sidney Keyes: *The Cruel Solstice*
C. Day Lewis: *Word Over All*
Edwin Muir: *The Narrow Place*
Kathleen Raine: *Stone and Flower*
Dylan Thomas: *New Poems* (U.S.)

Rayner Heppenstall

Forrest Reid: translation of *Poems from the
Greek Anthology*

NON-FICTION

Max Beerbohm: *Lytton Strachey*
Joyce Cary: *Process of Real Freedom*
David Cecil: *Hardy the Novelist*
Robert Graves and Alan Hodge: *The Reader
Over Your Shoulder: A Handbook for Writers
of English Prose*
Hugh MacDiarmid: *Lucky Poet*
William Plomer: *Double Lives*
Victoria Sackville-West: *The Eagle and the
Dove: A Study in Contrasts, St. Teresa of Avila
and St. Thérèse of Lisieux*
Edith Sitwell: *A Poet's Notebook*
Denton Welch: *Maiden Voyage* (dedicated to
Edith Sitwell, with a Foreword by her)
Charles Williams: *The Figure of Beatrice*

 "*. . . if you want to create life the
one way not to set about it is by
explanation.*"

HENRY GREEN

Walter de la Mare

VERSE AND DRAMA

T. S. Eliot: *Four Quartets*
Kenneth Fearing: *The Afternoon of a
Pawnbroker and Other Poems*
Edna St. Vincent Millay: *Collected Lyrics*
Kenneth Patchen: *Cloth of the Tempest*
Delmore Schwartz: *Genesis*
Oscar Williams, ed.: *New Poems, 1943*
Yvor Winters: *The Giant Weapon*

Allen Tate: translation of *Pervigilium Veneris*
(*The Vigil of Venus*)

NON-FICTION

Ellen Glasgow: *A Certain Measure: An
Interpretation of Prose Fiction*
H. L. Mencken: *Heathen Days, 1890–1936*
Albert J. Nock: *The Memoirs of a
Superfluous Man*

United States

FICTION

Dorothy Baker: *Trio*
Jane Bowles: *Two Serious Ladies*
John Dos Passos: *Number One*
James T. Farrell: *My Days of Anger*
Sinclair Lewis: *Gideon Planish*
H. P. Lovecraft: *Beyond the Wall of Sleep*
William Saroyan: *The Human Comedy*
Caroline Slade: *Lilly Crackell*
Robert Penn Warren: *At Heaven's Gate*
Eudora Welty: *The Wide Net and Other Stories*

James Thurber: *Men, Women and Dogs, a Book of Drawings*

Edmund Wilson, ed.: *The Shock of Recognition*

Yvor Winters: *The Anatomy of Nonsense*

Thomas Wolfe: *Letters to His Mother* (edited by John Skalley Terry)

❧ ❧ *"The answer is in the back of the book but the page is gone."*

ROBERT PENN WARREN

Eudora Welty

Related Events

DEATHS

Sidney Keyes: British poet; 21; "of unknown causes," after being taken prisoner on a dawn patrol during the Tunisian campaign; on April 29. "O it is terrible to dream of angels."

Simone Weil: French diarist and self-questioner; 34; of exhaustion due to fasting; at a sanatorium in Ashford, Kent, on August 29. "It is wrong to be an 'I', but it is worse to be a 'we'."

Other Deaths:

Stephen Vincent Benét

Laurence Binyon

Sergei Rachmaninoff

Mrs. G. B. Shaw

IN OTHER LANGUAGES

Colette: *Gigi* (Geneva)

André Gide: *Interviews Imaginaires* (New York)

Hermann Hesse: *Das Glasperlenspiel* (*Magister Ludi*)

André Malraux: *Les Noyers de l'Altenburg* (Switzerland)

Henri de Montherlant: *Fils de Personne*

Jean-Paul Sartre: *Les Mouches; L'Être et le Néant*

Yvor Winters

Plebejus (Lysandra) cormion *Nabokov*

IN OTHER ARTS

Sean O'Casey: *Red Roses for Me*
Carl Dreyer: *Day of Wrath*
Alfred Hitchcock–Thornton Wilder: *The Shadow of a Doubt*
Jackson Pollock and Robert Motherwell exhibit their first collages at Peggy Guggenheim's "Art of This Century" gallery in New York

IN THE MARGIN

In the District Court of the United States for the District of Columbia, a Grand Jury indicts Ezra Pound, 58, for "overt acts contrary to his duty of allegiance to the United States . . . and against the peace and dignity of the United States"
Vladimir Nabokov is appointed Research Fellow at Harvard University's Agassiz Museum, in charge of Lepidoptera
Quarterly Review of Literature, edited by Theodore Weiss
Laurels: Hawthornden Prize to Sidney Keyes, for *The Iron Laurel* || Pulitzer Prizes for Poetry to Robert Frost, for *A Witness Tree;* for Drama to Thornton Wilder, for *The Skin of Our Teeth;* for Fiction, to Upton Sinclair, for *The Dragon's Teeth*
Jacques Ducour, editor of the French underground newspaper, *Lettres Françaises*, is executed by the Nazis

Joyce Cary is sent by the Ministry of Information to East Africa to write a film, *Man of Two Worlds*
In the Wings: Gore Vidal, 18, graduates from Philips Exeter Academy and joins the U. S. Army, writing his first novel the following year aboard a supply freighter in the Aleutians || Indicted for failing to obey the Selective Service Act, Robert Lowell, 26, declares at his

Simone Weil

trial that the Allied bombing of European civilians seems to him morally indefensible, and is sentenced to one year and a day at the Federal Prison in Danbury, Connecticut || Philip Larkin, 21, just out of Oxford and inelligible for military service, is employed as a librarian and working evenings on his first book of poems, "equally compounded of W. B. Yeats and of having nothing to say"
Wyndham Lewis begins a year's lectureship at

Sidney Keyes

Assumption College, in Windsor, Ontario, teaching five days a week, at $200 a month, "the philosophic principles implicit in various works of fiction, from *War and Peace* to *Of Mice and Men*"

In the Great World: July: Allied invasion of Sicily and Italy; Mussolini arrested, then rescued by Nazi paratroopers in September

1944

Great Britain

FICTION

H. E. Bates: *Fair Stood the Wind for France*
Joyce Cary: *The Horse's Mouth*

Alex Comfort: *The Power House*
Ivy Compton-Burnett: *Elders and Betters*
Robert Graves: *The Golden Fleece* (U.S. title: *Hercules, My Shipmate*)
L. P. Hartley: *The Shrimp and the Anemone*
Aldous Huxley: *Time Must Have a Stop*
James Joyce: *Stephen Hero: Part of the First Draft of 'Portrait of the Artist as a Young Man'* (Introduction by Theodore Spencer)
W. Somerset Maugham: *The Razor's Edge*
Frank O'Connor: *Crab Apple Jelly*
Forrest Reid: *Young Tom; or, Very Mixed Company*
William Sansom: *Fireman Flower*
Denton Welch: *In Youth Is Pleasure*
Virginia Woolf: *A Haunted House and Other Short Stories*

VERSE AND DRAMA

W. H. Auden: *For the Time Being*; ed.: *A Selection from the Poems of Alfred, Lord Tennyson*
George Barker: *Eros in Dogma*
Laurence Binyon: *The Burning of the Leaves and Other Poems* (edited by Cicely Margaret Binyon)
Edmund Blunden: *Shells by a Stream*
Walter de la Mare: *Collected Rhymes and Verses*
Laurie Lee: *The Sun My Monument*
Louis MacNeice: *Springboard: Poems 1941–1944*
Edith Sitwell: *Green Song and Other Poems*; ed.: *Planet and Glow-Worm: A Book for the Sleepless*
Charles Williams: *The Region of the Summer Stars*

Rex Warner: translation of the *"Medea"* of Euripides

Louis MacNeice: *Christopher Columbus: A Radio Play*
Anne Ridler: *Cain*

NON-FICTION

Palinurus (Cyril Connolly): *The Unquiet Grave: A Word Cycle*
D. S. Savage: *The Personal Principle*

Louis MacNeice

Cyril Connolly

Saul Bellow

G. B. Shaw: *Everybody's Political What's What*
Osbert Sitwell: *Left Hand, Right Hand!*
J. B. Yeats: *Letters to His Son W. B. Yeats and Others*
W. B. Yeats: *Pages from a Diary Written in Nineteen Hundred and Thirty* (Cuala Press)

Christopher Isherwood and Swami Prabhavananda: translation of *The Bhagavad-Gita* (Introduction by Aldous Huxley; Hollywood)

 ". . . sometimes I see a giant lion-paw on my windowsill . . ."

EDITH SITWELL

United States

FICTION

Saul Bellow: *Dangling Man*
James T. Farrell: *To Whom It May Concern and Other Stories*
Ernest Hemingway: *The Portable Hemingway* (edited by Malcolm Cowley)
John Hersey: *A Bell for Adano*
Charles Jackson: *The Lost Weekend*
Henry James: *Stories of Writers and Artists* (edited by F. O. Matthiessen)
Anaïs Nin: *Under a Glass Bell*
Katherine Anne Porter: *The Leaning Tower and Other Stories*
Jean Stafford: *Boston Adventure*
James Thurber: *The Great Quillow*

W. Somerset Maugham

Karl Shapiro

VERSE AND DRAMA

Conrad Aiken: *The Soldier: A Poem*
e. e. cummings: *1 × 1*
H.D.: *The Walls Do Not Fall* (dedicated to Bryher)
Babette Deutsch: *Take Them, Stranger*
Rolfe Humphries: *The Summer Landscape*
Robert Lowell: *Land of Unlikeness* (Introduction by Allen Tate)
Marianne Moore: *Nevertheless*
Kenneth Rexroth: *The Phoenix and the Tortoise*
Muriel Rukeyser: *Beast in View*
Karl Shapiro: *V-Letter and Other Poems*
Allen Tate: *The Winter Sea*
Mark Van Doren: *The Seven Sleepers*
Robert Penn Warren: *Selected Poems 1923–1943*

William Carlos Williams: *The Wedge* (dedicated to Louis Zukofsky)
Marya Zaturenska: *The Golden Mirror*

Vladimir Nabokov: translation of *Three Russian Poets*

NON-FICTION

Van Wyck Brooks: *The World of Washington Irving*
Janet Flanner: *Pétain: The Old Man of France*
Horace Gregory: *The Shield of Achilles: Essays on Beliefs in Poetry*
A. J. Liebling: *The Road Back to Paris*
Henry Miller: *Sunday After the War*
Vladimir Nabokov: *Nikolai Gogol, a Biography*
George Santayana: *Persons and Places: The Background of My Life*
Thornton Wilder: *James Joyce* (Aurora, N.Y.)

Malcolm Cowley: translation of André Gide's
    Interviews Imaginaires (*Imaginary Interviews*)

❧❧ *". . . you don't devise a rhythm, the
rhythm is the person, and the sentence but
a radiograph of personality."*
                                    MARIANNE MOORE

Related Events

DEATHS

John Peale Bishop, American poet and
    man-of-letters
George Herriman, American poet and creator of
    Krazy Kat
Alun Lewis, British poet, accidentally killed while
    on Army duty in India

Other Deaths:

Jean Giraudoux
Aristide Maillol
Piet Mondrian
Thomas Sturge Moore
Romain Rolland
Antoine de Saint-Exupéry

IN OTHER LANGUAGES

André Breton: *Arcane 17* (U.S.)
Albert Camus: *Caligula; Le Malentendu*
Jean Genet: *Notre Dame des Fleurs*
André Gide: *Pages de Journal: 1939–1942* (U.S.);
    Hamlet (French translation; U.S.)
Alberto Moravia: *Agostino*
Ezra Pound: *L'America, Roosevelt e le Cause
    della Guerra Presente* (*America, Roosevelt and
    the Cause of the Present War; Venice*); *Oro e
    Lavoro* (*Gold and Labor; Rapallo*);
    *Introduzione alla Natura Economica degli
    S.U.A.* (*Introduction to the Economic Nature
    of the United States; Venice*)

Jean Genet

IN OTHER ARTS

Sean O'Casey: *Purple Dust*
Robert Motherwell edits "Documents of Modern
    Art" series in New York
Pablo Picasso: *L'Homme à l'agneau*

IN THE MARGIN

Settled in Big Sur, California, **Henry Miller**
writes an open letter to the world: "In order to
finish two important books I will need $2,500 in
weekly or monthly installments over a period of
fifty weeks. Do not know how long it will take to
pay off the loan but will give $3,000 for the sum
demanded. Arrangements and guaranties can be
made through my agents in N.Y. Over a dozen of
my books are being published this year here and
in England. Will some one take a chance on me?"

At work in Glampton, Devonshire, on a book about Jason and the Argonauts, **Robert Graves** suddenly realizes that "the Triple Goddess" ("there is none greater in the universe") is the ruling force of all pure poetry, and within three weeks develops his insight into 70,000 words of manuscript which become *The White Goddess*.

In Florida, recovering from a nearly fatal bout of pneumonia, **Robert Frost**, 70, writes to a friend reassuring of his good health: "The pneumonia didn't hurt my wind that I can see. I felled a pine tree today and swung the pick ax half an hour enlarging pot holes."

Asked to choose one of his works for the 500th volume of the World's Classics, **G. B. Shaw** selects *Back to Methuselah*—"a world classic or it is nothing." In this same year, Shaw's Corner, his house at Ayot St Lawrence, is given to the National Trust.

Krazy Kat, by George Herriman

Van Wyck Brooks

Allen Tate assumes editorship (until 1948) of the *Sewanee Review*.

After two uneventful years of hunting German submarines in the waters off Cuba, **Ernest Hemingway** docks his "destroyer" (a 42-foot fishing boat armed with a machine gun and high explosives) and heads for the European front as a correspondent.

Edna St. Vincent Millay in Doctor's Hospital, New York, recovering from a nervous breakdown, the result, she told Edmund Wilson, of five years of "writing almost nothing but propaganda."

In the Great World:

June 6: "D-day" invasion of Normandy by Allied Forces

June 13: First Nazi V-1 or "buzz" bomb strikes London

August 25: Liberation of Paris after more than four years of Nazi occupation

November: Franklin D. Roosevelt elected to a fourth term as President of the United States

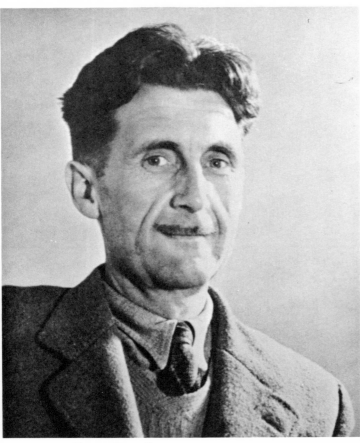

George Orwell

Great Britain

FICTION

Elizabeth Bowen: *The Demon Lover* (U.S. title: *Ivy Gripped the Steps and Other Stories*)

Walter de la Mare: *The Scarecrow and Other Stories*

Henry Green: *Loving*

Christopher Isherwood: *Prater Violet*

C. S. Lewis: *That Hideous Strength: A Modern Fairy-Tale for Grown-Ups*

Nancy Mitford: *The Pursuit of Love*

George Orwell: *Animal Farm: A Fairy Story*

V. S. Pritchett: *It May Never Happen*

Evelyn Waugh: *Brideshead Revisited: The Sacred and Profane Memories of Captain Charles Ryder*

Charles Williams: *All Hallows' Eve*

VERSE AND DRAMA

W. H. Auden: *Collected Poetry* (U.S.)

John Betjeman: *New Bats in Old Belfries*

Joyce Cary: *Marching Soldier*

Walter de la Mare: *The Burning-Glass*

Robert Graves: *Poems 1938–1945*

Sidney Keyes: *Collected Poems*

Philip Larkin: *The North Ship*

Alun Lewis: *Ha! Ha! Among the Trumpets* (Foreword by Robert Graves)

Ruth Pitter: *The Bridge: Poems 1939–1944*

William Plomer: *The Dorking Thigh and Other Satires*

Edith Sitwell: *The Song of the Cold*

Henry Treece: *The Black Seasons*

Sean O'Casey

Rex Warner: *Poems and Contradictions*
Vernon Watkins: *The Lamp and the Veil*

Arthur Koestler: *Twilight Bar: An Escapade in Four Acts*

NON-FICTION

Cyril Connolly: *The Condemned Playground: Essays, 1927–44*
Lawrence Durrell: *Prospero's Cell*
E. M. Forster: *The Development of English Prose between 1918 and 1939* (W. P. Ker Memorial Lecture)
Aldous Huxley: *The Perennial Philosophy*
Christopher Isherwood, ed.: *Vedanta for the Western World*
Arthur Koestler: *The Yogi and the Commissar*
Sean O'Casey: *Drums Under the Windows*
Peter Quennell: *Four Portraits* (U.S. title: *The Profane Virtues*)
Siegfried Sassoon: *Siegfried's Journey, 1916–1920*
H. G. Wells: *Mind at the End of Its Tether*

❧ ❧ *"All writers are vain, selfish and lazy, and at the very bottom of their motives lies a mystery. Writing a book is a horrible, exhausting struggle, like a long bout of some painful illness. One would never undertake such a thing if one were not driven on by some demon whom one can neither resist nor understand."*

GEORGE ORWELL

Theodore Dreiser

Ben Hecht: *Collected Stories*
Sinclair Lewis: *Cass Timberlane*
William Maxwell: *The Folded Leaf*
Wright Morris: *The Man Who Was There*
John O'Hara: *Pipe Night*
John Steinbeck: *Cannery Row*
Glenway Wescott: *Apartment in Athens*

Marianne Moore and Elizabeth Mayer: translation of Adalbert Stifter's *Bergkristall* (*Rock Crystal*)

United States

FICTION

James T. Farrell: *Bernard Clare*
Caroline Gordon: *The Forest of the South*

VERSE AND DRAMA

H.D.: *Tribute to the Angels*
Emily Dickinson: *Bolts of Melody: New Poems* (edited by Mable Loomis Todd and Millicent Todd Bingham)
Richard Eberhart and Selden Rodman, eds.: *War and the Poet*

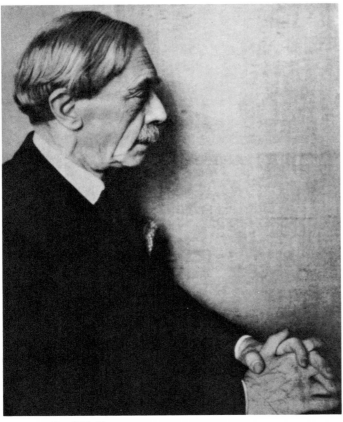

Paul Valéry

❦ ❦ *"Modernism, like Spinoza's substance, is the den from which no tracks return . . ."*

RANDALL JARRELL

Related Events

DEATHS

Paul Valéry: French poet and man-of-letters; 74; of cancer of the throat; in Paris, on July 21

Theodore Dreiser: American novelist; 74; of a heart attack; in Hollywood, California, on December 28; leaving his estate to his wife, with the request that after her own death, whatever remained should go to Negro orphans

Other Deaths:

Ellen Glasgow: American novelist

Anton Webern, Austrian composer

Charles Williams, British novelist and man-of-letters

Robert Frost: *A Masque of Reason*

Randall Jarrell: *Little Friend, Little Friend*

Alfred Kreymborg: *Selected Poems*

John Crowe Ransom: *Selected Poems*

Karl Shapiro: *Essay on Rime*

Wallace Stevens: *Esthétique du Mal*

NON-FICTION

Kenneth Burke: *A Grammar of Motives*

T. S. Eliot: *What Is a Classic?*

James T. Farrell: *The League of Frightened Philistines and Other Papers*

F. Scott Fitzgerald: *The Crack-Up* (edited by Edmund Wilson)

Henry Miller: *The Air-Conditioned Nightmare*

George Santayana: *The Middle Span*

Gertrude Stein: *Wars I Have Seen*

Richard Wright: *Black Boy*

Mrs. Marguerite Young: *Angel in the Forest: A Fairy Tale of Two Utopias*

IN OTHER LANGUAGES

Hermann Broch: *Der Tod des Vergil* (*The Death of Virgil*)

Antoine de Saint-Exupéry: *Le Petit Prince*

Jean-Paul Sartre: *Les Chemins de la Liberté* (*L'Âge de Raison; Le Sursis*); *Huis-Clos*

First issue of *Les Temps Modernes*, edited by Jean-Paul Sartre

IN OTHER ARTS

Films: Sergei Eisenstein: *Ivan the Terrible, Part I* ‖ Vittorio De Sica: *Sciuscià* (*Shoeshine*) ‖ Roberto Rossellini: *Roma, Città Aperta* (*Open City*)

Richard Wright

Ezra Pound

Stage: Tennessee Williams: *The Glass Menagerie* || Tennessee Williams and Donald Windham: *You Touched Me!* (based on the story of the same title by D. H. Lawrence)

Music: Benjamin Britten: *Peter Grimes*

Patronage: Arnold Schoenberg, 70 and obliged to retire from his position as professor of music at the University of California, applies for a Guggenheim Fellowship to finish his opera *Moses und Aron*, his oratorio *Die Jakobsleiter*, and three theoretical works in progress. His application is rejected

IN THE MARGIN

Laurels: Nobel Prize for Literature to Gabriela Mistral, of Chile || Pulitzer Prizes for Fiction to John Hersey, for *A Bell for Adano*; for Poetry to Karl Shapiro, for *V-Letter and Other Poems* || James Tait Black Prize to Forrest Reid, for *Young Tom*

London: W. H. Auden, in the uniform of an American Army major, arrives as an observer for the United States Strategic Bombing Survey, "to study the effects of bombing on the civilian population in Germany" (John Lehmann)

Rapallo, Italy: On May 8, Ezra Pound is taken into custody by the United States Army, and incarcerated in a cage at the Disciplinary Training Center near Pisa: "A special guard stood outside his cage which, at night, was brightly lighted. Everyone looked at him. The trainees marching by or working in the area considered Pound with awe, taking the reinforced cage as evidence that he was a particularly tough customer . . . As shelter, a piece of tar paper was thrown over the top . . . He was permitted books and writing materials, but refused a typewriter because, he said, the 'damned rust would ruin it . . ." (Robert L. Allen). Six months later, Pound was flown to Washington, D.C., to stand trial for treason

Hollywood: Katherine Anne Porter, as of January, is under contract to Paramount Studios: ". . . my part is to tell him [producer Sidney Franklin] stories I remember from books I have read, to give him the germ of the idea and the plot and theme; he is desperate for material, and I am supposed to know where it is. I do know, too, that is the lovely part about that. And before I mention the author I tell him a story of Henry James' and he is ringing up and sending for the book before I have finished."

Washington, D.C.: Louise Bogan appointed to the Chair in Poetry at the Library of Congress

Publishing: John Farrar and Roger Straus, Jr., launch their publishing house   ‖   First issue of *Orion: A Miscellany,* edited by C. Day Lewis, Rosamond Lehmann, etc., and containing an unprecedented interview with Ivy Compton-Burnett: "I cannot tell you why I write as I do, as I do not know. I have even tried not to do it, but find myself falling back into my own way . . . I think people's style, like the way they speak and move, comes from themselves and cannot be explained."

In the Great World:

April: The advancing Allied Armies reach Buchenwald and Belsen, revealing the Nazi concentration camps to the world for the first time

April 12: Franklin D. Roosevelt dies at Warm Springs, Georgia, and Harry S. Truman becomes the 33rd President of the United States

Tennessee Williams

April 28: Benito Mussolini and his mistress Clara Petacci executed by Italian partisans

April 30: suicide of Adolf Hitler in the ruins of Berlin

May 8: V-E day, following the surrender of the German Army at Rheims

August 6: A U. S. Army Air Force B-29 Superfortress releases a uranium bomb of the type called "Little Boy," which detonates at an altitude of 2,000 feet over the Japanese city of Hiroshima at 9:15 a.m. local time

August 15: V-J day, marking the surrender of Japan and the end of World War II

Great Britain

FICTION

Joyce Cary: *The Moonlight*
Walter de la Mare: *The Dutch Cheese and Other Stories*
Robert Graves: *King Jesus*
Henry Green: *Back*
L. P. Hartley: *The Sixth Heaven*
Arthur Koestler: *Thieves in the Night*
Philip Larkin: *Jill*
W. Somerset Maugham: *Then and Now*
William Sansom: *Three*

Christopher Fry

VERSE AND DRAMA

Ronald Bottrall: *Selected Poems* (Preface by Edith Sitwell)
Roy Campbell: *Talking Bronco*
Walter de la Mare: *The Traveller*
Lawrence Durrell: *Cities, Plains and People*
Rayner Heppenstall: *Poems, 1933–1945*
Edwin Muir: *The Voyage and Other Poems*
Kathleen Raine: *Living in Time*
Herbert Read: *Collected Poems*
Henry Reed: *A Map of Verona*
Dylan Thomas: *Deaths and Entrances; Selected Writings* (U.S.)
Christopher Fry: *A Phoenix Too Frequent* (produced 1946)
C. Day Lewis: translation of Paul Valéry's *Le Cimetière Marin* (*The Graveyard by the Sea*)
Anne Ridler: *The Shadow Factory* (produced 1945)
G. B. Shaw: *Cymbeline Refinished* (produced 1937)

NON-FICTION

W. H. Auden: Preface to Henry James's *The American Scene* (U.S.)
Max Beerbohm: *Mainly on the Air*
Joyce Cary: *Britain and West Africa*
Norman Douglas: *Late Harvest*
Lady Gregory: *Journals* (edited by Lennox Robinson)
Aldous Huxley: *Science, Liberty and Peace*
George Orwell: *Critical Essays* (U.S. title: *Dickens, Dali, and Others*)
V. S. Pritchett: *The Living Novel*
Forrest Reid: *The Milk of Paradise: Some Thoughts on Poetry*
Edith Sitwell: *Fanfare for Elizabeth*
Osbert Sitwell: *The Scarlet Tree*
Stephen Spender: *European Witness*
Ruthven Todd: *Tracks in the Snow*
Rex Warner: *The Cult of Power*

❧ ❧ *"My advice to young people who wish to earn their living by writing is: DO."*

DYLAN THOMAS

United States

FICTION

Isabel Bolton (Mary Britton Miller): *Do I Wake or Sleep?*

Kay Boyle: *A Frenchman Must Die; Thirty Stories*

Theodore Dreiser: *The Bulwark*

James T. Farrell: *When Boyhood Dreams Come True*

William Faulkner: *The Portable Faulkner* (edited by Malcolm Cowley)

Carson McCullers: *The Member of the Wedding*

Wright Morris: *The Inhabitants*

Anaïs Nin: *Ladders of Fire*

Conrad Richter: *The Fields*

William Saroyan: *The Adventures of Wesley Jackson*

Gertrude Stein: *Selected Writings* (edited by Carl Van Vechten); *First Reader and Three Plays* (Dublin); *Brewsie and Willie*

Gore Vidal: *Williwaw*

Robert Penn Warren: *All the King's Men; Blackberry Winter*

Eudora Welty: *Delta Wedding*

Edmund Wilson: *Memoirs of Hecate County*

VERSE AND DRAMA

Elizabeth Bishop: *North and South*

H.D.: *The Flowering of the Rod*

Robert Lowell: *Lord Weary's Castle*

Genevieve Taggard: *Slow Music*

William Carlos Williams: *Paterson, Book I*

e. e. cummings: *Santa Claus: A Morality*

Robinson Jeffers: *Medea* (an adaptation from Euripides; produced 1947)

Tennessee Williams: *27 Wagons Full of Cotton and Other One-Act Plays*

NON-FICTION

Horace Gregory and Marya Zaturenska: *A History of American Poetry, 1900–1940*

Peggy Guggenheim: *Out of This Century*

Robert Penn Warren

John Hersey: *Hiroshima*

Henry Miller: *Maurizius Forever*

Yvor Winters: *Edwin Arlington Robinson*

❧❧ *"Say it, no ideas but in things . . ."*
WILLIAM CARLOS WILLIAMS

Related Events

DEATHS

Gertrude Stein: American autobiographer, novelist, and explorer of new possibilities in English grammar; age 72; of cancer; at the

Jean-Paul Sartre

René Char: *Feuillets d'Hypnos*
Colette: *L'Étoile Vesper*
Jean Genet: *Le Miracle de la Rose*
André Gide: *Thésée*
Carlo Levi: *Cristo si é fermato a Eboli (Christ Stopped at Eboli)*
Cesare Pavese: *Feria d'Agosto (August Holiday)*
Jacques Prévert: *Paroles*
Jean-Paul Sartre: *Morts sans Sépulture; La Putain Respectueuse*

Music: Aaron Copland: *Third Symphony* || Igor Stravinsky: *Symphony in Three Movements*

Films: Jean Cocteau: *Belle et la Bête* || Sergei Eisenstein: *Ivan the Terrible, Part II* (censored by the Central Committee of the Communist Party)

Stage: Robinson Jeffers: *Medea* || Eugene O'Neill: *The Iceman Cometh*

American Hospital in Neuilly, France, on July 27. Buried in the 94th Division of the Père Lachaise Cemetery in Paris, with a tombstone designed by her friend, Sir Francis Rose. "I am not sure that anything but a lifework has meaning."

Other Deaths:

Damon Runyon, American short-story writer (*Guys and Dolls*, 1931)
May Sinclair, British novelist (*The Divine Fire*, 1904)
Logan Pearsall Smith, American belletrist (*Trivia*, 1902)
Booth Tarkington, American novelist (*Penrod*, 1914)
H. G. Wells, British novelist (*Kipps*, 1905)

Robert Lowell

Laurels: The Nobel Prize for Literature to
Hermann Hesse, of Switzerland || The
Pulitzer Prize for History to Arthur M.
Schlesinger, Jr., for *The Age of Jackson*

New Publishers: In London, Rupert Hart-Davis
and John Lehmann; in New York, William
Sloane and Bantam Books

In January, Jean-Paul Sartre arrives in New York
to lecture at Princeton and Yale

On February 13, after deliberating for three
minutes, a Washington District Court Jury
reaches a verdict on Ezra Pound: "Unsound
mind." Pound is sent to St. Elizabeth's
Hospital until the treason charges are dropped
in April 1958

In March, Ernest Hemingway, 47, is married for
the fourth time to journalist Mary Welsh in
Havana

William Carlos Williams, trying to find time to
continue work on *Paterson*, reports business as
usual: "At 4:30 this morning a woman—age
26, Para I, whose last period occurred January
26, 1946, and whose Wassermann was negative
5–16–46, who weighs 137 lbs, whose urine is
normal, whose blood pressure is 110 over 80
and the heart tones of whose belly-borne fetus
are at 128 in the ROA position—called me on
the phone to say she was having pains every
ten minutes"

On advice from his psychotherapist, Angus
Wilson, 31, begins writing: ". . . I sat down,
as they say in faith-healing testimonials, and
'just wrote a story one Sunday' "

Norman Mailer, 23, is discharged after eighteen
months with the U. S. Army in the
Philippines, having sustained himself by
listening to GI's "beating their gums about
how when they got out they were going to
write a fugging book which would expose the
fugging army, and I would think in my
fatigue-slowed brain that if they only knew
what I was going to do, they would elect me
sergeant on the spot"

Randall Jarrell serves as literary editor of *The
Nation* for the year, giving veteran Margaret
Marshall a sabbatical

Gertrude Stein

In November, Cyril Connolly arrives in New
York: "Walking back from the subway station
at two in the morning, I find a second-hand
bookstore open all night in Eighth Street, I go
in and buy more Cummings. To purchase the
early works of Cummings in the small hours
. . . and march home with them in the frosty
night, while the tugs hoot and central heating
plants under the long black street puff away
through its many manholes like geysers on the
moon, that is to enjoy that anonymous urban
civilization that Auden has chosen, and of
which Baudelaire dreamed and despaired!"

In the Great World: In Nuremberg, Germany,
the leaders of the Third Reich are tried as war
criminals || In San Francisco, the first
United Nations Assembly meets

Ivy Compton-Burnett

Great Britain

FICTION

Ivy Compton-Burnett: *Manservant and Maidservant* (U.S. title: *Bullivant and the Lambs*)

Lawrence Durrell: *Cefalù*

E. M. Forster: *Collected Tales*

Graham Greene: *Nineteen Stories*

L. P. Hartley: *Eustace and Hilda*

Philip Larkin: *A Girl in Winter*

Malcolm Lowry: *Under the Volcano*

W. Somerset Maugham: *Creatures of Circumstance*

Frank O'Connor: *The Common Chord*

Forrest Reid: *Denis Bracknel* (revised version of

The Bracknels, 1911)

C. P. Snow: *The Light and the Dark*

Elizabeth Taylor: *A View of the Harbour*

Philip Toynbee: *Tea with Mrs. Goodman* (U.S. title: *Prothalamium*)

Evelyn Waugh: *Scott-King's Modern Europe*

VERSE AND DRAMA

W. H. Auden: *The Age of Anxiety* (dedicated to John Betjeman)

John Betjeman: *Slick but Not Streamlined* (edited by W. H. Auden; U.S.)

Joyce Cary: *The Drunken Sailor*

Edward Lear: *The Complete Nonsense* (edited by H. Jackson)

John Lehmann, ed.: *A Greek Poet in England: Demetrios Capetanakis*

Siegfried Sassoon: *Collected Poems*

Edith Sitwell: *The Shadow of Cain*

Stephen Spender: *Returning to Vienna; Poems of Dedication*

Henry Treece: *The Haunted Garden*

Louis MacNeice: *The Dark Tower and Other Radio Scripts*

NON-FICTION

Rayner Heppenstall: *The Double Image*

C. Day Lewis: *The Poetic Image; Enjoying Poetry: A Reader's Guide*

Robert Liddell: *A Treatise on the Novel*

Percy Lubbock: *Portrait of Edith Wharton*

George Orwell: *The English People*

Osbert Sitwell: *Great Morning!*

Rebecca West: *The Meaning of Treason*

Virginia Woolf: *The Moment and Other Essays*

❧❧ *". . . it seems to me that this is a prose age because it requires us to be terribly explicit. And the serious possibilities of prose narrative have only just become known."*

RAYNER HEPPENSTALL

Philip Toynbee

United States

FICTION

Saul Bellow: *The Victim*
Vance Bourjaily: *The End of My Life*
John Horne Burns: *The Gallery*
Theodore Dreiser: *The Stoic*
Sinclair Lewis: *Kingsblood Royal*
Andrew Lytle: *A Name for Evil*
Willard Motley: *Knock on Any Door*
Vladimir Nabokov: *Bend Sinister; Nine Stories*
Anaïs Nin: *Children of the Albatross* (Preface by Lawrence Durrell)
Jean Stafford: *The Mountain Lion*
John Steinbeck: *The Wayward Bus*
Lionel Trilling: *The Middle of the Journey*
Gore Vidal: *In a Yellow Wood*
Calder Willingham: *End as a Man*

VERSE AND DRAMA

Conrad Aiken: *The Kid*
R. P. Blackmur: *The Good European and Other Poems*
Richard Eberhart: *Burr Oaks*
Robert Frost: *Steeple Bush; A Masque of Mercy*
Jean Garrigue: *The Ego and the Centaur*
Langston Hughes: *Fields of Wonder*
Rolfe Humphries: *Forbid Thy Ravens: Didactic and Lyrical Poems*
Karl Shapiro: *Trial of a Poet and Other Poems*
Wallace Stevens: *Transport to Summer*
Allen Tate, ed.: *A Southern Vanguard* (in memory of John Peale Bishop)
Richard Wilbur: *The Beautiful Changes and Other Poems*

Ezra Pound: translation of Confucius's, *The Unwobbling Pivot and the Great Digest*

NON-FICTION

Van Wyck Brooks: *The Times of Melville and Whitman*
T. S. Eliot: *Milton* (G.B.)
Henry James: *Notebooks* (edited by F. O. Matthiessen and Kenneth B. Murdock)

Jean Stafford, with Robert Lowell and Robert Giroux

Sarah Orne Jewett: *Letters* (edited by Carl J. Weber)

A. J. Liebling: *The Wayward Pressman;* ed.: *The Republic of Silence*

Henry Miller: *Remember to Remember*

E. A. Robinson: *Untriangulated Stars* (letters, edited by Denham Sutcliffe)

Gertrude Stein: *Four in America* (Preface by Thornton Wilder)

Wallace Stevens: *Three Academic Pieces* (essay and poems)

Edmund Wilson: *Europe Without Baedeker*

Yvor Winters: *In Defense of Reason*

André Gide

Lionel Trilling

❧❧ *"You must become an ignorant man again*
And see the sun again with an ignorant eye."

WALLACE STEVENS

Related Events

DEATHS

Willa Cather: American novelist and short-story writer; 74; in New York City, on April 24. "The artist spends a lifetime in loving the things that haunt him, in having his mind 'teased' by them, in trying to get these conceptions down on paper exactly as they are to him . . . And at the end of a lifetime he emerges with much that is more or less happy experimenting, and comparatively little that is the very flower of himself and his genius"

Other Deaths:

Pierre Bonnard

Mrs. Belloc Lowndes (*The Lodger*)

Maxwell Perkins

Forrest Reid

Alfred North Whitehead

1947

IN OTHER LANGUAGES

Antonin Artaud: *Van Gogh ou le Suicide de la Société*

Albert Camus: *La Peste*

André Gide: *Et Nunc Manet in Te* (private edition)

Thomas Mann: *Doktor Faustus: Das Leben des Deutschen Tonsetzers Adrian Leverkühn . . .* (*Doctor Faustus*)

Alberto Moravia: *La Romana* (*The Woman of Rome*)

Cesare Pavese: *Il Compagno* (*The Comrade*); *Dialoghi con Leucò* (*Dialogues with Leucò*)

Jean-Paul Sartre: *Baudelaire*

Simone Weil: *La Pesanteur et la Grâce*

IN OTHER ARTS

May: Virgil Thomson's opera *The Mother Of Us All*, with a libretto by Gertrude Stein, has its première in New York

August: Bertolt Brecht's epic drama *Galileo* is produced in Hollywood by Charles Laughton

December: Tennessee Williams' play *A Streetcar Named Desire* opens in New York

Jackson Pollock makes his first "drip" or "Action" paintings: "When I am *in* my painting, I am not aware of what I am doing . . . the painting has a life of its own. I try to let it come through"

IN THE MARGIN

Laurels: The Nobel Prize for Literature to André Gide ‖ Pulitzer Prizes for Fiction to Robert Penn Warren (*All the King's Men*) and for Poetry to Robert Lowell (*Lord Weary's Castle*) ‖ The first W. Somerset Maugham Trust Fund Award to A. L. Barker for *Innocents*

In Hollywood to negotiate a film contract for *Brideshead Revisited*, Evelyn Waugh discovers Forest Lawn. After seven weeks of trying to persuade moguls and censors to come to terms, he rejects an offer of $150,000 and returns to England convinced that cemeteries are "the only real thing in Hollywood"

Bertolt Brecht

In Florence for the first time, Dylan Thomas finds himself "very witty in Italian, though a little violent . . . I have to stand on my head, fall in the pool, crack nuts with my teeth, and Tarzan in the cypresses . . ."

In the Hebrides, his health failing, George Orwell is at work on *1984* in a farmhouse on the northernmost tip of Jura, 25 miles from the island's only port and the nearest store: ". . . quite an easy journey really, except that you have to walk the last eight miles"

In England, Christopher Isherwood arrives on his first visit in eight years, very much a U.S. citizen: "Throughout the years I had spent in Hollywood, I had never tired of protesting against the American film presentation of English life. . . . But now . . . even the bus which took us from the airport into London seemed grotesquely 'in character' . . . And then we would pass through an English village complete with a village church in a country churchyard; so absurdly authentic that it might have been lifted bodily off a movie-lot at MGM . . ."

Ladies in the Wings: After brief stints with *Argentor* (a jewelry house organ) and the Soldiers, Sailors and Airmen's Families Association (as press officer), Muriel Spark takes over the editorship of the Poetry Society's *Review* || Flannery O'Connor, 22, is a graduate student at the University of Iowa, studying creative writing with Paul Engle || After two years on the Continent, Iris Murdoch, 28, returns to her alma mater, Oxford, as a tutor in philosophy at St. Anne's College

Truman Capote

Great Britain

FICTION

H. E. Bates: *The Jacaranda Tree*
Henry Green: *Concluding*
Graham Greene: *The Heart of the Matter*
Aldous Huxley: *Ape and Essence*
Robin Maugham: *The Servant*
W. Somerset Maugham: *Catalina*
William Sansom: *Something Terrible, Something Lovely*
Evelyn Waugh: *The Loved One: An Anglo-American Tragedy* (dedicated to Nancy Mitford)
Denton Welch: *Brave and Cruel*

VERSE AND DRAMA

Richard Aldington: *Complete Poems*
John Betjeman: *Selected Poems*
Lawrence Durrell: *On Seeming to Presume*
Robert Graves: *Collected Poems 1914–1947*
C. Day Lewis: *Poems 1943–47*
Louis MacNeice: *Holes in the Sky: Poems 1944–1947*
Vernon Watkins: *The Lady with the Unicorn*

Aldous Huxley

Laurie Lee: *Voyage of Magellan* (radio play)

NON-FICTION

Harold Acton: *Memoirs of an Aesthete*

W. H. Auden, ed.: *The Portable Greek Reader* (U.S.)

Elizabeth Bowen, Graham Greene, and V. S. Pritchett: *Why Do I Write?*

Jocelyn Brooke: *The Military Orchid*

David Cecil: *Two Quiet Lives: Dorothy Osborne, Thomas Gray*

Winston S. Churchill: *The Gathering Storm*

Alex Comfort: *The Novel and Our Time*

Robert Graves: *The White Goddess: A Historical Grammar of Poetic Myth*

Rayner Heppenstall, ed.: *Imaginary Conversations*

D. H. Lawrence: *Letters to Bertrand Russell* (edited by Harry T. Moore)

Alun Lewis: *In the Green Tree* (letters and stories)

Wyndham Lewis: *America and Cosmic Man*

Richard March and Prince Tambimuttu, eds.: *T. S. Eliot: A Symposium*

W. Somerset Maugham: *Great Novelists and Their Novels* (U.S.)

William Sansom: *South: Aspects and Images from Corsica, Italy and Southern France*

Siegfried Sassoon: *Meredith*

Edith Sitwell: *A Notebook on William Shakespeare*

Osbert Sitwell: *Laughter in the Next Room*

Francis Thompson: *Literary Criticisms Newly Discovered and Collected* (edited by T. L. Connolly)

❧❧ *"A man may rebel against the current morality of his age and still be a true poet, because a higher morality than the current is entailed on all poets whenever and wherever they live: the morality of love. Though the quality of love in a painter's work, or a musician's, will endear him to his public, he can be a true painter or*

Robert Graves

musician even if his incapacity for love has turned him into a devil. But without love he cannot be a poet in the final sense."

ROBERT GRAVES

United States

FICTION

Truman Capote: *Other Voices, Other Rooms*

Willa Cather: *The Old Beauty and Others*

William Faulkner: *Intruder in the Dust*

Ross Lockridge: *Raintree County*
Norman Mailer: *The Naked and the Dead*
William Maxwell: *Time Will Darken It*
Henry Miller: *The Smile at the Foot of the Ladder*
Merle Miller: *That Winter*
Wright Morris: *The Home Place*
Carl Sandburg: *Remembrance Rock*
Delmore Schwartz: *The World Is a Wedding*
Irwin Shaw: *The Young Lions*
Gore Vidal: *The City and the Pillar*
Robert Penn Warren: *The Circus in the Attic and Other Stories*
Thornton Wilder: *The Ides of March*
Tennessee Williams: *One Arm and Other Stories*

VERSE AND DRAMA

John Berryman: *The Dispossessed*
John Peale Bishop: *Collected Poems* (Preface and memoir by Allen Tate)
Robert P. Tristram Coffin: *Collected Poems*

Norman Mailer

Kenneth Fearing: *Stranger at Coney Island and Other Poems*
Ruth Herschberger: *A Way of Happening*
Barbara Howes: *The Undersea Farmer*
Randall Jarrell: *Losses*
Robinson Jeffers: *The Double Ax and Other Poems*
Archibald MacLeish: *Actfive and Other Poems*
Ezra Pound: *Cantos; The Pisan Cantos*
Muriel Rukeyser: *The Green Wave*
Winfield Townley Scott: *Mr. Whittier and Other Poems*
Wallace Stevens: *A Primitive Like an Orb*
Allen Tate: *Poems: 1922–1947*
Peter Viereck: *Terror and Decorum: Poems 1940–1948*
William Carlos Williams: *Paterson, Book II; The Clouds*

Tennessee Williams: *American Blues: Five Short Plays*
William Carlos Williams: *A Dream of Love*

NON-FICTION

John Peale Bishop: *Collected Essays* (edited by Edmund Wilson)
Louis Bromfield: *Malabar Farm*
T. S. Eliot: *Notes Toward a Definition of Culture*
Henry James and Robert Louis Stevenson: *A Record of Friendship and Criticism* (edited by Janet Adam Smith)
Alfred C. Kinsey, Wardell B. Pomeroy, and Clyde G. Martin: *Sexual Behavior in the Human Male*
F. O. Matthiessen: *From the Heart of Europe*
John Steinbeck: *A Russian Journal* (photographs by Robert Capa)
Allen Tate: *On the Limits of Poetry*
James Thurber: *The Beast in Me and Other Animals: A New Collection of Pieces and Drawings about Human Beings and Less Alarming Creatures*

❦❦ *"We were fishers, weren't we? And
tried to fish
The egoed belly's dry
cartograph . . ."*

ALLEN TATE

Related Events

DEATHS

Antonin Artaud: French actor and theorist of
"the theater of cruelty"

Georges Bernanos: French novelist and political
polemicist

Sergei Eisenstein: Russian film maker

Zelda (Mrs. F. Scott) Fitzgerald, American
legend and life model for the Great Gatsby's
Daisy

Denton Welch, British writer of autobiographical
short stories

IN OTHER LANGUAGES

Gottfried Benn: *Statische Gedichte* (*Static
Poems*)

Albert Camus: *L'État de Siège*

Jean Genet: *Pompes Funèbres*

Elsa Morante: *Menzogna e Sortilegio* (*The
House of Liars*)

Cesare Pavese: *Prima Che Il Gallo Canti*

Georges Simenon: *Pedigree*

IN OTHER ARTS

Stage: Tennessee Williams: *Summer and Smoke*

Music: Igor Stravinsky: *Mass*

Painting: Painters who come to be identified as
the "New York School" of abstract
expressionists begin to gather at a cold-water
loft on Manhattan's East 8th Street called
"The Club"

IN THE MARGIN

Laurels: The Nobel Prize for Literature to
T. S. Eliot ‖ Pulitzer Prizes for Poetry to
W. H. Auden, for *The Age of Anxiety*; for
Drama, to Tennessee Williams, for *A Streetcar
Named Desire* ‖ The James Tait Black
Prize to L. P. Hartley, for *Eustace and Hilda*

William Empson, again teaching at the University
of Peking, flies to Gambier, Ohio, to join the
staff of the Kenyon Summer School and
lecture on "The Key Word in the Long Poem"

Lawrence Durrell, recently arrived in Buenos
Aires for the British Council, finds that his
new ambient leaves something to be desired:
"The interesting thing is the queer lightness of
the spiritual atmosphere: one feels buoyant,
irresponsible, like a hydrogen balloon. One
realizes too that the personal sort of European
man is out of place here: one cannot suffer
from angst here, only cafard."

Victor Weybright begins the New American
Library

Possibilities (*An Occasional Review*) is edited in
New York by Robert Motherwell, Harold
Rosenberg, John Cage, and Pierre Chareau

T. S. Eliot accepts his Nobel Prize unaware that it,
along with the O.M. and the future Broadway
success of *The Cocktail Party*, is a reward from
the White Goddess, bestowed on him for
having been the editor who had decided that
Robert Graves's book about Her had to be
published "at all costs." (The first editor to
whom Graves sent the manuscript rejected it,
regretfully; he died of a heart attack a month
later. The second decided the book would be
of interest to no one; he presently hanged
himself from a tree, attired in a woman's bra
and panties. Fortunately for Publishers Row,
Eliot was the third.)

In the Great World: Harry S. Truman elected to
a term of his own as 33rd President of the
United States ‖ Mahatma Gandhi
assassinated in New Delhi, India, January 30

Allen Tate and T. S. Eliot

Great Britain

FICTION

Elizabeth Bowen: *The Heat of the Day*
Joyce Cary: *A Fearful Joy*
Ivy Compton-Burnett: *Two Worlds and Their Ways*
Nigel Dennis: *Boys and Girls Come Out to Play* (U.S. title: *Sea Change*)
Robert Graves: *Seven Days in New Crete* (U.S. title: *Watch the North Wind Rise*); *The Islands of Unwisdom*
L. P. Hartley: *The Boat*
Nancy Mitford: *Love in a Cold Climate*
Olivia (Dorothy Bussy): *Olivia*
George Orwell: *Nineteen Eighty-Four*
William Sansom: *The Body*
C. P. Snow: *Time of Hope*
Angus Wilson: *The Wrong Set*

VERSE AND DRAMA

Edmund Blunden: *After the Bombing*
Roy Campbell: *Collected Poems* (Vol. I)
William Empson: *Collected Poems* (U.S.)
Roy Fuller: *Epitaphs and Occasions*
Louis MacNeice: *Collected Poems: 1925–1948*
Edwin Muir: *The Labyrinth*
Kathleen Raine: *The Pythoness and Other Poems*
Edith Sitwell: *The Canticle of the Rose: Selected Poems: 1920–1927*
Stephen Spender: *The Edge of Being*
W. B. Yeats: *Collected Poems* (Definitive Edition)

Dorothy Sayers: translation of Dante's *Inferno* (*Hell*)

Christopher Fry: *The Lady's Not for Burning* (produced 1948)

C. P. Snow

William Empson

NON-FICTION

C. M. Bowra: *The Creative Experiment; The Romantic Imagination*

Winston S. Churchill: *Their Finest Hour*

Kenneth Clark: *Landscape into Art*

Robert Graves: *The Common Asphodel: Collected Essays on Poetry, 1922–1949*

Christopher Isherwood: *The Condor and the Cows*

John Maynard Keynes: *Two Memoirs* (Introduction by David Garnett)

Arthur Koestler: *Promise and Fulfillment: Palestine, 1917–1949; Insight and Outlook: An Inquiry into the Common Foundations of Science, Art, and Social Ethics*

W. Somerset Maugham: *A Writer's Notebook*

Harold Nicolson: *Benjamin Constant*

Sean O'Casey: *Inishfallen Fare Thee Well*

G. B. Shaw: *Sixteen Self Sketches*

Henry Treece: *Dylan Thomas: "Dog Among the Fairies"*

❧ ❧ *"The best autobiographies are confessions; but if a man is a deep writer, all his works are confessions."*

G. B. SHAW

United States

FICTION

Nelson Algren: *The Man with the Golden Arm*

Isabel Bolton: *The Christmas Tree*

Paul Bowles: *The Sheltering Sky*

John Horne Burns: *Lucifer with a Book*

Paul Bowles

Truman Capote: *A Tree of Night and Other Stories*
John Dos Passos: *The Grand Design*
William Faulkner: *Knight's Gambit*
Shirley Jackson: *The Lottery; or, the Adventures of James Harris*
Sinclair Lewis: *The God-Seeker*
H. P. Lovecraft: *Something About Cats and Other Pieces*
Mary McCarthy: *The Oasis*
Henry Miller: *Sexus* (Paris)
Gore Vidal: *The Season of Comfort*
Eudora Welty: *The Golden Apples*

VERSE AND DRAMA

Conrad Aiken: *The Divine Pilgrim*
Arna Bontemps and Langston Hughes, eds.: *The Poetry of the Negro: 1746–1949*
Rolfe Humphries: *The Wind of Time*
Kenneth Rexroth: *The Art of Worldly Wisdom*; ed.: *New British Poets*

Theodore Roethke: *The Lost Son and Other Poems*
William Carlos Williams: *Paterson, Book III; The Pink Church; Selected Poems* (Introduction by Randall Jarrell)

Henry James: *Complete Plays* (edited by Leon Edel)
Gertrude Stein: *Last Operas and Plays* (edited by Carl Van Vechten)

NON-FICTION

Willa Cather: *On Writing*
H.D.: *By Avon River* (dedicated to Bryher)
H. L. Mencken: *A Mencken Chrestomathy*
Allen Tate: *The Hovering Fly and Other Essays*
Mark Twain: *Love Letters* (edited by Dixon Wecter)

❧ ❧ *"My time for reading is short, limited. I don't want to keep informed, or abreast of the times. I have time now only to reread my favorites and to taste the flavor of those whom I deliberately and sedulously ignored hitherto . . . I am becoming more prejudiced, instead of less. I grow more ignorant every day— purposely so!"*

HENRY MILLER

Related Events

DEATHS

Count Maurice Maeterlinck: Belgian dramatist (*L'Oiseau Bleu*, 1909) and Nobel Laureate, 1911
Klaus Mann: German man-of-letters (*The Turning Point*, 1942)
Margaret Mitchell: American popular novelist (*Gone With the Wind*, 1936)

Richard Strauss: Austrian composer and operatic collaborator with Hugo von Hofmannsthal (*Der Rosenkavalier*)

Simone de Beauvoir: *Le Deuxième Sexe*
Colette: *Le Fanal Bleu*
André Gide: *Feuillets d'Automne; Anthologie de la Poésie Française*
Jean Genet: *Journal du Voleur; Haute Surveillance*
Thomas Mann: *Die Entstehung des "Doktor Faustus"* (*The Story of a Novel*)
Cesare Pavese: *La Belle Estate* (*The Beautiful Summer*)
Nathalie Sarraute: *Portrait d'un Inconnu*
Jean-Paul Sartre: *La Mort dans l'Âme*
Simone Weil: *L'Enracinement*

Stage: Arthur Miller: *Death of a Salesman* || Sean O'Casey: *Cock-a-Doodle-Dandy* || T. S. Eliot: *The Cocktail Party*

Films: Carol Reed–Graham Greene: *The Third Man* || Vittorio De Sica: *Ladri di Bicicletti* (*Bicycle Thief*) || Robert Rossen–Robert Penn Warren: *All the King's Men*

Laurels: The Nobel Prize for Literature to William Faulkner, who accepted it in Stockholm one year later || Pulitzer Prizes for Poetry to Peter Viereck, for *Terror and Decorum*; for Drama to Arthur Miller, for *Death of a Salesman*; for Music to Virgil Thomson, for the score to *Louisiana Story* || The James Tait Black Prize to Graham Greene, for *The Heart of the Matter* || The first annual Partisan Review Award of $1,000 to George Orwell || The Bollingen Poetry Prize to Ezra Pound, for *The Pisan Cantos*

In the Wings: On the Campus: Bernard Malamud, 35, at Oregon State College; Kingsley Amis, 27, at University College, Swansea; John Wain, 24, at Reading University || On the Move: Doris Lessing, 30, arrives in England from Southern Rhodesia; Jack Kerouac, 26, somewhere between New York and Mexico; James Baldwin, 25, "after living in Paris for a little over a year," is arrested on December 19 "as a receiver of stolen goods" (a bed sheet) and spends eight days in prison

Publishing: General Mills commissions John Dos Passos to write a "humane and objective" report on its operations which is published the following year in its employees' magazine *The Modern Millwheel* || The Grove Press founded on August 1, Melville's 130th birthday || In London, the final issue of Cyril Connolly's *Horizon* appears in December, with an Augustan *vale* from the editor: ". . . 'Nothing dreadful is ever done with, no bad thing gets any better, you can't be too serious.' This is the message of the Forties from which, alas, there seems no escape, for it is closing time in the gardens of the West and

William Faulkner with his daughter Jill

Mary McCarthy

James Baldwin

from now on an artist will be judged only by the resonance of his solitude or the quality of his despair" ‖ The British Book Center opens in New York at 122 East 55th Street

Visitors: In California and celebrating his 75th birthday (January 25), W. Somerset Maugham admits that "the nicest compliment ever paid to me was a letter from a G.I. in the Pacific during the war, who wrote me that he had read an entire story of mine without having to look up a single word in the dictionary" ‖ On a lecture tour of the U.S., Evelyn Waugh is disconcerted by the listening habits he encounters: ". . . looking around I notice on every face . . . a rapt nun-like contemplative calm. They are paying no attention at all" ‖ On his second American visit in two years, E. M. Forster addresses the American Academy of Arts and Letters in New York: "Ancient Athens made a mess—but the Antigone stands up. Renaissance Rome made a mess—but the ceiling of the Sistine got painted. James I made a mess—but there was *Macbeth*. Louis XIV—but there was *Phèdre*. Art for art's sake? I should just think so . . ."

In the Great World: Communist People's Republic (October 1) with poet Mao Tse-tung as leader

Great Britain

FICTION

George Barker: *The Dead Seagull*
Jocelyn Brooke: *The Image of a Drawn Sword*
Henry Green: *Nothing*
Graham Greene: *The Third Man and The Fallen Idol*
Doris Lessing: *The Grass Is Singing*
P. H. Newby: *The Young May Moon*
William Sansom: *The Passionate North*
Evelyn Waugh: *Helena*
Denton Welch: *A Voice Through a Cloud*
Angus Wilson: *Such Darling Dodos*

Robert Graves: translation of *The Transformations of Lucius, Otherwise Known as The Golden Ass*, by Lucius Apuleius

VERSE AND DRAMA

W. H. Auden: *Collected Shorter Poems, 1930–44*
W. H. Auden and Norman Holmes Pearson, eds.: *Poets of the English Language*
George Barker: *News of the World; The True Confession of George Barker*
Walter de la Mare: *Inward Companion*
David Gascoyne: *A Vagrant and Other Poems*
Ruth Pitter: *Urania: Collected Poems*
Edith Sitwell: *Poor Men's Music*
Dylan Thomas: *Twenty-Six Poems*

Stephen Spender and Frances Cornford: translation of Paul Éluard's *Le Dur Désir de Durer (The Dour Desire to Endure)*

Lawrence Durrell: *Sappho*
Christopher Fry: *Venus Observed* (produced 1950)
Rayner Heppenstall and Michael Innes: *Three Tales of Hamlet*
G. B. Shaw: *Buoyant Billions* (produced 1948, Zurich); *Farfetched Fables; Shakes versus Shav* (ten-minute puppet play, produced 1949)

W. H. Auden

NON-FICTION

Richard Aldington: *Portrait of a Genius But . . . (The Life of D. H. Lawrence 1885–1930)* (U.S.)
W. H. Auden: *The Enchafèd Flood* (U.S.)
James Boswell: *London Journal, 1762–63* (edited by Frederick Pottle)
Elizabeth Bowen: *Collected Impressions*
Winston S. Churchill: *The Grand Alliance*
R. H. S. Crossman, ed.: *The God That Failed* (Silone, Koestler, Gide, Spender, Fischer, Wright)
Robert Graves: *Occupation: Writer*
Aldous Huxley: *Themes and Variations*
Wyndham Lewis: *Rude Assignment*
George Orwell: *Shooting an Elephant*
Bertrand Russell: *Unpopular Essays*
Edith Sitwell, ed.: *A Book of the Winter*

Angus Wilson

Osbert Sitwell: *Noble Essences*
Kenneth Tynan: *He That Plays the King*
Virginia Woolf: *The Captain's Death Bed and
    Other Essays*

❧❧ *"To be able to speak in one's own
person, and directly in terms of one's own
experience without making a fool of
oneself requires a wisdom and assumed
authority which is more likely to come, if
it comes at all, in later life."*

W. H. AUDEN

Ernest Hemingway

Richard Wilbur

United States

FICTION

Paul Bowles: *The Delicate Prey and Other Stories*
Frederick Buechner: *A Long Day's Dying*
Edward Dahlberg: *The Flea of Sodom*
William Faulkner: *Collected Stories*
Paul Goodman: *The Break-Up of Our Camp; The Dead of Spring*
William Goyen: *The House of Breath*
Ernest Hemingway: *Across the River and Into the Trees*
Mary McCarthy: *Cast a Cold Eye*
Anaïs Nin: *The Four-Chambered Heart*
Gertrude Stein: *Things as They Are* (written in 1903 as *Quod Erat Demonstrandum*)
Peter Taylor: *A Woman of Means*
James Thurber: *The 13 Clocks*

Gore Vidal: *Dark Green, Bright Red; A Search for the King*
Robert Penn Warren: *World Enough and Time*
Tennessee Williams: *The Roman Spring of Mrs. Stone*
William Carlos Williams: *Make Light Of It*
Donald Windham: *The Dog Star*

VERSE AND DRAMA

e. e. cummings: *XAIPE: Seventy-One Poems*
F. O. Matthiessen, ed.: *The Oxford Book of American Verse*
Ogden Nash: *Family Reunion*
Kenneth Rexroth: *The Signature of All Things*
Carl Sandburg: *Complete Poems*
Delmore Schwartz: *Vaudeville for a Princess and Other Poems*
Wallace Stevens: *The Auroras of Autumn*
Peter Viereck: *Strike Through the Mask!*
Richard Wilbur: *Ceremony and Other Poems*
William Carlos Williams: *Collected Later Poems*

T. S. Eliot: *The Cocktail Party* (produced 1949)
Edmund Wilson: *The Little Blue Light*

NON-FICTION

John Berryman: *Stephen Crane*
Kenneth Burke: *A Rhetoric of Motives*

Dylan Thomas

G. B. Shaw

Truman Capote: *Local Color*
Ezra Pound: *Patria Mia; Letters, 1907–1941*
    (edited by D. D. Paige)
Lionel Trilling: *The Liberal Imagination*
Norbert Wiener: *The Human Use of Human
    Beings: Cybernetics and Society*
William Carlos Williams: *A Beginning on the
    Short Story: Notes*
Edmund Wilson: *Classics and Commercials*

❧❧ "*. . . criticism is as inevitable as
breathing . . .*"

T. S. ELIOT

Related Events

D E A T H S

George Orwell (Eric Arthur Blair): Bengal-born
    novelist and autobiographer; 47; of
    tuberculosis, the day before he was to have left
    for a Swiss sanatorium; in London, on January
    23
F. O. Matthiessen: American literary historian
    and anthologist; 48; suicide, by leaping from a
    hotel window in Boston, on April 1
Cesare Pavese: Italian (Piedmontese) novelist,
    poet, translator, and man-of-letters; 42; suicide,
    by taking poison; in a hotel room in Turin, on
    August 27
Edna St. Vincent Millay: American poet; 58; of a
    heart attack, at her home near Austerlitz, New
    York, on October 19
George Bernard Shaw: Irish dramatist, essayist,
    and gadfly-of-letters; 94; of complications
    following a broken hip; at his home in Ayot
    St Lawrence, on November 2

Other Deaths:

Edgar Rice Burroughs
John Gould Fletcher
Edgar Lee Masters
Waslaw Nijinsky

I N   O T H E R   L A N G U A G E S

Gottfried Benn: *Doppelleben (Double Life)*
Albert Camus: *Les Justes*
André Gide: *Journal: 1942–1949*
Marcel Jouhandeau: *L'Imposteur*
Cesare Pavese: *La Luna e i Falo (The Moon and
    the Bonfires); Verrà la Morte e Avrà i Tuoi
    Occhi (Death Will Come and It Will Have
    Your Eyes)*
Simone Weil: *La Connaissance Surnaturelle*

I N   O T H E R   A R T S

Jean Cocteau: film adaptation of his play *Orphée*
Aaron Copland: *Twelve Poems of Emily
    Dickinson*
Carson McCullers: stage adaptation of her
    novel, *The Member of the Wedding*

IN THE MARGIN

Laurels: The Nobel Prize for Literature to
   Bertrand Russell || Bollingen Prize to
   Wallace Stevens || Academy of American
   Poets Fellowship to e. e. cummings ||
   National Book Awards (for the first time) to
   William Carlos Williams for Poetry and to
   Nelson Algren for Fiction || In Resolution
   No. 224, the United States Senate cites Robert
   Frost for having written poems which
   "have helped to guide American thought with
   humor and wisdom, setting forth to our minds
   a reliable representation of ourselves and of all
   men"—and extends him felicitations of the
   Nation on the occasion of his 75th birthday
Publishing: Karl Shapiro assumes editorship of
   Poetry magazine || Lillian Ross's portrait of
   Ernest Hemingway appears in *The New
   Yorker* || Frederick A. Praeger inaugurates
   his publishing house || A symposium,
   "Religion and the Intellectuals," with Allen
   Tate, W. H. Auden, James Agee among the
   contributors, is convened in *Partisan Review*
In the Great World: The U.N. Building is
   completed in New York || Korean War
   (June) || U. S. Senator Joseph McCarthy
   charges Communist infiltration in State
   Department
On the Move: James Agee to California, to
   collaborate with director John Huston on a
   film version of C. S. Forester's *The African
   Queen:* "The work is a great deal of fun:
   treating it fundamentally as high comedy with
   deeply ribald undertones . . ." || Dylan
   Thomas to America for the first of his three
   transcontinental reading tours: "If people like
   my poetry, if they like my reading of it, if they
   like me, that is success, and that is bad for me.
   I should be what I was . . . arrogant and lost.
   Now I am humble and found. I prefer that
   other" || Henry Green (Henry Yorke) to
   New York for the U.S. publication of *Nothing*,
   registering at the Hotel Gotham as "Mr.
   H. V. Yonge": "I prefer the oblique approach"

|| Thornton Wilder to Cambridge,
Massachusetts, to deliver the Charles Eliot
Norton lectures at Harvard University: "I
must remember to maintain the tone of a
personal deposition"

ENVOI

Cyril Connolly: "Flaubert, Henry James, Proust,
Joyce and Virginia Woolf have finished off the
novel. Now all will have to be re-invented as from
the beginning."

Glenway Wescott: "It shall be an age of telling
the truth . . . An age of confessions and
curiosities; yes, it must shock some people."

Sources and Acknowledgments

We would especially like to offer our thanks to the following friends and associates for various forms of help, including books, letters, photographs, hot meals, quick loans, veteran patience, and abounding good will: Mrs. Elizabeth Ames, Miss Nathalie Babel, Miss Rosemarie Beck, Miss Louise Bogan, James Oliver Brown, Mr. and Mrs. Albert Deane, Mrs. Linda Deane, Michael di Capua, Miss Janet Flanner, Miss Dolly Gattozzi, Robert Giroux, Miss Gloria Glikin, Miss Carmen Gomezplata, Rayner Heppenstall, William T. LaMond, Miss Evelyn Lauer, Misses Delia and Jennifer Lauve, Michael Lebeck, William Miller, Mrs. Natalia Danesi Murray, Miss Anaïs Nin, Bernard Perlin, Roger Phelps, Miss Katherine Anne Porter, Dolph Rijkers, Mr. and Mrs. Joseph Rogers, Mrs. Marilyn Schwartz, Gunther Stuhlmann, Lionel Trilling, Hal D. Vursell, Glenway Wescott, Monroe Wheeler, and Mrs. William Carlos Williams.

TEXTS

Foreword: Herman Melville: from *Moby Dick.* W. H. Auden: from his Foreword to *W. H. Auden: A Bibliography,* by B. C. Bloomfield (The University of Virginia Press, 1964)

1900 W. B. Yeats: from "The Song of the Happy Shepherd," in *Poems* (T. Fisher Unwin, London, 1895); reprinted in *The Collected Poems of W. B. Yeats* (Macmillan, London, 1950). Stephen Crane: as quoted by John Berryman in *Stephen Crane* (William Sloane, 1950). Willa Cather: from a memorial note on Stephen Crane, originally published under the pseudonym of Henry Nicklemann, in *Library*, June 23, 1900. André Gide: from "In Memoriam: Oscar Wilde," in *Prétextes* (Mercure de France, 1913). Joseph Conrad: from his letter of July 20, to John Galsworthy, in G. Jean-Aubry's *Joseph Conrad: Life and Letters* (Doubleday, Page & Co., 1927). Henry Adams: from *Letters of Henry Adams (1892–1918)*, edited by Worthington Chauncey Ford (Houghton Mifflin, 1938)

1901 George Gissing: from *The Private Papers of Henry Ryecroft*. Frank Norris: from *The Responsibilities of the Novelist and Other Literary Essays*. James Joyce: from "The Day of the Rabblement," as quoted in Herbert Gorman's *James Joyce* (Farrar & Rinehart, 1939)

1902 W. H. Hudson: from *A Hind in Richmond Park* (J. M. Dent & Sons, Ltd., 1922). William Dean Howells: as reported by Edith Wharton in *A Backward Glance* (Charles Scribner's Sons, 1934). Sarah Orne Jewett: from her letter of August 17, 1908, to Willa Cather, in *Letters of Sarah Orne Jewett,* edited by Annie Fields (Houghton Mifflin, 1911). Amy Lowell: from a letter to Eunice Tietjens, as quoted in S. Foster Damon's *Amy Lowell* (Houghton Mifflin, 1935)

1903 Ambrose Bierce: from an entry under the letter *I* in *The Cynic's Wordbook* (*The Devil's Dictionary*)

1904 Joseph Conrad: from his letter of December 5, 1903, to A. K. Waliszewski, in *Lettres Françaises* (Gallimard, 1929). Henry Adams: from *The Life of George Cabot Lodge* (Houghton Mifflin, 1911). W. B. Yeats: from "Advice to Playwrights Who Are Sending Plays to the Abbey, Dublin," as quoted in Lady Gregory's *Our Irish Theatre* (G. P. Putnam's Sons, 1913). Arnold Bennett: from his *Journal* (Viking Press, 1933). Henry Adams: from *Letters of Henry Adams (1892–1918)*, edited by Worthington Chauncey Ford (Houghton Mifflin, 1938). E. M. Forster: from *Marianne Thornton, 1797–1887: A Domestic Biography* (Edward Arnold, 1956)

1905 Ford Madox Hueffer: from a letter to Mrs. C. F. G. Masterman, as quoted in *Critical Writings of Ford Madox Ford,* edited by Frank MacShane (University of Nebraska Press, 1964). Edith Wharton: from *A Backward Glance* (Charles Scribner's Sons, 1934). E. A. Robinson: from his letter of July 22, 1908, to Daniel Gregory Mason, in *Selected Letters of Edwin Arlington Robinson* (Macmillan, New York, 1940). W. H. Hudson: from a letter to Edward Garnett, in *Letters from W. H. Hudson, 1901–1922,* edited by Edward Garnett (E. P. Dutton & Co., 1923). Wallace Stevens: from an excerpt of a letter to Elsie Moll, in *Letters of Wallace Stevens,* edited by Holly Stevens (Knopf, 1966)

1906   H. G. Wells: from his letter of July 8, 1915, to Henry James, in *Henry James and H. G. Wells,* edited by Leon Edel and Gordon N. Ray (University of Illinois Press, 1958). Jack London: from *The Cruise of the Snark* (Macmillan Co., New York, 1960). H. G. Wells: from his letter of January 25, 1906, to Henry James, in *Henry James and H. G. Wells,* edited by Leon Edel and Gordon N. Ray (University of Illinois Press, 1958). Ford Madox Hueffer: from a letter to J. B. Pinker, in *Letters of Ford Madox Ford,* edited by Richard M. Ludwig (Princeton University Press, 1965). James Joyce: from a letter to Grant Richards, in *Letters,* edited by Stuart Gilbert (Viking, 1957). Hilaire Belloc: as reported by Robert Speaight in *The Life of Hilaire Belloc* (Hollis & Carter, 1957). Winston S. Churchill: as quoted by Upton Sinclair in his *Autobiography* (Harcourt, Brace & World, 1962)

1907   Rudyard Kipling: from *Something of Myself* (Doubleday, Doran, 1937). Henry James: from his letter of July 28, 1883, to Grace Norton, in Vol. I of *Letters of Henry James,* edited by Percy Lubbock (Charles Scribner's Sons, 1920). E. A. Robinson: from *The New York Times Book Review,* February 22, 1925. Thomas Hardy: as quoted in *The Life of Thomas Hardy, 1840–1928,* by Florence Emily Hardy (St. Martin's Press, New York, 1962). Ezra Pound: from *Indiscretions, or Une Revue de Deux Mondes* (Three Mountains Press, Paris, 1923; reprinted in *Quarterly Review of Literature,* Vol. V, No. 2, 1949)

1908   E. M. Forster: from "Howard Overing Sturgis," in *Abinger Harvest* (Edward Arnold, 1936). O. Henry: in *The Bookman;* July, 1910. G. B. Shaw: from his letter to Maurice Lindsay, as quoted in the latter's Introduction to *John Davidson: A Selection of His Poems* (Hutchinson of London, 1961). T. E. Hulme: from "Notes on Language and Style," edited by Herbert Read, *The Criterion,* July, 1925

1909   Thomas Hardy: as quoted in *The Life of Thomas Hardy, 1840–1928,* by Florence Emily Hardy (St. Martin's Press, New York, 1962). William James: as quoted by Randall Jarrell, in "On Preparing to Read Kipling," in *A Sad Heart at the Supermarket* (Eyre & Spottiswoode, 1965). John Davidson: from *Sentences and Paragraphs.* John Millington Synge: from his Preface to *The Playboy of the Western World* (John W. Luce, 1911). George Meredith: from his last letter, of April 13, 1909, in Vol. XXIX of the Memorial Edition (Charles Scribner's Sons, 1912); and as reported by Desmond MacCarthy and quoted by Siegfried Sassoon in *Meredith* (Constable, 1948). Siegfried Sassoon: from *Meredith* (Constable, 1948). Sarah Orne Jewett: from a letter to Willa Cather, in *Letters of Sarah Orne Jewett,* edited by Annie Fields (Houghton Mifflin, 1911). Sigmund Freud: as reported by Ernest Jones in Vol. II of *The Life and Work of Sigmund Freud* (Basic Books, 1955)

1910   John Millington Synge: from his Preface to *Poems and Translations* (Cuala Press, 1909). William Dean Howells: as quoted by John Berryman in *Stephen Crane* (William Sloane, 1950). G. B. Shaw: from his letter of July 3, 1907, to Mark Twain, as quoted in Justin Kaplan's *Mr. Clemens and Mark Twain* (Simon & Schuster, 1966). Jules Renard: from his *Journal* (Gallimard, 1935). William Carlos Williams: as reported by Charles Norman in *Ezra Pound* (Macmillan, New York, 1960). Henry James: as reported by W. Somerset Maugham in "Some Novelists I Have Known," in *The Vagrant Mood* (Heinemann, 1952). Sinclair Lewis–Jack London: from *Letters from Jack London,* edited by King Hendricks and Irving Shepard (Odyssey Press, 1965)

1911   G. B. Shaw: from Prefatory Note to *The Six of Calais,* in *Complete Plays with Prefaces* (Dodd, Mead and Co., 1962). Theodore Dreiser: from *Jennie Gerhardt* (Harper & Bros., 1911). Ronald Firbank: as quoted by Ifan Kyrle Fletcher in *Ronald Firbank: A Memoir* (Brentano's, New York, 1932)

1912   Max Beerbohm: from *A Variety of Things* (Knopf, 1928). Ezra Pound: from "A Stray Document," in *Make It New* (Faber and Faber, 1934). Leonard Woolf: from *Beginning Again* (The Hogarth Press, 1964). Robert Frost: from his letter of September 15, 1912, to Susan Hayes Ward, in *Selected Letters of Robert Frost,* edited by Lawrance Thompson (Holt, Rinehart and Winston, 1964)

1913   D. H. Lawrence: from his letter of December 16, 1915, to J. B. Pinker, in *The Letters of D. H. Lawrence,* edited by Aldous Huxley (Viking Press, 1932). Robert Frost: from his letter of February 22, 1914, to John T. Bartlett, in *Selected Letters of Robert Frost,* edited by Lawrance Thompson (Holt, Rinehart and Winston, 1964). Ford Madox Hueffer: from a Dedicatory Letter, dated 1927, to later editions of *The Good Soldier.* Joseph Conrad: from his letter of July 20, 1913, to Alfred A. Knopf, in Vol. II of *Joseph Conrad: Life and Letters,* by G. Jean-Aubry (Doubleday, Page & Co., 1927). Rupert Brooke: from a letter to Edward Marsh, included in *Letters from America* (Charles Scribner's Sons, 1916). Leonard Woolf: from *Beginning Again* (The Hogarth Press, 1964)

1914   Gertrude Stein: from *Everybody's Autobiography* (Random House, 1937)

1915   Virginia Woolf: from her letter of January 28, 1909, to Lytton Strachey, in *Letters of Virginia Woolf and Lytton Strachey* (The Hogarth Press and Chatto & Windus, 1956). Willa Cather: from "Miss Jewett," in *Not Under Forty* (Alfred A. Knopf, 1936). Rupert Brooke: as quoted in Christopher Hassal's *Rupert Brooke* (Harcourt, Brace and World, 1964).

H. G. Wells: from *Boon,* as reprinted in *Henry James and H. G. Wells,* edited by Leon Edel and Gordon N. Ray (University of Illinois Press, 1958). Henry James: from his letter of July 10, 1915, to H. G. Wells, and from his letter of July 26, 1915, to Edmund Gosse, both in Vol. II of *Letters of Henry James,* edited by Percy Lubbock (Charles Scribner's Sons, 1920); as reported by Edith Wharton in *A Backward Glance* (Charles Scribner's Sons, 1934)

1916   H. G. Wells: from the Introduction to *George Meek, Bathchairman,* by Himself (Constable, 1910). Henry James: from *The Golden Bowl* (Charles Scribner's Sons, 1905). Henry James epitaph: from the plaque on the wall of Chelsea Old Church, in Chelsea, London.

1917   Thomas Hardy: as quoted in *The Life of Thomas Hardy, 1840–1928,* by Florence Emily Hardy (St. Martin's Press, New York, 1962). T. S. Eliot: from "The Music of Poetry," in *On Poetry and Poets* (Farrar, Straus & Giroux, 1957). e. e. cummings: from the Foreword by Edward Cummings, the poet's father, to *The Enormous Room* (Boni and Liveright, 1922). John H. Watson: from *His Last Bow,* by Arthur Conan Doyle (George H. Doran, 1917)

1918   Lytton Strachey: as quoted in *Lytton Strachey: His Mind and Art,* by Charles Richard Sanders (Yale University Press, 1957). Logan Pearsall Smith: from *Afterthoughts* (Harcourt, Brace, 1931). Aldous Huxley: from his letter of September 14, 1918, to Juliette Huxley, his sister-in-law, as printed in *Aldous Huxley, 1894–1963: A Memorial Volume,* edited by Julian Huxley (Harper & Row, 1966)

1919   W. Somerset Maugham: from *The Summing Up* (Doubleday, Doran, 1938). H. L. Mencken: from *Prejudices: First Series* (Knopf, 1919). Robert Graves: from *Good-bye to All That* (Jonathan Cape, 1929). Roy Campbell: from *Light on a Dark Horse: An Autobiography (1901–1935)* (Regnery, 1952). Elizabeth Bowen: from the Preface to *Encounters* (Sidgwick & Jackson, 1949); reprinted in *Afterthought* (Longmans, 1962)

1920   Norman Douglas: from *An Almanac,* as quoted in *Grand Man: Memoirs of Norman Douglas,* by Nancy Cunard (Secker & Warburg, 1954). George Santayana: from *Character and Opinion in the United States* (Charles Scribner's Sons, 1920). Robert Graves: from a letter to Eleanor Ruggles, as quoted by her in *The West-Going Heart* (W. W. Norton, 1959). Katherine Anne Porter: from "Why I Write About Mexico," in *The Days Before* (Harcourt, Brace, 1952)

1921   Walter de la Mare: from "Mr. Kempe," in *The Connoisseur and Other Stories* (Knopf, 1926). Sherwood Anderson: as reported by Hart

Crane in an article in *The Double Dealer,* July, 1921. E. M. Forster: from *The Hill of Devi* (Edward Arnold, 1953). Ernest Hemingway: as reported by Lincoln Steffens in his *Autobiography* (Harcourt, Brace, 1931). Ford Madox Ford: from *It Was the Nightingale* (J. P. Lippincott, 1933)

1922 Virginia Woolf: from the entry for June 4, 1923, in *A Writer's Diary* (Harcourt, Brace, 1953, 1954). Ezra Pound: from a letter to T. S. Eliot, in *Letters of Ezra Pound 1907–1941,* edited by D. D. Paige (Harcourt, Brace, 1950). "Bel Esprit": see pp. 174–75 of *Letters of Ezra Pound 1907–1941,* edited by D. D. Paige (Harcourt, Brace, 1950). Ronald Firbank: as reported by Osbert Sitwell in *Ronald Firbank* (Brentano's, 1932). W. H. Auden: from Part IV of "Letter to Lord Byron," in *Letters from Iceland,* by W. H. Auden and Louis MacNeice (Random House, 1937). V. S. Pritchett: from an untitled essay in *Beginnings* (Thomas Nelson & Sons, 1935). "A Novelist's Symposium": Virginia Woolf: from the entry for September 6, 1922, in *A Writer's Diary* (Harcourt, Brace, 1953, 1954); Ford Madox Ford: from *Thus To Revisit* (Chapman & Hall, 1921); D. H. Lawrence: from his letter of August 15, 1928, to Aldous Huxley, in *Letters of D. H. Lawrence,* edited by Aldous Huxley (Viking, 1932); E. M. Forster: from a review of *Ulysses* in the *New Leader* (England), March 12, 1926, as quoted in *The Cave and the Mountain,* by Wilfred Stone (Stanford University Press, 1966)

1923 Joseph Conrad: from Author's Note to *Chance* (Doubleday, Page & Co., 1924). Marianne Moore: from "A Burning Desire To Be Explicit," in *Tell Me, Tell Me* (Viking Press, 1966). Katherine Mansfield: from "The Canary," as quoted by Katherine Anne Porter in "The Art of Katherine Mansfield," in *The Days Before* (Harcourt, Brace, 1952). Henry Green: from *Pack My Bag* (Hogarth Press, 1940). Allen Tate: from *"The Fugitive 1922–25: A Personal Recollection Twenty Years After,"* in *The Princeton University Library Chronicle,* April, 1942. Ford Madox Ford: on pronouncing his name: from *It Was the Nightingale* (J. P. Lippincott, 1933); on Jules Renard: as quoted by Douglas Goldring, in *Trained for Genius* (E. P. Dutton & Co., 1949). Ronald Firbank: from a letter to his mother, as quoted in *A Bibliography of Ronald Firbank,* by Miriam J. Benkovitz (Rupert Hart-Davis, 1963)

1924 W. B. Yeats: as reported by Lady Gregory in her *Journal,* edited by Lennox Robinson (Macmillan Co., New York, 1947). Ernest Hemingway: from Chapter I of *Death in the Afternoon* (Charles Scribner's Sons, 1932). Franz Kafka: from "Reflections on Sin, Pain, Hope, and the True Way," in *The Great Wall of China: Stories and Reflections,* translated by Willa and Edwin Muir (Shocken Books, 1946). W. H. Auden on Kafka: from "The Wandering Jew," in *The New Republic,* February 10, 1941. "On Conrad": Norman Douglas: from *D. H. Lawrence and Maurice Magnus: A Plea for*

Better Manners, as reprinted in *Norman Douglas: A Selection from His Works,* edited by D. M. Low (Chatto & Windus, Secker & Warburg, 1955); Ernest Hemingway: from the *transatlantic review,* pp. 341–42, October, 1924; Paul Valéry: from "Sujet d'une Conversation avec Conrad," in *La Nouvelle Revue Française,* December 1, 1924; André Gide: from "Joseph Conrad," in *Feuillets d'Automne* (Mercure de France, 1949). André Breton: from *Manifeste du Surréalisme* (Éditions Kra, 1929). Richard Hughes: from *Richard Hughes: An Omnibus* (Harper and Bros., 1931)

1925 D. H. Lawrence: from his letter of January 20, 1930, to Mrs. Caresse Crosby, in *Letters of D. H. Lawrence,* edited by Aldous Huxley (Viking Press, 1932). Gertrude Stein: from *The Making of Americans: The Hersland Family* (abridged edition, Harcourt, Brace, 1934). G. B. Shaw: as quoted in Archibald Henderson's biography *George Bernard Shaw: Man of the Century* (Appleton-Century-Croft, 1956). Langston Hughes: from *The Big Sea* (Knopf, 1940). "Progress Report on the Great American Novel": E. M. Forster: from *Aspects of the Novel* (Harcourt, Brace, 1927); James Agee: from his letter of April 20, 1927, in *Letters to Father Flye* (Braziller, 1962); T. S. Eliot: from his letter of December 31, 1925, to F. Scott Fitzgerald, as printed in *The Crack-Up,* edited by Edmund Wilson (New Directions, 1945)

1926 Robert Graves: from *Good-bye to All That* (Jonathan Cape, 1929). e. e. cummings: from his Foreword to *Is 5* (Boni and Liveright, 1926). Ronald Firbank: from Chapter II of *Vainglory* (1915), as reprinted in *Three Novels of Ronald Firbank* (New Directions, no date). Rainer Maria Rilke: from Letter Three, of April 3, 1903, in *Letters to a Young Poet,* translated by M. D. Herter Norton (W. W. Norton, 1934, 1954). W. B. Yeats: as reported in the *Irish Times,* February 12, 1926, and reprinted in *Sean O'Casey: The Man and His Work,* by David Krause (MacGibbon & Kee, 1960). Virgil Thomson: from his autobiography, *Virgil Thomson* (Knopf, 1966). Gertrude Stein: from *The Autobiography of Alice B. Toklas* (Harcourt, Brace, 1933)

1927 E. M. Forster: from *Aspects of the Novel* (Harcourt, Brace, 1927). Thornton Wilder: from *The Cabala* (Albert & Charles Boni, 1926). Hilaire Belloc: from his letter to Maurice Baring, as quoted in *The Life of Hilaire Belloc,* by Robert Speaight (Hollis and Carter, 1957). Christopher Isherwood: from *Lions and Shadows* (New Directions, 1947). Cyril Connolly: from "England Not My England," in *The Condemned Playground: Essays: 1927–1944* (Routledge, 1945)

1928 James Joyce: from "Anna Livia Plurabelle," in *Finnegans Wake* (Viking Press, 1939). Glenway Wescott: from "Fiction Writing in a Time of Troubles," in *Images of Truth: Remembrances and Criticism* (Harper & Row, 1962). Aldous Huxley: from a letter to Victoria Ocampo, editor of *Sur,* in *Aldous Huxley, 1894–1963: A Memorial Volume,* edited by Julian Huxley (Harper & Row, 1966). W. B. Yeats: from his letter of May 22, 1933, to Olivia Shakespear, in *Letters of W. B. Yeats,* edited by Allen Wade (Macmillan Co., New York, 1954). Rebecca West: from *Ending in Earnest* (Doubleday, Doran, 1931). Thomas Wolfe: from his letter of November 17, to Maxwell Perkins, in *The Letters of Thomas Wolfe,* edited by Elizabeth Nowell (Charles Scribner's Sons, 1956). W. H. Auden: from "I Like It Cold," in *House and Garden,* December, 1947

1929   William Faulkner: from *Faulkner at West Point,* edited by Joseph L. Fant and Robert Ashley (Random House, 1964). William Faulkner: from his Introduction to *Sanctuary* (Modern Library, 1932)

1930   D. H. Lawrence: as quoted by Aldous Huxley in his Introduction to the *Letters of D. H. Lawrence* (Viking Press, 1932). Katherine Anne Porter: from "Why I Write About Mexico," in *The Days Before* (Harcourt, Brace, 1952). E. M. Forster: from two letters to *The Nation and Athenaeum,* as quoted in *The Cave and the Mountain,* by Wilfred Stone (Stanford University Press, 1966). Sergei Eisenstein: from the contract of November 24, 1930, between Eisenstein and Mrs. Upton Sinclair, as quoted by Marie Seton in *Sergei M. Eisenstein* (A. A. Wyn, no date). Sinclair Lewis: from his Nobel Acceptance Speech, as printed in *Sinclair Lewis: An American Life,* by Mark Schorer (McGraw-Hill, 1961). Willa Cather: from "A Chance Meeting," in *Not Under Forty* (Knopf, 1936). James Agee: from his letter of November 19, 1930, in *Letters to Father Flye* (Braziller, 1962)

1931   Virginia Woolf: from "Reading," in *The Captain's Death Bed* (Harcourt, Brace, 1950). Edmund Wilson: from "A Modest Self-Tribute," in *The Bit Between My Teeth: A Literary Chronicle of 1950–1965* (Farrar, Straus & Giroux, 1965). Arnold Bennett: as quoted in *Arnold Bennett,* by Frank Swinnerton (Longmans, Green & Co., 1950). Vachel Lindsay: as quoted in *The West-Going Heart,* by Eleanor Ruggles (W. W. Norton, 1959). Virginia Woolf: from the entry for February 7, 1931, in *A Writer's Diary* (Harcourt, Brace, 1953, 1954). Forrest Reid: from *Private Road* (Faber and Faber, 1940). Theodore Dreiser: as quoted in *Dreiser,* by W. A. Swanberg (Charles Scribner's Sons, 1965)

1932   Aldous Huxley: from *Texts and Pretexts* (Harper and Bros., 1932). James Thurber: as reported by George Plimpton and Max Steele in "James Thurber," in *Writers at Work: The Paris Review Interviews,* edited by Malcolm Cowley (Viking Press, 1958). Katherine Anne Porter: as quoted in *Hart Crane,* by Philip Horton (W. W. Norton, 1937)

1933   Stephen Spender: from *World Within World* (Harcourt, Brace, 1951).

Hart Crane: from his letter to Gorham Munson, in *Letters of Hart Crane,* edited by Brom Weber (University of California Press, 1959). Sigmund Freud: as reported by H.D. in *Tribute to Freud* (Pantheon, 1956). Hon. John M. Woolsey: from "U.S. District Court (Southern District of New York) Opinion A.110–59," as reprinted (pp. 317–20) in *James Joyce,* by Herbert Gorman (Farrar & Rinehart, 1939). George Barker: from an untitled essay (#4) in *Coming to London,* edited by John Lehmann (Phoenix House, Ltd., London, 1957)

1934 Evelyn Waugh: *A Little Learning* (Little, Brown and Co., 1964). F. Scott Fitzgerald: from his Introduction to *The Great Gatsby* (Modern Library, 1934). Gertrude Stein: from *Narration* (University of Chicago Press, 1935). C. Day Lewis: from *The Buried Day* (Chatto & Windus, 1960). Ezra Pound: as reported (p. 469) in *W. B. Yeats: 1865–1939,* by Joseph Hone (Macmillan Co., New York, 1943)

1935 Christopher Isherwood: from *A Single Man* (Methuen, 1964). Ernest Hemingway: from *The Green Hills of Africa* (Charles Scribner's Sons, 1935). Pablo Picasso: as reported by Christian Zervos, in "Conversation avec Picasso," translated by Myfanwy Evans, and reprinted in *Picasso: Forty Years of His Art,* edited by Alfred H. Barr, Jr. (Museum of Modern Art, 1939). E. M. Forster: from "Liberty in England," in *Abinger Harvest* (Edward Arnold, 1936). Katherine Anne Porter: from "E. M. Forster," in *The Days Before* (Harcourt, Brace, 1952). Sigmund Freud: as reported by Thornton Wilder, in his letter of October 14, 1935, to Gertrude Stein and Alice B. Toklas, in *The Flowers of Friendship,* edited by Donald Gallup (Knopf, 1953)

1936 W. Somerset Maugham: from *The Summing Up* (Doubleday, Doran, 1938). T. S. Eliot: from "Mélange adultère de Tout," in *Collected Poems 1909–1962* (Farrar, Straus and Giroux, 1963). André Gide at Gorky's Moscow funeral: from *Littérature Engagée: Textes Réunis et Présentés par Yvonne Davet* (Gallimard, 1950). A. E. Housman: as quoted (p. 610) by Louis Untermeyer in *Lives of the Poets* (Simon & Schuster, 1959). "Writers in Action": André Gide: from an unpublished text quoted by Jean-Jacques Thierry in *Gide* (La Bibliothèque Idéale, Gallimard, 1962); Graham Greene: from *Journey Without Maps* (Heinemann, 1936); Robert Graves: from *Majorca Observed* (Doubleday, 1954)

1937 W. H. Auden: from Part III of "Letter to Lord Byron," in *Letters from Iceland,* by W. H. Auden and Louis MacNeice (Random House, 1937). Louise Bogan: from "The Quest of W. H. Auden," in *Selected Criticism* (Noonday Press, 1955). Max Eastman: from "Bull in the Afternoon," *New Republic,* June 7, 1933; reprinted in *Art and the Life of Action* (George

Allen & Unwin, Ltd., 1935). Graham Greene: as quoted in *Graham Greene,* by John Atkins (Humanities Press, New York, 1966). Ford Madox Ford: from Dedication and Introduction to *The March of Literature: From Confucius' Day to Our Own* (Dial Press, 1938). Dylan Thomas: from his letter of July 15, 1937, to Vernon Watkins, in *Selected Letters of Dylan Thomas,* edited by Constantine Fitzgibbon (J. M. Dent & Sons, 1966). Saul Bellow: as reported by Harvey Breit in *The New York Times Book Review,* September 20, 1953

1938   Graham Greene: from "Walter de la Mare's Short Stories," in *The Lost Childhood* (Viking Press, 1951). Thornton Wilder: from "The American Loneliness," in *Atlantic Monthly,* August, 1952. Thomas Wolfe: from his letter of September 22, 1937, to Sherwood Anderson, in *Story,* September–October, 1941. Virginia Woolf: from the entry for November 1, 1938, in *A Writer's Diary* (Harcourt, Brace, 1953, 1954)

1939   Louis MacNeice: from "Thomas Malory," in *The English Novelists,* edited by Derek Verschoyle (Harcourt, Brace, 1936). Thomas Wolfe: from his letter of July 26, 1937, to F. Scott Fitzgerald, in *The Crack-Up,* edited by Edmund Wilson (New Directions, 1945). W. H. Auden: from "In Memory of W. B. Yeats," in *Another Time* (Random House, 1940) and *The Collected Poetry of W. H. Auden* (Random House, 1945). Graham Greene: from "Ford Madox Ford," in *The Lost Childhood* (Viking Press, 1952). Thornton Wilder: from his letter of October 14, 1935, to Gertrude Stein and Alice B. Toklas, in *The Flowers of Friendship,* edited by Donald Gallup (Knopf, 1953). T. S. Eliot: from *The Criterion,* January, 1939

1940   William Empson: from "Missing Dates," in *The Gathering Storm* (Faber and Faber, 1940). Glenway Wescott: from "The Moral of Scott Fitzgerald," as reprinted in *The Crack-Up,* edited by Edmund Wilson (New Directions, 1945). Arthur Koestler: from *The Invisible Writing* (Macmillan Co., New York, 1954). Louis MacNeice: from *The Strings Are False: An Unfinished Autobiography,* edited by E. R. Dodds (Faber and Faber, 1965)

1941   Joyce Cary: from *Herself Surprised* (Michael Joseph, 1941). James Agee: from "Verses: To Walker Evans," in *Let Us Now Praise Famous Men* (Houghton Mifflin, 1941). James Joyce: from *A Portrait of the Artist as a Young Man* (B. W. Huebsch, 1916). Sherwood Anderson: from *A Story Teller's Story* (B. W. Huebsch, 1924). Isaac Babel: details of his death, as reported by his daughter, Nathalie Babel, in her Introduction to *The Lonely Years 1925–1939,* by Isaac Babel (Farrar, Straus & Co., 1964); epitaph quotation from "Guy de Maupassant," in Isaac Babel's *Collected Stories,* translated by Walter Morison (Criterion Books, 1955). Virginia Woolf: from "The Novels of Turgenev," in *The Captain's Death Bed* (Harcourt, Brace,

1950). Graham Greene: from "Convoy to West Africa," in *The Mint,* edited by Geoffrey Grigson (Routledge & Sons, 1946). Bennett Cerf: as quoted (p. 238) in *Gertrude Stein: Her Life and Work,* by Elizabeth Sprigge (Harper and Bros., 1957)

1942 E. M. Forster: from "Jane Austen," in *Abinger Harvest* (Edward Arnold, 1936). Mary McCarthy: from "The Fact in Fiction," in *On the Contrary* (Farrar, Straus and Cudahy, 1961). Jean Cocteau: from *La Difficulté d'Être* (Paul Morihien, 1947)

1943 Henry Green: from "A Novelist to his Readers," in *The Listener,* November 9, 1950. Robert Penn Warren: from "The Ballad of Billie Potts," in *Selected Poems 1923–1943* (Harcourt, Brace, 1944). Simone Weil: as quoted by Leslie Fiedler in his Introduction to *Waiting For God,* by Simone Weil (G. P. Putnam's Sons, 1951). District Court of U.S.: as quoted by Charles Norman in *Ezra Pound* (Macmillan Co., New York, 1960)

1944 Edith Sitwell: from *Taken Care Of* (Atheneum, 1965). Marianne Moore: from *Predilections* (Viking Press, 1955). Robert Frost: from a letter of March 7, to Earle J. Bernheimer, in *Selected Letters of Robert Frost,* edited by Lawrance Thompson (Holt, Rinehart and Winston, 1964)

1945 George Orwell: from "Why I Write," in *England Your England* (Secker & Warburg, 1953). Randall Jarrell: from "A Note on Poetry," in *The Rage for the Lost Penny,* in *Five Young American Poets* (New Directions, 1940). John Lehmann: from *I Am My Brother* (Reynal & Co., 1960). Robert L. Allen on Ezra Pound at Pisa: from "The Cage," *Esquire,* February, 1958. Katherine Anne Porter: from an unpublished letter of January 23, 1945, to Monroe Wheeler

1946 Dylan Thomas: from a response to a questionnaire on "The Cost of Letters," in *Horizon,* June, 1946; reprinted in *Ideas and Places,* by Cyril Connolly (Weidenfeld & Nicolson Ltd., 1953). William Carlos Williams: from *Paterson: Book I* (New Directions, 1946). Gertrude Stein: as reported by John Preston in "A Conversation with Gertrude Stein," reprinted in *The Creative Process: A Symposium,* edited by Brewster Ghiselin (New American Library, 1955). William Carlos Williams: from a letter to Kenneth Burke, in *The Selected Letters of William Carlos Williams,* edited by John C. Thirlwall (McDowell, Obolensky, 1957). Angus Wilson: from *The Wild Garden* (University of California Press, 1963). Norman Mailer: from *Advertisements for Myself* (G. P. Putnam's Sons, 1959). Cyril Connolly: from "American Injection," in *Ideas and Places* (Weidenfeld & Nicolson Ltd., 1953)

1947 Rayner Heppenstall: from *The Double Image* (Secker & Warburg,

1947). Wallace Stevens: from *Notes Toward a Supreme Fiction* (Cumming-ton Press, 1942); reprinted in *The Collected Poems of Wallace Stevens* (Knopf, 1954). Willa Cather: from "Miss Jewett," in *Not Under Forty* (Knopf, 1936). Jackson Pollock: from "My Painting," as quoted in *Jackson Pollock*, by Frank O'Hara (Braziller, 1959). Dylan Thomas: from his letter of May 29, 1947, to John Davenport, in *Selected Letters of Dylan Thomas*, edited by Constantine Fitzgibbon (J. M. Dent & Sons, 1966). George Orwell: from a letter to Richard Rees, quoted in his *George Orwell: Fugitive from the Camp of Victory* (Secker & Warburg, 1961). Christopher Isherwood: from "Coming to London," in *Exhumations* (Simon & Schuster, 1966)

1948 Robert Graves: from "The Ghost of Milton," in *The Common Asphodel: Collected Essays on Poetry 1922–1949* (Hamish Hamilton, 1949). Allen Tate: from "The Trout Map," in *Poems: 1922–1947* (Charles Scribner's Sons, 1948). Lawrence Durrell: from a letter to Henry Miller, in *A Private Correspondence*, edited by George Wickes (E. P. Dutton & Co., 1963). Robert Graves: from *Steps* (Cassell, 1958)

1949 G. B. Shaw: from *Sixteen Self Sketches* (Dodd, Mead, 1949). Henry Miller: from Vol. I of *Hamlet*, by Henry Miller and Michael Fraenkel (Carrefour, 1939). James Baldwin: from "Equal in Paris," in *Notes of a Native Son* (Beacon Press, 1955). Cyril Connolly: from "Hail and Farewell — II," *Horizon*, November–December, 1949. W. Somerset Maugham: from *A Writer's Notebook* (Doubleday, 1949). E. M. Forster: from "Art for Art's Sake," in *Two Cheers for Democracy* (Edward Arnold, 1951)

1950 W. H. Auden: from his Preface to *A Mask for Janus*, by W. S. Merwin (Yale Series of Younger Poets, Vol. 49, Yale University Press, 1952). T. S. Eliot: from "Tradition and Individual Talent," in *The Sacred Wood* (Methuen, 1920). U.S. Senate on Robert Frost: from the *Congressional Record*, Vol. 96, Pt. 3, p. 3997, Resolution No. 244. James Agee: from his letter of December, 1950, in *Letters to Father Flye* (Braziller, 1962). Dylan Thomas: as reported by Harvey Breit, in *The New York Times Book Review*, May 14, 1950. Henry Green: from "A Novelist to His Readers: II," in *The Listener*, March 15, 1951. Thornton Wilder: from "Toward an American Language," in *Atlantic Monthly*, July, 1952

Envoi: Cyril Connolly: from *The Unquiet Grave* (Harper and Bros., 1945). Glenway Wescott: from *Fear and Trembling* (Harper and Bros., 1932)

ILLUSTRATIONS

1900 Joseph Conrad: Keating Collection, Yale. Mark Twain: Yale Uni-

versity Library. Stephen Crane: Frances Cabani Scovel Saportas. Oscar Wilde: William Andrews Clark Library. Ernest Dowson: Lessing F. Rosenwald Collection, Library of Congress

1901 Thomas Hardy: Rev. T. Perkins; Dorset Natural History and Archaeological Society. G. B. Shaw: Histed, London

1902 Illustration for *The Hound of the Baskervilles:* Sidney Paget. John Masefield: Elliot and Fry. Illustration for *The Virginian:* Arthur I. Keller

1903 Samuel Butler: Alfred Emery Cathie

1904 W. H. Hudson: Oil portrait by Frank Brooks; Royal Society for the Protection of Birds. G. K. Chesterton: Alvin Langdon Coburn. Henry James: Alice Boughton. E. M. Forster: E. M. Forster Collection

1905 H. G. Wells: Elliot and Fry. Ronald Firbank: Kaulak

1906 Ford Madox Hueffer and his daughter Christina: Katherine Lamb Collection. Upton Sinclair: Lilly Library, Indiana University. Paul Cézanne: Émile Bernard

1907 Pablo Picasso: Canals

1908 W. B. Yeats: Times Hulton Picture Library. Ezra Pound: Elliot and Fry

1909 Lady Gregory, as seen by Jacob Epstein: Dublin Municipal Gallery of Modern Art. Gertrude Stein, as seen by Pablo Picasso: Metropolitan Museum of Art. Algernon Charles Swinburne: B. J. Poole

1911 Max Beerbohm: Alvin Langdon Coburn. Sarah Teasdale: Williamina and Grace Parrish

1912 Walter de la Mare: Elliot and Fry

1913 Robert Frost: Dartmouth College Library. William Carlos Williams: Mrs. William Carlos Williams Collection. Igor Stravinsky: Sergei Diaghilev

1914 Thomas and the second Mrs. Hardy: Hermann Lea

1915 Rupert Brooke: Scherril Schell. Henry James: E. G. Hoppé

1916 Ronald Firbank: Bertram Park. Sherwood Anderson: Sue de Lorenzi. Eugene O'Neill: Muray

1917   Joseph Conrad: G. C. Beresford

1918   Henry Adams: Marian Adams; Massachusetts Historical Society. Guillaume Apollinaire: Librairie Gallimard. Wilfred Owen: John Gunston

1919   James Branch Cabell: Foster Studio. Sylvia Beach: Gisèle Freund

1920   H. G. Wells: G. C. Beresford. Sinclair Lewis: Underwood and Underwood. Vachel Lindsay: Herbert Georg Studio. Katherine Anne Porter: Robert A. Turnbull

1921   Walter de la Mare: Herbert Lambert. Marianne Moore: G. Maillard Kesslère

1922   T. S. Eliot: Maurice Beck, London. e. e. cummings: Dr. Edward Cummings

1923   Edith Sitwell: Elliot and Fry. Louise Bogan: Bruhlmeyer. Robert Penn Warren: Isabell Howell Collection. Katherine Mansfield: Ida Baker

1924   E. M. Forster: Russell. Herman Melville: Rodney Dewey. Robert Frost: Doris Ulmann

1925   Virginia Woolf: Agnès Varda. Theodore Dreiser: Robert H. Davis

1926   D. H. Lawrence and Frieda in Mexico: D. H. Lawrence Collection, University of Texas. Ernest Hemingway: Sylvia Beach Collection. Isaac Babel: Nathalie Babel Collection. Sergei Eisenstein: Kenneth MacPherson Collection

1927   Glenway Wescott: George Platt Lynes

1928   Siegfried Sassoon: G. C. Beresford. Allen Tate: Isabell Howell Collection. Djuna Barnes: United Press International. Eugene O'Neill: Muray

1929   Richard Hughes: Hay Wrightson. Thomas Wolfe: Doris Ulmann

1930   W. Somerset Maugham: Carl Van Vechten. Katherine Anne Porter: M. Alvarez Bravo. D. H. Lawrence: Robert H. Davis. Sinclair Lewis receiving the Nobel Prize for Literature in Stockholm: Underwood-Stratton. Willa Cather: H. Foster Ensminger

1931   C. Day Lewis: Howard Coster

1932 Aldous Huxley: Bassano and Vandyk Studios

1933 Gertrude Stein: Man Ray Collection. Stephen Spender: O. Wild. Archibald MacLeish: Robert Disraeli. André Malraux: Roger Parry. H.D.: Man Ray

1934 Henry Miller: Anaïs Nin Collection. *Four Saints in Three Acts:* White, New York

1935 Louis MacNeice: W. H. Auden. William Carlos Williams: Charles Sheeler. Marianne Moore: Gotham Book Mart Collection. e. e. cummings: Associated Press. T. E. Lawrence: Lionel Curtis Collection. E. M. Forster: E. M. Forster Collection

1936 E. M. Forster and Forrest Reid: E. M. Forster Collection. Djuna Barnes: Berenice Abbott. *The Dog Beneath the Skin, or Where Is Francis?:* Pollard Crowther

1937 Edna St. Vincent Millay: Nation-Wide News Service. Dylan and Caitlin Thomas: Mrs. Harry Locke Collection. Frederic Prokosch: George Daniell. Ernest Hemingway: United Press International

1938 Lawrence Durrell: Anaïs Nin Collection. George Orwell: O. Wild. Delmore Schwartz: Polly Storey. Edmund Wilson and Mary McCarthy: Sylvia Salmi; Mary McCarthy Collection

1939 Roy Campbell: Imperial War Museum Collection. Christopher Isherwood: John Lehmann. W. B. Yeats: Howard Coster. Anaïs Nin: Anaïs Nin Collection. Ford Madox Ford: *Daily News,* Greensboro, N.C.

1940 Arthur Koestler: Fred Stein. Graham Greene: Howard Coster. Janet Flanner (Genêt): John Deakin. Glenway Wescott: Wilbur Pippin. F. Scott Fitzgerald: Carl Van Vechten

1941 W. H. Auden: George Platt Lynes. Rebecca West: B.B.C. Collection. Carson McCullers: Louise Dahl-Wolfe. James Agee: Father Flye Collection. Isaac Babel: Nathalie Babel Collection. Virginia Woolf: Gisèle Freund. Sherwood Anderson: Wide World

1942 Thornton Wilder: Sam Rosenberg

1943 Walter de la Mare: Bassano

1944 W. Somerset Maugham: Balkin—Pix. Jean Genet: Douchan Stanimirovitch. Van Wyck Brooks: Spotpix. Krazy Kat by George Herriman: King Features Syndicate, Inc.

1945 Theodore Dreiser: Lotte Jacobi. Ezra Pound: Wide World

1946 Christopher Fry: Picture Post. Jean-Paul Sartre: Bildarchiv Süddeutscher Verlag. Robert Lowell: Robert Giroux. Gertrude Stein: André Ostier

1947 Ivy Compton-Burnett: Camera Press. Philip Toynbee: Vogue Studios, London. Lionel Trilling: Robert Christie. André Gide: Miller, Oxford

1948 Truman Capote: Holmes-Lebel. Aldous Huxley: George Platt Lynes. Robert Graves: William J. Sumits. Norman Mailer: G. Maillard Kesslère

1949 William Faulkner and his daughter Jill: Wide World. Mary McCarthy: Mary McCarthy Collection. James Baldwin: William Cole

1950 W. H. Auden: William Miller. Angus Wilson: Maurice Ambler. Ernest Hemingway: Agence Intercontinentale. G. B. Shaw: Felix H. Man—Picture Post